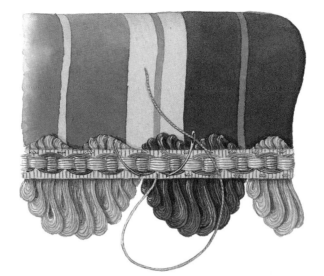

THE ESSENTIAL GUIDE TO
UPHOLSTERY

DEDICATION To all my family for their help and support:
my dear husband John; our sons Matthew and Jonathan and their
wives Debbie and Jacqui; our grandchildren Jacob, Georgia, Joshua
and Thomas; and my sisters, Patricia, Margaret and Rosemary.

Published in 2000 by Merehurst Limited
Ferry House, 51–57 Lacy Road, Putney, London, SW15 1PR

Copyright © 2000 Merehurst Limited

ISBN 1-85391-757-5

A catalogue record of this book is available from the British Library.

Senior Commissioning Editor: Karen Hemingway
Editors: Geraldine Christy and Justine Upex
Concept and Art Direction: Marylouise Brammer
Designer: Caroline Verity
Principal Photography: Andrew Newton-Cox
Additional Photography: Graeme Ainscough, Dominic Blackmore
and Joe Filshie
Styling and Additional Text: Deena Beverley
Additional Styling: Georgina Dolling
Illustrations: Carolyn Jenkins

Publishing Manager: Fia Fornari
Production Manager: Lucy Byrne
Marketing & Sales Director: Kathryn Harvey
International Sales Director: Kevin Lagden
CEO: Robert Oerton
Publisher: Catie Ziller
Group CEO & Publisher: Anne Wilson

Colour separation by Colourscan in Singapore

THE ESSENTIAL GUIDE TO
UPHOLSTERY

Dorothy Gates

Principal photography by Andrew Newton-Cox

MEREHURST

CONTENTS

DISCOVER UPHOLSTERY

Discover Upholstery

Whether revamping furniture to give it a new lease of life or re-covering it to fit in with a change of decoration, upholstery gives an opportunity to stamp style and character on your home. As well as explaining the traditional and modern techniques needed for a result worthy of a professional upholsterer, this book gives advice on assessing furniture and presents a wealth of possibilities to help you decide on the final finish.

GOOD-QUALITY UPHOLSTERY brings a comfort and style into the home that is a real pleasure to live with and can be tangibly appreciated. If you are practically minded, you will no doubt be eager to learn the skills of upholstery for yourself and enjoy the sense of satisfaction and achievement that can be gained from completing a job that is worthy of a professional upholsterer.

The craft and skills of upholstery have been passed down the generations through families and apprenticeships. My father started as an apprentice in 1925 and by the time he retired he was responsible for two more generations of upholsterers in our family. Having grown up in an upholstery environment, it was natural for me to spend all my working life in the same trade, reupholstering clients' furniture and teaching the skills to generations of new students, and my two sons and youngest sister have done the same. I have certainly found it to be a very satisfying occupation and hope that this book will pass on those skills to amateur upholsterers who wish to approach their work in a professional manner and perhaps seek out courses in colleges and workshops to extend their knowledge and practical abilities.

The Essential Guide to Upholstery

This book guides you through all the processes involved in upholstery, from assessing the condition of the furniture you want to work on, through rebuilding the upholstery from the frame upwards if necessary, to covering it with fabric and embellishing it with trimmings. It suggests where you might find suitable pieces to upholster if you do not already have a project of your own, as well as giving advice on all the tools you will need and on creating a suitable work space.

The Techniques & Materials section features a button-back armchair in order to demonstrate the traditional skills needed to upholster a chair from the bare frame to the top cover and trimming. This will help you to thoroughly understand the practical aspects of each procedure and you can follow this chair through right from the ripping out stage to the trimmed top fabric. Other additional techniques, such as upholstering wings, applying different trimmings and making cushions, are also explained. The techniques employed on the button-back chair are all traditional ones, using traditional materials as close as possible to the originals, but bearing modern health and safety recommendations in mind. As each type of material, from webbing and tacks to hessian and gimp, is needed in the upholstery process, they and the choices available are explained. Although some of the materials originally used on antique pieces are not

This page & opposite: Upholstery has developed with furniture-making over centuries. Classic upholstery shapes and techniques flourished in the eighteenth century, as on this Hepplewhite gilt settle in the French style, re-covered in silk. circa 1770, Clandon Park (The National Trust).

Right: Traditionally a male domain, more women are taking up upholstery either as a business or as a leisure pursuit.

available now, you can still find high-quality alternatives and good upholstery suppliers will be able to advise you. For example, although a wide variety of materials including alva (seaweed) were once used as stuffings, you must now use modern fibres and horsehair, which are more ecologically friendly and fire retardant. The Techniques & Materials section is your guide and you will find it invaluable as a reference tool as you build up your repertoire of skills and work on your own projects.

There are many types of furniture that you might choose to upholster, and the Projects section of the book presents a variety of both traditional and modern pieces to illustrate the wide range of approaches possible. Each project has been carefully selected to demonstrate different methods, whether that is to use modern materials like foam on the Tapestry fireside stool, different traditional constructions such as a tack roll on the Chippendale-style stool or adventurous choices of top fabric such as those on the Modern sofa or the Blanket box.

They all show what can be achieved with confident skills, imagination and flair, and it is hoped that they will provide practical solutions to the decisions that you will need to make on your own projects.

Comprehensive advice is also offered on how to select top fabrics that will wear well and look stunning. There are ideas on colour schemes, and how to use different patterns and textures to create combinations that suit the piece of furniture and the rest of your home. These ideas are initiated in the section on Decorative Choices and then further developed on special feature spreads throughout the book that aim to fire your imagination and give you inspiration. Style is an individual matter and some of the ideas may seem strange at first, but try putting samples together *in situ* on the furniture, live with them a little, and you will learn to gain confidence with more innovative approaches.

The History of Upholsterers

As you practise your upholstery skills and begin to appreciate the excitement of being able to give pieces of furniture a new lease of life, you will be following in the steps of a long tradition of skilled upholsterers practising their time-honoured craft. Over the centuries, as the trade of the upholsterer became established, upholstery evolved into a distinct craft with traditionally accepted practical and decorative techniques. In England, for instance, the trade guilds were established to set standards, arrange apprenticeships and look after the welfare of their members. In the City of London many of these guilds for different types of crafts eventually became known as livery companies, deriving that name from the livery or distinctive ceremonial dress worn on official occasions. An upholsterer was originally known as an upholder and The Worshipful Company of Upholders was granted a Royal Charter in 1626, although they first came into existence in the fourteenth century. The Company is still very active today in the training of upholstery and soft-furnishing students, supporting those who wish to train as professional upholsterers with grants and bursaries.

The role of the upholsterer has changed quite considerably over the centuries. In the seventeenth century, the upholsterer was a vital member of the household, responsible for all the textile furnishings. At that time the main responsibility was for wall and bed hangings, but also included upholstered seating and even coffin interiors. Gradually the role of the upholsterer has become rather more fragmented, largely due to the diminishing availability and length of apprenticeships. This has led craftspeople to specialize in furniture, carpeting, soft furnishings or wall covering, rather than to be thoroughly trained in all the traditional areas of upholstery as they were up until two generations ago. The production of new domestic seating, with its modern processes and use of the sewing machine, has led to even more specialization. The machining on modern furniture can be a vital part of the design, but not all upholsterers are confident of using a machine and so the separate role of machinist is now important. Although the furniture industry pursues its mass-market approach, there is still a demand for traditional upholstery techniques, often met by small businesses or by those learning the skills for their own pleasure. As a result, the stereotypical male and female roles no longer apply. Many women are now involved in traditional upholstery and many men make good machinists and soft furnishers.

Below: A good example of early upholstery, this English oak chair retains its original leather cover, which is simply stuffed and held in place with nails. The decorative nailing is extended to all parts of the frame. circa 1660, Geffrye Museum.

This page & opposite: This William and Mary walnut chair, with its contemporary needlework cover and silk fringe, is typical of the elaborately decorated seating owned by the wealthy classes. Upholstery and chair manufacturing techniques were still in their infancy, but the cover proclaims status even now. circa 1700, Clandon Park (The National Trust).

A Brief History of Upholstery

The desire to create attractive and comfortable surroundings in which to live is a universal characteristic of human nature and has naturally encompassed domestic furniture. As ideas on the style and shape of furniture have developed, the skills and techniques available to the upholsterer have also evolved. However, no doubt there were very simple beginnings, probably when the first cave dwellers hung animal skins over the door to make a curtain. Having provided a little privacy and extra warmth, they would have wished for yet more comfort and rolled a skin into a bundle to make a soft seat.

In the Middle Ages, domestic interiors were considerably more comfortable than that and upholstery was playing an important part in the interior decoration of wealthy homes. These decorations were mainly what would now be considered soft furnishings, in the shape of bed and wall hangings and padded cushions to soften wooded frames, although there were also simple platforms of webbing, canvas or leather for stools, chairs and, elaborately decorated, even for thrones that already demonstrated the rudimentary beginnings of upholstered furniture.

By the beginning of the seventeenth century, chair seats were being padded, but this form of upholstery was still fairly basic. All sorts of stuffing from sawdust, grass or feathers to deer, goat or horse hair were used, although in England, the Livery Company forbade the use of goat and deer hair and imposed fines for misdemeanours. The stuffing was heaped on the wooden platform and held in place with a decorative top fabric and nails. This produced a characteristic simple domed shape, sloping towards the edges of the seat, that was embellished with very elaborate fabrics and trimmings depending on the wealth of the owner.

Only towards the end of the century did upholsterers start to develop the techniques that would distribute and shape the stuffing into more controlled shapes. Curled horsehair was being used more consistently for stuffing and was easier to hold in place with stitches in twine that were developed from saddlery techniques. Thus layers of stuffing could be distributed evenly and secured to stay in place. On a basic level, squab cushions were made more stable with tufting ties and were used, not only as loose cushioning, but as a padding structure under the fixed top fabric on a seat. Stuffed edge rolls appeared on seat fronts, providing support at first for a cushion to be retained and later for deeper stuffing to be held in place under a fixed top fabric.

This gradual growth of technical expertise gave upholsterers much more control over their materials and allowed upholstery to be used along the sloping shapes of backs and arms as furniture developed more curvilinear lines.

Classic upholstery

What we now think of as classic upholstery shapes and techniques flourished in the eighteenth century as furniture frames of elegant line and proportion were sympathetically partnered by expertly executed upholstery. Previously, luxurious fabrics and trimmings had concealed crude underpinnings, but now the upholsterer's technical knowledge meant that stuffing could be controlled along upright and sloping lines, giving new levels of comfort and a simply stated elegance. The upholstery followed the smoothly flowing lines of the furniture with a confidence built on techniques that were by then much closer to those in use today. On chairs with curved seats, backs and arm pads, stuffed edge rolls held in place by a mattress stitch gave a compact, but soft, shape that followed the curves of the frame. Another style was characterized by straighter lines and the upholstery on these chairs and sofas had a much squarer profile. A border was added to create height and the edge roll was very firmly stitched to give it a square edge.

By the end of the century, the techniques used to create this style had developed to be even more like those used today. The border was replaced by a single piece of linen or scrim taken over the stuffed seat and tacked to the frame. At the same time, the locked blind stitch and top stitching combination that pulled the side and top surfaces together and brought the stuffing up to make a firm top edge had evolved. Beautiful top fabrics in silks and damasks were popular in wealthy homes, although plainer and cheaper fabrics in complementary colours were often used on the outside backs. Trimmings were also expertly used to enhance the shape of the furniture and included tufting, close nailing (often in complex patterns), piping and braid.

At the beginning of the nineteenth century, the preoccupation with minimalist style was reaching such an extreme that furniture as well as clothing became the victim of fashion. A sense of austerity prevailed in the Regency, Empire and Federal periods that could be seen in the very taut lines of furniture based on ancient Greek and Egyptian styles. Shapes became extremely angular, surfaces hard and flat, edges uncomfortably sharp and even cushions were only added for effect. Trimmings also emphasized this minimal approach with cord picking out a line, tassels accentuating a focal point, and fringe, although popular, hanging like fragile cobwebs.

Opposite & left: The sinuous lines and padded back of this gilt settle were made possible by the growing technical expertise of upholsterers. A typically French style, this type of seating was usually covered in silk. circa 1770, Clandon Park (The National Trust). Below: A different eighteenth century style can be seen in this English mahogany chair. The contemporary needlework cover has been specially designed to fit the straight, square lines of the frame. circa 1720, Clandon Park (The National Trust).

Right & below: The close nailing used to fix the new silk cover on this gilt, French-style chair accentuates the elegant lines of the frame. circa 1770, Clandon Park (The National Trust).

Victorian opulence

As the century progressed, a more relaxed style and a desire for comfort returned, giving rise to what we now consider to be the characteristic overstuffed look of Victorian upholstery. With the advent of mass production, upholstered furniture was available in huge quantities and to all sections of society, middle and working class, as it never had been before. The availability of better quality steel springs and the development of lashing techniques to keep them in position meant upholstery could be built up on seats, backs and arms quite independently of the frame shape. Stuffing became ever more complex, edges became elaborately shaped into rolls and scrolls, and buttoning folded fabrics into soft, padded shapes. Elaborate top fabrics with heavy patterning and brilliant colours were popular, sometimes with contrasting plain velvets for borders, outside surfaces and vallances. Every conceivable type of trimming was used, not just to attach fabric or hide seams and edges, but for the sheer exuberance of decoration and its perceived added value, from gathered ruche edges to vallances and copious amounts of passementerie. The result was an indulgence of swelling curves and an opulence of fabric and adornment that often overwhelmed the profile of the piece of furniture underneath, but was deemed to proclaim the wealth and social standing of the owner.

Although this style was evocative of an era, a reaction to it was beginning to emerge at the end of the century. Simpler, more fluid lines, lighter colours, and understated trimmings such as brass nails and gimp began to have an impact, with the interest in Japanese design and the influence of the Arts and Crafts Movement.

Modern developments

As the twentieth century progressed, the focal point of the average living room was a three-piece suite, typically with a cover of leather, damask, moquette or printed cotton. Furniture with an upholstered shape was still most prevalent and traditional materials and methods were still used.

Shortage of materials resulting from war restricted industry and in England, for example, furniture manufacture was subject to the Utility Scheme until the early 1950s. Although styling was simple to the point of austerity, strict government standards had to be followed, ensuring good quality and durability.

In the second half of the century, new materials inspired more experimental design, often with sculptural shapes. Fibreglass shells padded with foam were fashioned into womb-like chairs and plywoods were moulded into fluid lines. Tubular steel and aluminium allowed new ideas for frames and the upholstery was reduced to a leather or

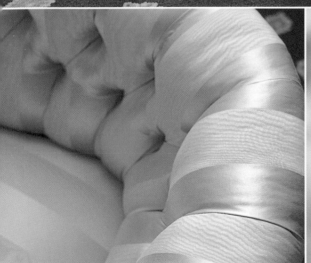

Left & above: Deep buttoning, well-padded shapes and elaborate trimmings were very popular in the Victorian era and all make an appearance, although in restrained form, on this English chaise, re-covered in silk with its contemporary tassels. circa 1840, Hughendon Manor (The National Trust).

Above: Victorian devotion to religion and splendour shows itself in the wool and bead work on the contemporary cover of this English prie-dieu. circa 1850, Geffrye Museum. Opposite: The simple sculptural shape of the 'Balzac chair' designed by Matthew Hilton in 1991 achieves an elegant style for the twentieth century. Geffrye Museum.

canvas sling. Other seating designs developed that needed no padding at all. By limiting the need for lengthy upholstery techniques, manufacturing times were slashed, costs reduced and furniture regarded as much more disposable.

Now, a rich diversity of furniture construction and design is available, from reproduction styles to those inspired by the Space Age. However, the most popular mass-produced upholstered furniture is influenced by demand for comfort at an affordable price, necessitating the use of spring units in seats, machine stitching of top covers and loose cushions in place of traditional fixed and stitched stuffings.

Return to traditions

New materials and manufacturing techniques have given us a huge choice of upholstered furniture that will bring comfort and a certain style into our homes. But we are now beginning to return to an appreciation of the benefits of the proven natural materials and traditional techniques. Even if it is becoming increasingly uneconomical for manufacturers to satisfy this shift in values, you can learn to perpetuate this rich tradition of craftsmanship yourself by upholstering your own pieces of furniture. With a wealth of historical and contemporary patterns from which to choose, your upholstery can be as individual as you are and need be bounded only by your imagination.

Whether you have just one or two pieces of furniture to complete or wish to take up upholstery more seriously, I hope that you enjoy this book and gain great satisfaction from a job well done.

GETTING STARTED

Getting Started

Recognizing the potential of a dilapidated piece of furniture and transforming it into

a beautifully upholstered treasure is one of the real joys of learning this craft. The

following pages give you tips on how to find something that will repay your efforts,

explain how to plan your working space, and describe the basic equipment that you

will need for both traditional and modern methods of upholstery.

Finding Furniture

Disregard the state of the previous upholstery when you are looking for furniture to reupholster. Instead, look for pieces that have a good frame, and your investment of time and money will be worthwhile.

Most of us inherit furniture from a variety of sources. Perhaps friends or relations are moving and have decided to buy brand-new furniture and to throw out the old. These pieces have usually been well cared for and will not need a great deal of work on them, but the top cover may be slightly worn or dated. With a little attention, you can restore the furniture to glory and acquire a treasured piece.

If you do not have furniture readily given to you, there are plenty of places where you might find interesting pieces that would reward work on them. Hunting out suitable projects is fun and you may

come up with some surprising bargains. Even a search in the loft or the garden shed may bring some forgotten pieces to light. Skips can yield a variety of items, including the odd chair, and the local tip may also be a good place to look. It is unlikely that you will discover a valuable antique piece, but you could find a very good solid frame that is worth upholstering.

Other sources are second-hand furniture shops or antique shops or auctions. Look in your local paper for details of forthcoming auctions and antique fairs. It is also worth searching out similar sources when you are on holiday and visiting car boot sales near home and further afield.

Choosing furniture

The button-back armchair chosen to demonstrate the techniques of traditional upholstery in this book is a good example of how to go about looking for a piece of furniture. This chair was found by venturing into a second-hand shop that had old furniture on the forecourt and simply asking the proprietor if he had something suitable that needed to be completely reupholstered. He produced this one, which was falling to pieces. While it was not exactly cheap, it was just what was needed and had a great deal of potential.

This style of easy chair has always been popular because of the depth and width of the seat, which affords a great deal of comfort as well as support. It is large enough for people of solid build to fit into, while small people can curl up cosily in it. The back has a good height to support the head, and the arms are substantial without being bulky.

This type of traditional easy chair can still be found in many homes. They are usually reupholstered using traditional methods and, apart from the cover wearing out, many still have the original upholstery and may only have been re-covered once. Others may have been poorly

upholstered, even more than once—our chair had three covers, one on top of the other. None of the old upholstery was worth saving, so it was a matter of buying new materials and reupholstering from scratch. In such a case it is worth asking yourself whether you like the chair enough to go to all this trouble or if it is worth the cost of refurbishment.

Assessing the frame

The first step to deciding if a reupholstery job will reward you financially or aesthetically is to check that the frame is good. Place your piece of furniture on the floor and push it from the back, then the sides, to see if it rocks or is unstable. This is not a definitive test as sometimes it is the fabric that is holding the frame together; however, it is a good general guide and this principle applies to both traditional and modern furniture.

If the frame has show wood, check to see if there are any carved areas missing. Consider if you can restore it yourself, or if you are willing to have it professionally restored and polished. If so, decide how much time and money you are willing to spend.

If you are satisfied that the frame is generally sound, take off all the coverings and stuffings before repairing or polishing the frame.

Making good the frame

Assemble your tools before starting, and proceed to rip out the frame (see page 50). Then check the frame thoroughly to investigate the extent of any damage and the source of any instability.

If the frame has damaged rails, consider having them professionally replaced. If it is unstable, clean the problem joints, reglue them and cramp back in position. Use a G-cramp to hold two pieces of wood together under pressure while the adhesive is drying.

This type of cramp is made of solid metal in the shape of a 'G' and is available in several sizes. Adjust the cramp to fit around the frame by tightening the screw. Use a sash cramp to hold a frame together or joints in place while the adhesive is drying. Position the locking pin along the length of the cramp and place the cramp around the damaged frame. Adjust the pressure applied by tightening the screw.

Otherwise, fill any large holes in the frame and rebate with an adhesive and sawdust mixture. Leave ordinary tack holes alone, as these will close up when the new tacks are hammered in. When the mixture is dry, rub off any excess filling with sandpaper until it is level with the surface.

Finishing the frame

If the frame or legs need polishing, waxing or painting, this should be done before attempting to reupholster. Clean off the old polish using a paint stripper or, if the surface only needs cleaning, use a mixture of vinegar and water. Sand the surface and stain or paint to the required colour.

In some cases, you may have to strip old paint off a frame. Use paint stripper and wire wool to remove some of the residue to restore the wood back to the original. If the furniture is in a very bad condition, ask advice before trying to restore it yourself.

Many frames, especially reproduction furniture, can be bought as white wood for you to stain and polish as you wish, or can be polished to order.

When the frame is down to the bare wood, it can be waxed, polished or painted. There are a number of finishes you can use, depending on your preference, the style of the furniture and its intended use. When dry, polish with a soft cloth or polishing pad. Wrap the legs with calico or stockinette if newly polished or painted to prevent damage during upholstering. If you are working on a chair with a drop-in seat, check that the seat still fits at this stage.

Obtaining Materials

The materials needed for upholstery are described in detail later in the book, in conjunction with the techniques for which they are used.

If they are in good condition, you may be able to save some of the materials to use again. However, you will often need to replace them and many of the materials and sundries are available from hardware stores. Most are also available from local upholsterers, although they may be reluctant to sell small quantities. A few upholstery wholesalers offer a mail order retail service, although they may also stipulate minimum quantities. If you have the storage or can group together with other upholstery students, consider buying larger quantities for convenience and economy. As a starting point, see the list of suppliers at the back of the book.

The Work Space

Making adequate space to work in is essential, especially if you want to upholster large pieces of furniture. If you have a large space, you need to plan its arrangement well or you will fill it in no time and still find that your actual working area is small. With a small work space, you will have to plan even more carefully at the outset.

If you are upholstering as a hobby, you will probably manage with whatever space you have available and be prepared to move your equipment daily from one place to another, for example back and forth from the dining room to the garage. It takes real commitment to complete a project in these circumstances, but the end results will be worth it. Most amateur upholsterers learn to make the most of their space and to improvise, though the ideal is to allocate an area such as a spare bedroom or a garage entirely to upholstery projects. The space really needs to be at least 3 x 3 m (10 x 10 ft) to allow enough room to work in comfortably, store materials and tools, and accommodate furniture as big as a sofa.

Above: Consider all of the area that is available when planning your work space, including the walls.

25

It is easier to work if you raise pieces off the ground. A pair of 94 cm (37 in) wide trestles at a height of 76 cm (30 in) are useful for this or a low table could be used. A table at least as wide as the average fabric width, 137 cm (54 in), and long enough to enable you to cut the fabric flat as you unroll it, minimum 137 cm (54 in), makes cutting easier. A table hinged to the wall so it can be stored flat when not in use is a great space saver. Alternatively, use plywood or chipboard on your trestles as a cutting surface, but remember you will still need floor space for your furniture when using the cutting board. If no table is available, use the floor for cutting, but make sure it is scrupulously clean.

To work safely and for ease of movement, leave at least 78 cm (31 in) of clear space all around your work piece. Remember you will probably also need space for a sewing machine and adequate electrical sockets if you are using power tools.

Many local colleges and schools hold upholstery classes. Generally these courses are well equipped, so before you disrupt the whole house in an effort to find space, try a project at a class first.

If you intend to set up an upholstery business, your work space will depend on the premises you can find and afford, and you will also have to comply with regulations that apply to commercial premises.

Below: Mounting your tools on the wall will keep them neat and tidy, and also in good condition.

Hand Tools

Upholstery does not require many hand tools. The essentials consist of a mallet, a ripping chisel, two hammers, scissors, a web stretcher for traditional work and a selection of upholstery needles. The list below describes each of these upholsterer's tools and includes useful additions, many of which can be collected over a period of time. Most modern professional upholsterers rely on some power tools as well, but still have a basic set of hand tools for use as required.

1. STEEL OR WOOD RULE A metre or yard stick used mainly when cutting out flat on the table.

2. RETRACTABLE STEEL MEASURE Used mainly for measuring larger areas.

3. SCISSORS Two pairs are useful. Use long blades for cutting fabrics on the table, and shorter blades for general cutting and shaping fabric on the furniture.

4. MALLET Used with the chisel for ripping out. Several types are available, with either square or round heads.

5. WEB STRETCHER The bat and peg type is most often used, but you may also see spiked stretchers. Hide strainers are sometimes used for stretching webs; they are especially useful for short ends of webbing as you do not need extra to thread through the stretcher.

6. TAILOR'S CHALK Used for marking. It is advisable to use it on the wrong side of the fabric, if possible, as it does not always rub off as intended.

7. CLAW HAMMER The claw at one end is for removing tacks or nails and the blunt end is for heavier work such as webbing.

8. RIPPING CHISEL (ripper) Used with the mallet to remove tacks when ripping out. Straight or cranked chisels are available.

9. TACK LIFTER This tool has a metal end that is split into a fork shape. The fork tucks under the tack, enabling you to lift and remove it.

10. MAGNETIC HAMMER This type of hammer is useful for leaving one hand free as the magnetic end picks up the tack, ready to place it. It requires some practice to use. (Upholsterers used to hold the tacks in their mouths and could work at great speed, pushing the tack onto the hammer with their

tongues—not recommended practice. The occasional tack was swallowed, but the supposed remedy was to eat a piece of bread immediately afterwards.)

11. *REGULATOR* This versatile tool is useful for holding the fabric in place while tacking, as well as regulating the stuffing on stitched edges. The flat blade is also used for placing pleats when deep buttoning.

12. *BRADAWL* Use the pointed end for making pilot holes or marking.

13. *WIRE CUTTERS* Can be used to remove staples by cutting them in the centre and then pulling them out of the wood. Wire cutters are available from an electrical or tool shop.

14. *PLIERS* Can be used as pincers. They have a better grip and a smaller nose.

15. *CRAFT KNIFE* Useful for cutting into edges and trimming the excess fabric away.

16. *CABRIOLE HAMMER* A hammer with a very small tip on one end used for working on show wood or delicate areas.

17. *TAPE MEASURE* Mostly used for measuring over and around objects when estimating for coverings.

PINCERS Used for removing old tacks and nails. Some pincers have a claw end for reaching into awkward places. *RASP* Used to chamfer the edges on chair frames prior to tacking down scrim.

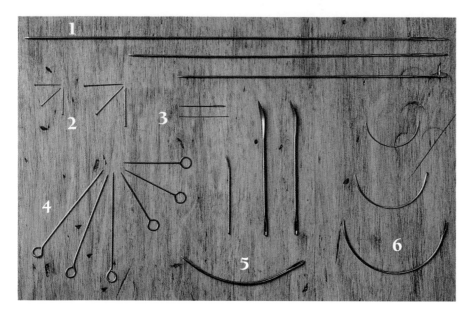

Needles and Pins

There are a number of specialist needles and pins made for use in upholstery. The needles are shaped for particular tasks and to allow you to sew through several layers of materials. Pins are designed to hold the bulk of upholstery securely while you are working on the different parts of a piece of furniture.

1. DOUBLE-ENDED NEEDLE (mattress needle) Has a round or bayonet point at each end, and an eye one end. Mainly used in stitching edges, stuffing ties and buttoning. Available in sizes from 20 cm (8 in) to 40 cm (16 in).

2. UPHOLSTERY PINS Thick and strong sharp steel pins. They are used mainly in 3 cm (1¼ in) and 4 cm (1½ in) sizes, for pinning and positioning fabric.

3. SEWING NEEDLES Straight sewing needles with sharp-pointed ends are useful in a variety of lengths and gauges. Use tapestry needles with rounded blunt ends when appropriate.

4. SKEWERS Used for the same purpose as pins, but are much larger and stronger. Available in various lengths from 10 cm (4 in) upwards.

5. SPRING NEEDLE (bottom) A curved needle with a bayonet end used to sew through webbing and hessian when sewing in springs. A *SACKING NEEDLE* is similar, but is straight with a curved top end.

6. CIRCULAR NEEDLE (cording needle) Actually half a circle, used for stitching through hessian and fabric, for slip stitching and cording. Made in various sizes and gauges to suit the work required.

Power Tools

Modern upholstery methods involve the use of a number of power tools to save time. In some cases they are also used with traditional methods because they cause less damage to frail parts of furniture.

Make sure that you have enough electrical sockets available, and that they are suitably placed for safe use while you are working. Unplug any power tools that are not actually in use.

1. GLUE GUN Hot-melt adhesive guns are used mostly for attaching trimmings. The sticks of adhesive melt, and as a trigger is pulled the adhesive is pushed out on to the trimming. The disadvantage is that the adhesive sets very quickly, so you need to place it accurately. (Fabric adhesives used from a tube are also available and also work well.)

2. STAPLE GUN An essential tool in most modern upholstery workshops. Even in traditional upholstery, staples can be used on a narrow rebate with much less damage to the wood than tacks. The staple gun is very accurate as the gun touches the wood when fired. (Tacks are still used, however, for temporary tacking in some cases, as they are easier to remove.)

Staples are available in 8 mm (³/₈ in), 10 mm (³/₈ in) and 14 mm (⁵/₈ in) widths. Different sizes and thicknesses are available depending on the manufacturer of the staple gun.

3. CORDLESS DRIVER This tool can be used as a screwdriver or drill with different tool attachments. It has to be charged up at intervals, but this is a very useful tool, particularly if you are working on a piece away from a suitable electrical socket.

Sewing Machines

With traditional upholstery, unless you need a seat cushion, piping or a fly, you can upholster a whole chair without touching a sewing machine. However, a machine is one of the most essential items needed for upholstering modern furniture as the covers are often sewn first and then capped on. All you need is a sturdy machine that produces a plain lock stitch.

A DOMESTIC SEWING MACHINE will suffice if you use a heavy-duty needle, but check that it will cope with the thickness of the fabric you are using before you start. For instance, the needle has to sew through at least four layers when piping. It may also be difficult to place a thick fabric under the foot of a domestic machine. Many fabrics have a fire-retardant back coating, and residue can soon build up under the foot, so try a sample first before you ruin your machine. It may be worth buying a second-hand machine especially for your upholstery.

INDUSTRIAL SEWING MACHINES are built to withstand heavy use, but are also very versatile and, with a fine needle, can sew delicate fabric. A machine with a walking foot is a good option because the foot grips and moves the fabric along, particularly useful where thick or piled fabric would otherwise slip. Alternatively, a machine needle feed has the same effect.

You can also buy *COMPUTERIZED SEWING MACHINES* that self-adjust for stitching.

Machine accessories

Whichever machine you use, you will need a selection of accessories for general use and to make specific jobs easier.

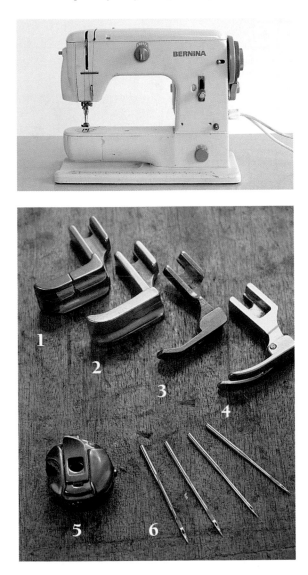

1. DOUBLE-GROOVED FOOT Ideal for making double piping in the most accurate way.

2. SINGLE-GROOVED PIPING FOOT Perfect for accurate single piping, this type of foot can also be used to make double piping and for sewing on flange cord.

3. ZIP FOOT A versatile tool used for inserting zips that can also double as a piping foot.

4. PRESSER FOOT (running foot) This basic foot is used for straight stitching.

5. BOBBIN Loosen or tighten the screw on the bobbin to adjust the tension on the lower thread. Always test the tension before starting.

6. NEEDLES Pointed needles in sizes 14–19 are most useful, but use ballpoints for synthetics or fabrics with a knitted backing and bayonets for leather. Always use a sharp needle to avoid pulling or breaking the threads in the fabric.

When machine stitching the top cover, pin the seams together, matching any notches and with the heads of the pins facing towards you so they are ready to pull out as the foot approaches. Always hold both sides of the fabric as it passes under the needle. The hand at the back keeps the fabric in line and keeps the tension on the fabric to prevent it gathering. The hand at the front holds the fabric taut and guides the fabric towards the needle.

Stitching a straight seam

Fit the presser foot to the sewing machine. Position the fabric so that the needle is 1.25 cm (½ in) away from the edge of the fabric. As you stitch, keep the side of the foot parallel to the raw edge. Stitch a straight row of stitches, keeping a uniform distance from the edge. The presser foot has a spring heel at the back so that when it crosses a seam or join it will ride up and over it.

Above: Take the time to align the pattern carefully for a perfect finish.

Machine Stitching

Before starting to stitch the actual top cover, always test out the stitching on a scrap of the top fabric first. Stitch through the same number of layers of fabric as the work in progress to ensure that the tension and the stitch length are appropriate. The requirements will depend on the weight of the fabric and the number of layers, but it is easier and less costly to make adjustments at this stage. If the top thread is loose, adjust the tension of the bobbin, and if the bottom thread is loose, adjust the upper tension control.

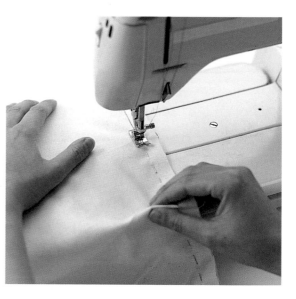

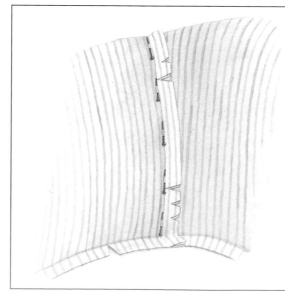

MAKING NOTCHES

When fitting two fabric sections together, position the fabric right-sides uppermost, and pin the pieces in place on the furniture. Make the notches by cutting halfway into the seams through both of the layers of fabric. Do not cut all the way down to the seam line. The notches can now be used as a guide to match the fabric pieces together when they are re-pinned, right-sides together, ready to stitch the seam.

Matching a pattern

Match the pattern on the two sections of the fabric. Pin the seam together, keeping the pins parallel to the raw edge. You can double check the alignment of the pattern at this stage by opening out and adjusting the fabric. Fit the presser foot to the sewing machine. Stitch the seam precisely along the line of the pins and the match will be perfect. Do not sew across the pins or you may damage the needle and upset the timing of the sewing machine.

Stitching a curved seam

Pin and stitch the fabric in the same manner as for the straight seam, but when stitching around the curve make a series of cuts from the raw edge up to the seam line. This will help the fabric spread around the curve, passing under the needle without pulling or gathering.

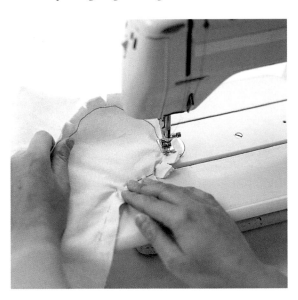

Preparing to make single piping

Fit the zip foot to the sewing machine. Set the machine stitch at a medium length (select the middle of the range of stitches on the sewing machine). Position the edge of the foot so it is just touching the encased cord. The needle will then stitch a fraction in from this edge. (See page 97 for the method of making piping.)

Preparing to make double piping

Fit the double-grooved foot to the machine. Turn the fabric over one length of cord in the fabric, position one of the grooves on the foot over the cord and stitch close to the cord to enclose it. Turn the fabric over the second length of cord and underneath the first cord. Position the centre of the two grooves of the foot between the cords and stitch along the original row of stitches. With practice, this procedure may be done in one process. (See page 100 for a more detailed method of making double piping.)

Ready to upholster

Good preparation is the basis for success in any craft, and upholstery is no exception. Having created a workable space in which to do your upholstery, gather all the tools and organise them so that they are readily available when needed. Check that all the tools are in good order and especially that your sewing machine is suitable for the job. With these basics in place, you are now ready to embark upon the exciting task of learning the skills involved and choosing the fabrics and trimmings to transform your piece of furniture.

DECORATIVE CHOICES

Decorative Choices

A well-upholstered piece of furniture adds both comfort and style to a room. There are many factors to bear in mind when choosing fabric, and this is all part of the fun of upholstery. Whether you wish to follow a traditional or modern style, there is a wealth of materials and trimmings to choose from. The following pages will help you consider colour, pattern and texture, and guide you in choosing a top cover that is right for your furniture, your room and your lifestyle.

Fabric Choices

Upholstery is not a quick or inexpensive craft and it is vital to put as much time and care into selecting the top fabric as in working on the various processes required for the upholstery. The result will be a piece of furniture that is not only comfortably upholstered, but which sits well in its chosen setting and adds to the ambience of your home for years to come. To achieve this, there are a number of simple factors to consider at the outset when selecting fabric.

Considering use

Functionality is the obvious place to start. If the fabric you have chosen is not practically suited to the job, your upholstery efforts will soon be showing signs of strain. For example, dining chairs that are in daily use demand a fabric that can withstand regular handling and, ideally, will tolerate being wiped over with a damp cloth in case of accidental food and drink spills. A robust, heavy-duty cotton, first sprayed with a fabric protector, would be a sensible choice in this situation.

Furnishing fabrics are generally marked with guidelines for suitability of use, and good shops and stores will have well-informed assistants who are familiar with the practical constraints of various fabrics. That is not to say that you cannot break the

Choose your fabric to suit the use and style of the chair. A hard-wearing cotton with a small repeat and subtle texture will prove much more practical than a lavish silk that will be better on best dining chairs. A simple checked fabric has a homely feel for a country chair, whereas the sharp citrus colours on white perfectly complement a metal frame.

rules, of course. If you are placing a dining chair primarily as a visual accent in a room that is rarely used, you can let your imagination run riot and use a less practical material as a top cover. Further guidance on selecting a fabric that is appropriate to the use to which you will put your furniture is given in the Techniques & Materials section (see page 74).

Considering style

Having considered the practicalities, look carefully at the style of the furniture you are upholstering. Its shape and finish will give valuable pointers as to possible fabric choices. A distressed painted chair in a simple, rustic shape might lend itself to a fabric with a suitably modest, country feel, such as natural unbleached linen. However, you can make a conscious decision to play dramatically against, rather than with, the inherent character of the piece. Throughout history, inventive decorators have enjoyed playing with design in this way. The same, simple painted chair can look equally stylish in cool striped cotton, or with details of the woodwork picked out in gilding, the seat could be covered in an elegant, silk Regency stripe strewn with dainty flowers.

Motifs in the carvings and mouldings on furniture can also suggest ideas to follow through in the patterns you choose for the fabric. A chair with beehive finials, for instance, upholstered in silk damask with a Napoleonic bee motif looks witty and sophisticated.

The overall shape of the piece can also be an influential factor. Upholstering a graphic-looking, straight-edged sofa in a crisp dobby-weave will emphasize its clean, geometric lines. If you want to disguise its hard-edged contemporary look, however, wrap it in a sinuously patterned, richly textured fabric to mute the angles, and add cushions covered in a variety of toning fabrics and soft shapes.

The historical period of the piece provides additional cues for fabric selection. You can play it safe and use the same kind of silk damask on a Georgian chair that would have originally dressed it or be adventurous and use an ultra-modern fabric such as neoprene or synthetic suede.

Where you want to place your piece of furniture will also influence your final choice of covering. You will need to decide whether you wish the piece to blend in quietly with its surroundings, or to make a powerful visual statement. If you have a disparate collection of furniture, built up over time, you could choose to upholster all the pieces in the same fabric to link them. Or perhaps you have an existing sofa in one colour, and an armchair in another; by combining the colours in a patterned fabric on a third armchair, and making some cushions from this fabric to add to the two existing pieces, you will attain a harmonious, co-ordinated look.

Mood and Atmosphere

Upholstered furniture can make a dramatic contribution to the mood of a room. Perhaps there is already a feeling or look that you want to reinforce. To do so, choose fabrics that work well within the existing scheme. Keep the colours, patterns and textures harmonious rather than aiming for a dramatic contrast. For example, an intimate, book-lined study filled with dark wood furniture, with deep-coloured walls and little natural light, cries out for sympathetic fabrics in muted shades and traditional heavy textures, such as woven woollens or fabrics with a pile.

Alternatively, you can lift or change the mood of a room by the introduction of a piece of furniture. A dingy living room that needs updating can be enlivened with vibrant hues in crisp, contemporary textures such as a zingy orange-ribbed Madras cotton or shocking pink cotton check.

The effects of light on colour should not be underestimated. Sometimes a room may have lighting that will virtually dictate a colour scheme,

Well-chosen fabric can reinforce the mood of a room. Create the feel of unashamed sumptuousness with plush animal print velvets or an understated air of quality with a simple floral sprig. Complement a delicate gilded antique frame with a dainty gold threaded fabric that reflects the light, or aim to surprise and lift the spirits with bold colour combinations.

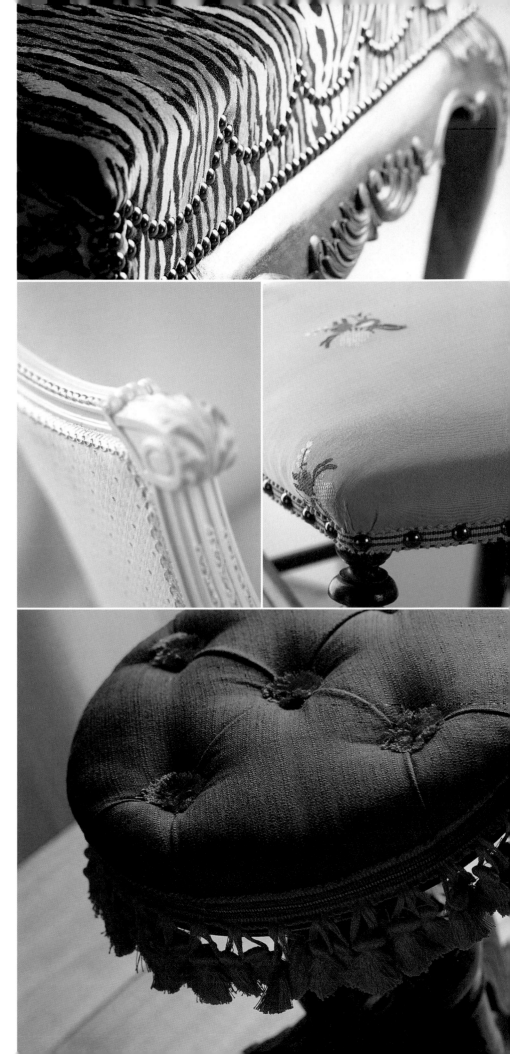

Even a restricted palette of reds and neutrals can be combined to very different effect. On this page, the harmony of a soft red with warm beige, further enhanced by the pile and texture of the fabric, produce a footstool that invites comfortable relaxation. The bold combination of neutrals on velvet make the animal print much more stimulating and the beading adds to the sense of decadent opulence.

unless you are planning a complete lighting overhaul. It is difficult to brighten some rooms that receive little natural light solely by using pale shades for paint, wall coverings and fabrics. White without light falling and reflecting on to it merely looks grey, so a wiser decision may be to emphasize the room's intimate nature by choosing a deep tone for the walls, adding warmth with pools of light from individual lamps. Use the upholstery and soft furnishing fabrics to intensify the feeling of comfort and intimacy. Velvets, brocades and damasks in rich jewel shades will add depth and warmth.

If you are fortunate enough to have a light-filled room, your choice of colours, patterns and textures is almost limitless. An airy feel can be further emphasized by keeping to clear colours, rather than muted shades, and by using crisp, clean-looking fabrics such as cottons and linens.

As well as the available light, you will need to consider the overall function of a room. Depending on your lifestyle, you may wish your dining room, for example, to be a calm, relaxing haven where you and your family can escape the stress and pressures of daily life. If this is the aim, use easy, comfortable toning colours. Or you may entertain on a regular basis and want to create a vibrant, stimulating room with a lively atmosphere,

so here is a chance to use bright colours and challenging combinations.

Choice of pattern and texture play a vital role in setting the tone of a room. Sumptuous velvets, silks and chenilles instantly spell luxury, comfort and relaxation, inviting you to curl up with a cushion and a good book. In a more workaday setting, such as a bathroom, a chair upholstered in a brisk cotton ticking will add a bright, uplifting note that seems to waft a fresh sea breeze into the morning washing routine.

Using Colour

Colour, of course, is all important. There are so many possibilities that many people become nervous about using colour in the home, and choose familiar combinations or fabrics, cushions, soft furnishings and bedding from co-ordinated ranges. Although this is a temptingly simple option, the end results can lack spontaneity and imagination. If you match your upholstery precisely to the other elements in your room, you may find the results disappointing. Happily, fabric manufacturers have been quick to respond to the growing trend for a relaxed approach and you will find some ranges of fabrics that do not necessarily

all bear exactly the same motif and precisely the same colourway, but that nevertheless have been designed to work well together.

A few simple guidelines will help you to make informed choices about colour that will transform your home, and even your wellbeing, since it is now widely accepted that colour can affect our emotional state. Colour can be stimulating, such as reds and oranges, or calming, such as blues and greens. Increasingly colour is used in a therapeutic way in public buildings, such as hospitals and offices. Treatment rooms are often painted soft pink to calm and reassure, while a café may have large amounts of red to encourage a lively, buzzing atmosphere. You can also fine tune the mood of a room in your own home by careful use of colour, evoking whatever atmosphere you wish, whether romantic, luxurious, sensual, or jolly.

Colour combinations

Although the colour wheel of primary and secondary colours is often quoted as the standard device for creating successful colour combinations, there is no substitute for your own instinct. Build up a visual dictionary of what works for you. Look at books, paintings, nature, and films. Collect paint swatches, tear sheets from magazines, scraps of

trimmings, anything that speaks to you. Patterns will begin to emerge. Although these will probably fall loosely into the theories demonstrated in the colour wheel, you will find it much easier to gain confidence by working with colour in this way rather than studying theory and trying to make decisions based on what can sometimes become a finely balanced calculation.

You will find that successful colour combinations generally fall into a few simple categories. Make a point of carefully looking at and interpreting colour combinations that you see, and you will soon be creating confident mixtures of your own. For instance, combinations of brown colours such as caramel, putty, fudge and chocolate instantly produce a sophisticated look of unstudied, effortless chic. This is an example of a monochromatic scheme—literally using mono, or single, colour.

Similarly elegant effects may be produced using tone on tone in any colour; for example, using shades of blue, from silvery or steely shades through to saturated inky cobalts. Using shades of black, through greys, to white in a classic monochromatic scheme can give a stylish, sleek look, but may be demanding to live with. If you are new to monochromatic scheming, it is advisable to start gently, by

Here, red is combined with its complementary green in a dark shade. The colours are in perfect balance, receive the gold stamp of approval and result in a confident statement that feels very smart. The last neutral combination is fairly monochromatic. In woven cotton with a grosgrain braid, this footstool has a simple look that would be easy to live with in a modern or country setting.

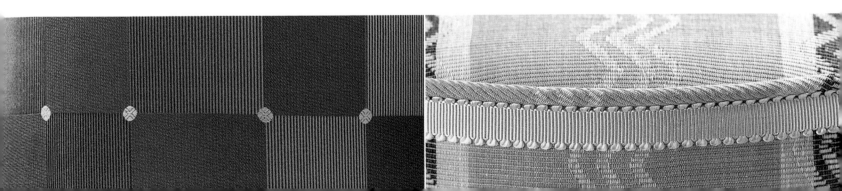

building tone on tone in a colour choice that is less confrontational, such as lilac through to deep purple, or a pale pistachio green through to a deep green.

Accent colours are widely used to enliven monochromatic schemes. These are especially useful for injecting life into an otherwise restricted palette. For example, imagine a room with walls papered in neoclassical lithographic images and sparsely furnished entirely in black and white. Placing a classically shaped chair upholstered in shocking Schiaparelli pink, or acid-lime green, in a prominent position can change the whole personality of the room from being elegant, maybe even a little daunting, to a room with a touch of humour and bravado. Of course, this is accent colour taken to extremes, but, even in a traditional domestic setting, accent colours can be used to liven up your existing scheme at minimal expense and effort. Adding cushions and throws to upholstered pieces is an easy way to experiment with bold colour choices before splashing out on metres of fabric.

Complementary colours are also widely used by designers. These schemes feature colours that are situated opposite each other on the colour wheel; for example, red and green, or blue and orange. Complementary colours contrast potently, emphasizing each other while retaining their own individual power. You can use this knowledge to create dramatically intense schemes by matching equal amounts of complementary colours. Or add small amounts of a complementary colour to magnify the effect of your predominant colour; for example, add a deep-red cushion to a wing chair upholstered in bottle green.

Using harmonizing colours is another winning designer recipe. These are colours that sit next to each other on the colour wheel and, like best friends who can sit in a room without the need for constant chatter, they get along in companionable, easy silence. Harmonizing colours promote a comfortable, restful effect and are ideal for a room in which you wish to relax totally, rather than where you want to make a big style statement. Reds and orange-golds, violets and blues, greens and blues are all examples of colour combinations that can work well.

Texture is exciting to play with as it evokes a mood literally by its feel and by the way light falls on it. From the extremes of cool, crisp cotton to the warm luxury of a deep faux fur, texture in all its different guises adds depth and richness to interior decor that can be followed through on to the upholstered furniture.

Neutral colours

Similarly restful, and increasingly popular in recent years, has been the use of neutral colours to invoke a pure, simple look that enhances a feeling of space in which to think and reflect. The use of fabrics in their natural state, and the emergence of shops specializing in these characterful materials, has led a design exodus into a land of non-colour. More restrained than monochrome, the neutral palette consists of 'barely there' colours such as stone, milk and putty. Even the names evoke a serene, contemplative mood. The effect is wonderfully peaceful, and works equally well in contemporary and period interiors.

Even when using a neutral colour scheme, there is no need for the result to be dull. Look closely at your growing pile of pictures and swatches and you will notice that as well as colour, pattern and texture are important features in maximizing decorative impact. For example, let us return to that hypothetical chair in the monochromatic room, upholstered in shocking pink or green. Use plain velvet, and you create a feeling of classical opulence, with a light-hearted edge given by the choice of colour. Use a crisp cotton plaid in lime green and fuchsia pink for a modern, casual look.

Combining Patterns

Many people shy away from mixing patterns and textures. Undeniably, some decorators, be they amateur or professional, have the happy knack of combining seemingly incongruous patterns effortlessly to great effect, but if you look at enough images you will notice that certain themes recur, and with such frequency simply because they are so effective. For example, checks and stripes in toning shades always look fresh and stylish, and have been used for centuries in endless variations.

Some classic combinations spring from historical contexts. When we mix striped silk with fabrics printed with ropes and tassels, a neoclassical look results, but we might not be aware that we are taking our lead from the striped bunting that adorned buildings to celebrate Napoleonic victory, and the military rope and tassels that prevailed on uniform and spilled over into decor. These associations, reinforced by all the pictorial imagery that surrounds us in the cinema, advertising and television, have formed an extensive visual vocabulary that summarizes an era and mood without needing precise historical explanation. We mix stylized, earthy floral patterns with self-patterned acanthus leaf damasks, and produce an Arts and Crafts look. William Morris may not have prescribed exactly the same combinations that we create today, but he would have approved of our increased courage in mixing and matching from the great diversity of patterns available to create an individual look.

Using Texture

Playing with texture is also great fun. When introducing new fabrics into your home, remember that as well as the wonderful array of colours and patterns you have to choose from, there is a feast of texture to experiment with. Use texture to emphasize the existing mood of a piece of furniture or room, or combine a variety of contrasting textures to create a witty statement. For example, a Victorian chaise lounge can be reupholstered in comfortable velvet as it was originally, in perfect keeping with its intended use and historical context. However, if you have inherited the piece and now need to fit it into your own, rather more modern setting, be bold and choose the new covering with a hint of irony. Traditional shapes can look stunning upholstered in seemingly incongruous choices, such as denim or ticking. Somehow, the contrast afforded by using such utilitarian fabrics only serves to further emphasize the elegant lines of classical furniture. Maybe we have become so accustomed to seeing such pieces dressed in more traditional choices that we have simply ceased to really appreciate their architectural form. The visual jolt of seeing a Biedermeier chair clad in fake cowhide, however, may be taking things a little too far.

Whatever the choice of pattern and texture, choose a scale that is appropriate to both the piece of furniture and the other soft furnishings in the room. Blending and balancing proportions is a skill that will develop with practice. Broadly speaking, the patterns need to have some kind of affinity or link, be it of colour, mood or type. Mix scales for a sympathetic result, rather than having many different patterns of similar size fighting for attention. Visit inspirational interiors on both grand and domestic scales for hints on how decorators through the ages have combined patterns to good effect.

Certain classic combinations of pattern work well. The busy effect of small repeats can be restrained by combining them with plain fabrics, and even larger patterns can work successfully together in colours that harmonize. Checks, stripes and other geometrics speak the same language and in toning shades produce a stylish feel that is easy to achieve.

Choosing Trimmings

The plain pink fabric on this nursing chair is the perfect canvas for exuberant trimmings. The tri-coloured cord and rosettes are used to create smart elegance, enhanced by association with the Empire style. In contrast, the pleated ribbon, sculpted into pretty forms, dresses the chair in a much more frivolous way.

Making the right choice of top fabric takes careful consideration. With such an important decision made, however, you can enjoy browsing through the vast array of trimmings that are on offer. That is not to say that they should be considered lightly, because to be used effectively they must be chosen to complement the piece of furniture and the top fabric. Trimmings can create a scrumptious visual feast, but they are also functional. Gimp, braid and decorative nails have traditionally been used to cover tacks and the edges of fabric. Piping and cord give definition to the lines of a piece of furniture and provide some protection for the edges that will receive the most wear and tear. More elaborate trimmings, such as tassels and rosettes, create a dramatic focal point that draws the eye to a

beautiful detail or shape, and fringes are often used around the bottom edge of a chair or sofa to hide the legs. Remember, if the trimmings are likely to need cleaning or replacing sooner than the top fabric, to sew rather than glue them in place.

The popularity of elaborate trimmings, or passementerie, has exploded in recent times. Classes in making passementerie are widely available, together with all the materials for making a rich array of tassels, fringes and other embellishments. At the top end of the market, passementières construct concoctions that are works of art, sculptural in their form, and with such mastery in blending colour and texture that they cannot fail to add quality to whatever they embellish.

However, trimmings need not necessarily be elaborate and fanciful. A simple band of grosgrain ribbon finishes a piece of furniture with

understated elegance, while the same furniture completed with a sumptuously elaborate braid has a more decadent look. As with the choice of top fabric, the choice of trimmings will to some extent be dictated by the end use of the piece. A piano stool that will be in constant use, handled by the edges of its seat, would not be best suited by an elaborate beaded fringe, whereas pieces that are made predominantly to be enjoyed visually, and with areas that will not need to withstand constant handling, can have intricate and fanciful decoration.

As well as the traditional options of gimp, braids, fringes, tassels and cords, designers are increasingly borrowing from the fashion world, and using more ephemeral materials such as ribbons and beads. Look at magazines and in designer trimmings shops for inspiration. These can be a rich source of ideas that you can adapt. Modern passementières have experimented with great success in using unusual objects and materials in their work; for example, making elaborate tassels from jute, which is normally used to make string. You can create simple tassels and plaited cords from materials as diverse as silk and jute, crystal beads and pebbles. The possibilities are limited only by your imagination. Rediscover the simple craft skills of childhood. Make bright wool pompoms to trim a nursery bedhead, or sculpt pleated ribbon into flower shapes to use instead of tassels.

Designers have been adapting materials to decorative effect for centuries. Creating your own style is all about such adaptation, mixing what you have available with what you can afford until you achieve an effect that pleases you. With instinct, experience, and a basic grasp of colour theory, you have all you need to create beautiful upholstery.

The extraordinary shape of a prie dieu calls for trimmings that make a statement. The elaborate braid is placed along simple outlines, emphasizing the shape of the chair with an understated luxury. The cord and tassel combination, perfectly colour co-ordinated with the fabric, are equally beautiful but in a more traditional way.

TECHNIQUES & MATERIALS

TYPICAL ORDER OF WORKING

Upholstery techniques usually follow one after another in a set pattern, so it is helpful to familiarize yourself with typical orders of working before looking at the techniques in detail.

Dimensions of Demonstration Button-back Armchair

height: 84 cm (33 in)
width: 74 cm (29 in)
depth: 76 cm (30 in)

EXPERT TIP

It is a good idea to take a photograph of the chair before you begin. This will give you a guide to the original outlines of the upholstery.

Forward planning is essential in upholstery so no processes are forgotten. Work in a logical order to allow access to all parts. One of the best ways to achieve this, detailed in the panel opposite, is to upholster the seat and inside arms first, up to securing the first stuffing, then to upholster the inside back, including starting the buttoning, up to calico. Then the seat and arms are brought up to calico, before proceeding to top cover the insides. Next the outsides are backed up and the top cover is fitted. Trimmings must be applied at the appropriate time and bottoming cloth fitted to the underside of the seat.

Another approach, followed on the demonstration chair, is to do each process on all the parts of the chair one after the other, as far as possible, to give repeated practice in each technique and reinforce your learning.

The order of working usually has to be adapted to the piece that you are working on. However, the basic principles apply. As you gain experience, you will learn to recognize the best order of working for each project.

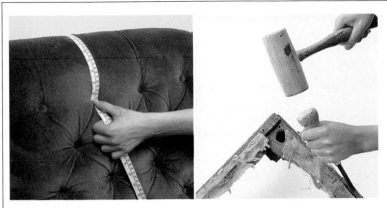

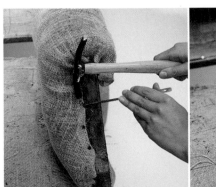

ESTIMATING MATERIALS

RIPPING OUT

WEBBING the base

SPRINGING and LASHING the base

Sewing springs through the HESSIAN

Stitching BRIDLE TIES into the hessian

Tacking on scrim after FIRST STUFFING

Putting STUFFING TIES into the arm

CHECK LIST

Listed below is a typical sequence of working and the techniques used for upholstering a button-back armchair, giving you a check list and a good understanding of how the processes build up.

The demonstration armchair in the rest of this section is done in a slightly different sequence to reinforce the techniques to be learnt, and very different orders of working are adopted in some of the projects to suit those particular types of furniture.

1. Estimate materials

Estimate the new materials and stuffings that you will need as you strip the old stuffing and cover from the chair.

2. Rip out

Remove the fabric, padding, tacks and staples from the frame.

3. Repair the frame

Clean and re-glue joints where necessary.

4. Strip off the old polish

Sand down until smooth, then either wax or polish the legs and make sure they are dry before continuing to upholster.

5. Build the seat to first stuffing

WEBBING Web the base of the seat.

SPRINGING Position and sew the springs in.

LASHING Lash the springs down.

HESSIAN Apply hessian over the springs and tack down. Sew the springs in place through the hessian.

BRIDLE TIES Stitch ties into the hessian.

FIRST STUFFING Tease in the stuffing and cover with scrim.

STUFFING TIES Put in the stuffing ties.

BLIND STITCHING Blind stitch along the front edge.

TOP STITCHING Top stitch along the front edge.

6. Build inside arms to first stuffing

WEBBING Web the arms.

HESSIAN Apply the hessian.

BRIDLE TIES Stitch ties into the hessian.

FIRST STUFFING Tease in the first stuffing; cover with scrim.

STUFFING TIES Put in the stuffing ties.

BLIND STITCHING Blind stitch around the front scrolls.

TOP STITCHING Top stitch around the scrolls.

continued over page >

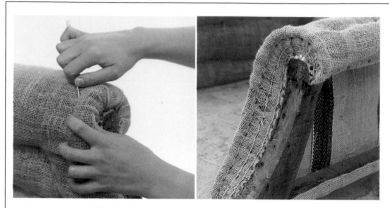

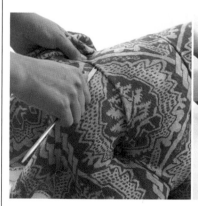

Preparing for BLIND STITCHING

STITCHED EDGE around scroll

FITTING CALICO on arm

BUTTONING IN CALICO on inside back

REGULATING top fabric into position

FITTING top fabric on inside back

BACKING UP arms with hessian

BLACK BOTTOM on base

CHECK LIST

7. Build inside back to calico

WEBBING Web the inside back.

HESSIAN Apply hessian. Mark top, side and lumbar panels in preparation for the first stuffing.

SCRIM Sew scrim in place, leaving a hollow centre panel.

BRIDLE TIES Stitch ties into the hessian.

FIRST STUFFING Tease in the first stuffing and cover with the scrim panels.

STUFFING TIES Put the stuffing ties in the top edge.

BLIND STITCHING Blind stitch around the back scrolls.

TOP STITCHING Top stitch around the back scrolls.

SECOND STUFFING Stitch in more bridle ties over the whole back and stuff.

BUTTON IN CALICO Mark button positions on the back hessian. Cover in calico, using calico washers for button markers, and stitch around the scrolls.

8. Finish arms to calico

SECOND STUFFING Stitch in more bridle ties, and stuff.

FIT CALICO Cover in calico and stitch around the scrolls.

9. Finish seat to calico

SECOND STUFFING Stitch in more bridle ties, and stuff.

FIT CALICO Cover the seat in calico and stitch along the front edge.

10. Top cover

CUT FABRIC Measure for the fabric. Plan the positioning of the pattern.

COVER INSIDE BACK Cover with wadding. Cover with top fabric, finishing the buttoning. Stitch around the scrolls.

COVER SEAT Cover with wadding. Cover with top fabric and stitch along the front edge.

COVER INSIDE ARMS Cover with wadding. Cover with top fabric and stitch around the scrolls.

11. Outsides

BACK UP Cover outside panels of frame with calico.

TOP COVER Trim and apply the scrolls. Cover all outside panels with top fabric.

12. Finishing

FINISH BASE Apply bottoming cloth to the underside of the seat.

LAYERS OF UPHOLSTERY

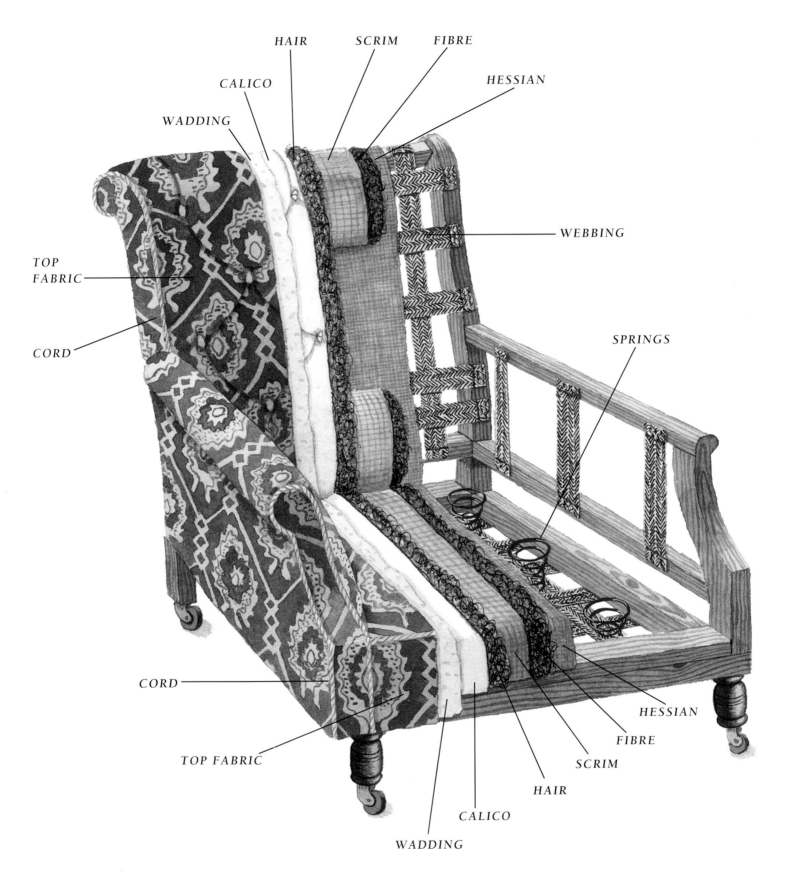

HAIR

SCRIM

FIBRE

CALICO

HESSIAN

WADDING

WEBBING

TOP
FABRIC

SPRINGS

CORD

CORD

HESSIAN

TOP FABRIC

FIBRE

SCRIM

HAIR

CALICO

WADDING

ESTIMATING MATERIALS

The techniques for the demonstration button-back armchair are now described in detail. While every piece of furniture will differ in exactly which techniques and materials are required, you will always need to start by estimating the quantities of the materials.

Unless your piece of furniture is in very good order underneath the cover, you will probably need to replace all the old materials, including the stuffings, with modern substitutes. In particular, alva (seaweed) or old flock (made out of surplus army greatcoats) are no longer available and would not pass modern safety regulations. Health and safety issues are now prime considerations and all new materials must comply with legal requirements.

It is important to plan ahead. Nothing is more annoying than stuffing a seat halfway, only to

TOOLS
Tape measure
Notebook
Pencil

find you have not allowed enough fibre or hair, particularly as this is not the type of item you can buy in an average local store.

It is usually best to start the process of estimating for most materials before you start to remove the existing cover, when you can still see the size and shape of the padding. However, do not estimate for the top fabric at this stage, which should be done when the newly upholstered chair is in calico. Do not be tempted to re-use the old hessian, scrim or calico, as they have already been trimmed.

1 Take the dimensions of each section of the chair. Measure across the widest point and down around the base rails on each section. For the dimensions of the inside back, measure down into the buttons. Add a handling allowance of 10 cm (4 in) to each dimension.

2 Estimate for wadding by adding the dimensions for all the inside and outside sections.

3 Estimate for hessian and scrim by adding the dimensions for all the inside sections, plus the scrolls and front border.

4 Estimate for calico by adding the dimensions as for scrim, plus enough to back up all the outside sections.

5 Estimate how much fibre and hair is needed as you rip out the old upholstery. As a guide, you will need about 450 g (1 lb) of fibre per 930 sq cm (1 sq ft) and 225 g (8 oz) of hair per 930 sq cm (1 sq ft) to be covered.

6 Write down all the dimensions and quantities in a notebook and keep a record for reference.

The quantities listed for this chair will give a good guide for an average easy chair, but every piece varies. The list of materials with each project in the book will give you further guidance for different types of furniture. It is always better to overestimate, rather than scrimp and find you cannot complete your piece. You can always keep any remaining materials for your next project.

SECTIONS TO MEASURE

OUTSIDE BACK

BACK SCROLL

INSIDE BACK

INSIDE ARM

OUTSIDE ARM

FRONT SCROLL

SEAT

FRONT BORDER

RIPPING OUT

The first step towards reupholstering a chair is to take the old cover off and assess how much of the upholstery can be left intact or if the chair needs taking back down to the frame.

It is possible to use good-quality horsehair again if it is springy and clean. If it is in good condition, tease and separate it by hand, but do not wash it. As a general rule, most materials will need to be replaced. This armchair was in such a state that no materials could be salvaged, and it needed to be upholstered from the frame.

The first task is to start ripping out in an organized manner.

1 Place the chair on a dust sheet, on its knees, with the front of the arms facing the floor. Take off the bottoming by removing all the old tacks and staples from the underside of the chair. Use your mallet and chisel, or a tack lifter if

TOOLS
Dust sheet
Mallet
Ripping chisel
Tack lifter
Staple remover
Pincers
Scissors

you prefer, for tack removal, or a staple remover and pincers if you are removing staples. Use your chisel along the grain of the wood to prevent splitting or knocking pieces out of the frame. Tuck the chisel under the tack, and hit it with the mallet so that the tack will lift out.

2 Remove the outside back cover by cutting the slip stitches around the outside edges, and remove all tacks and staples. Remove all fabric, hessian, scrim or ties from the outside back, and any materials tucked in and tacked to the rails; in fact, anything attached to the frame.

3 Turn the chair on its side and start removing fabric and materials from the outside arms then the inside arms in the same manner as the outside back. Cut any ties holding the materials. Lever off the front scrolls using a mallet and chisel, if they have been nailed on, or remove bolt fixings if this method was used. Keep the bolts in a safe place for later. Finish removing the arm fabrics and materials.

4 Remove all the stuffings and the old cover from the inside back.

5 Remove tacks and ties from the front border. The whole of the seat should now fall to the floor onto your dust sheet, leaving a bare frame.

BACK UPRIGHT RAIL

HEAD RAIL

INSIDE BACK RAIL

BACK RAIL

TOP ARM RAIL

BOTTOM ARM RAIL

SIDE RAIL

FRONT UPRIGHT RAIL

FRONT RAIL

WEBBING

Webbing is used for the base or foundation of a chair and it is most important to apply it properly. A strong seat depends on a good foundation with webbing that is spaced to support an even distribution of weight and the diameter of the springs used.

There are several types of webbing, all with individual uses. Use the best you can afford. English webbing, with a black and white herringbone weave, is the best quality, has the strongest construction and is recommended for all traditional upholstery. It is the best webbing for seats, but jute webbing can be used on backs and arms for economy.

TOOLS

Web stretcher
Magnetic hammer
Scissors

in a line close to the fold. Hammer in two more tacks towards the inner edge of the rail, spaced between the first ones, to form a 'W'. This arrangement of tacks will prevent the wood from splitting.

Seat

Every chair is webbed to suit the size and shape of its frame. On a seat, leave a gap of no more than three finger widths between each webbing. An average seat will take five webs each way. The seat may be webbed underneath the base rails when depth is needed for springs, or across the top of the rails when no springs are needed.

1 Turn the chair over and ensure it is supported. Mark the centre of the underside of the back rail.

2 Fold the end of the webbing over about 2.5 cm (1 in). Place it on the centre mark, just in from the edge of the rail. Hammer three 16 mm (5/8 in) improved tacks into the webbing

3 Bring the webbing to the centre of the front rail. Fold the webbing to make a loop and push it into the web stretcher. Put the peg through the loop. Hold the padded end of the web stretcher under the centre of the front rail. Keeping it against the frame, push the handle down until the webbing is drum tight.

WEBBING

Webbing is stretched over the frame to form a foundation to hold the springs and hessian in place. Various types of webbing are available, suitable for different applications.

1. BLACK AND WHITE ENGLISH WEBBING, 5 cm (2 in) wide, with a herringbone weave, is the strongest.
2. JUTE WEBBING, 5 cm (2 in) wide, a beige colour, is also strong. It is widely used on backs, arms and some seats.
3. PIRELLI WEBBING is a rubber webbing used as a flat spring on seats and backs. Clips or wire hooks fix the webbing to the chair frame, or it can be tacked in place. The standard size is 5 cm (2 in). This type of webbing makes a firm and resilient base for a seat cushion. Other makes of rubber webbing are also available.
POLYPROPYLENE WEBBING (not shown) can be found on modern items and is much cheaper than the other types.

EXPERT TIP

Use your webbing from the roll. Do not cut it into lengths as you will waste a piece every time you thread it through the web sretcher.

TACKS, GIMP PINS AND STAPLES

Tacks, gimp pins and staples are used to attach webbing, fabrics and trimmings to the frame of the furniture.

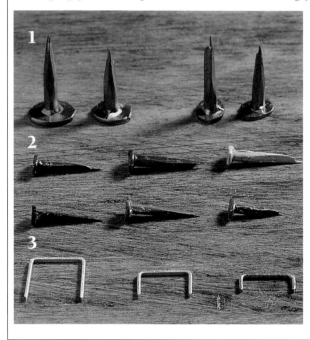

1. TACKS Fine tacks with a small head and improved tacks with a large head are used in traditional upholstery. Blued rough-cut tacks are most suitable as they hold the wood best and tend not to rust. The most useful sizes are 10 mm (³⁄₈ in) (improved for hessian and scrim and fine for calico and black bottom), 13 mm (¹⁄₂ in) (improved for webbing, and fine for temporary tacking and top fabric) and 16 mm (⁵⁄₈ in) (improved for webbing), all available in boxes of 500 g (1 lb).

2. GIMP PINS are available in many colours in 10 mm (³⁄₈ in) and 13 mm (¹⁄₂ in) sizes, and 16 mm (⁵⁄₈ in) in black only. They are small fine pins with a flat head, used for attaching gimp and braids, as well as for delicate areas where a tack would be too heavy. They are sold in boxes of 500 g (1 lb).

3. STAPLES are used with modern materials and inserted with a staple gun. They can also be used on delicate rebates where tacks would damage the wood and on fine fabrics to avoid pulling or splitting the threads. The most useful sizes are 8 mm (³⁄₈ in) (for covering scrolls), 10 mm (¹⁄₂ in) (for foam, calico, black bottom and top fabric) and 14 mm (⁵⁄₈ in) (for webbing), sold in boxes of 5000.

4 Temporary tack three tacks in a line on the webbing towards the front edge.

EXPERT TIP

If the frame is frail, use 13 mm (¹⁄₂ in) improved tacks instead of 16 mm (⁵⁄₈ in). A staple gun will often do less damage to the wood than tacks.

5 Tack home, then cut the webbing with 2.5 cm (1 in) to fold over. Tack home with two tacks, forming a 'W' formation.

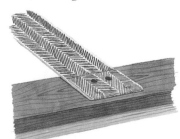

6 Position the next piece of webbing on the back rail, leaving a gap of 5 cm (2 in) or three finger widths. Fix the webbing with tacks as before and bring it forward, positioning it on the front rail, leaving a slightly larger gap than on the back one. This is because the front of a chair is usually wider and you need to space the webbing evenly on both rails, following the shape of the seat so that you do not end up with a gap between the front of the seat and the arm. Continue in this way until all the webs are in place from front to back.

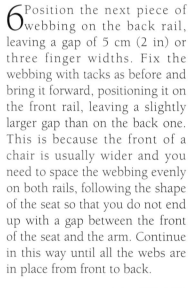

7 Before starting to web from side to side, work out the spacing required to hold the springs and provide support where it is needed. Then weave the webbing from the roll, taking it through the webs already there, under the first, over the next and so on. Do not fix the webbing at this stage so that it can be woven with ease. Then, leaving a gap between the web and the back rail, tack it in place across the frame. Repeat the same process with the next web, weaving it over and under alternative webs to start creating a basketweave pattern. Leaving a gap between it and the first web, fix it in position. Continue to complete webbing the seat.

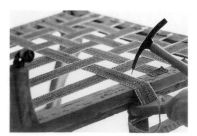

Arms

The inside arm is webbed to support the hessian and stuffings. The webbing folded in half near the inside back acts as an extra rail to which the upholstery materials and fabric can be sewn.

1 Fold the first webbing in half lengthways. Place the folded edge towards the back of the arm, to make a firm upright. Tack the raw edge flat to the bottom arm rail about 5 cm (2 in) in from the back, stretch the webbing up to the top arm rail and tack three tacks in a line. Cut off 2 cm (1 in) from the tacks, leaving a raw edge.

2 Place another unfolded length of webbing midway along the arm. Tack home in the same manner as on the seat. Add a final web 5 cm (2 in) from the front upright and tack in place. Repeat on the other arm.

Back

1 Place webbings across the inside back, positioning two close together in the lumbar region. Add one centrally just above arm level, one at the top just below the head rail and one exactly between these two.

2 Tack the first upright web in the centre of the inside back rail. To avoid distorting the contours of the chair, do not weave the webbing, but take it behind the existing webs. Stretch it around the front of the head rail and tack in place. Continue to web the inside back, keeping the webs evenly spaced and starting on each side of the centre web.

EXPERT TIP

For a more pronounced lumbar support, place the lower webs on the inside of the back and weave the upright webs under and over them basketweave fashion.

Temporary tacking

Tacks are hammered halfway into the frame to hold materials or fabric in place. They are easily removed when materials need re-tensioning, or can be tacked home.

Tacking home

The new tacks are hammered flat to the frame and the temporary tacks are removed.

SPRINGING

Having completed the webbing, you can now tackle the springing. Not all seating has to be sprung, but the springs add depth and comfort and are an important feature of traditional upholstery.

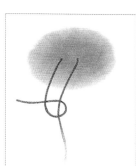

The springs form part of the foundation and need to be set in the correct way so that they do not buckle. The lashings that hold them to the frame play an important role in keeping them in the best position to absorb weight. The lashings hold the springs down around the sides of the frame, but allow the springs to form a slight dome in the middle of the seat. When sat on, all the springs are depressed to the same level and the weight is evenly distributed.

1 The seat is the only part that needs springs on this armchair, and in this case requires nine 9-gauge 17.5 cm (7 in) double-cone springs for a fairly firm seat.

| TOOLS |
| Chalk |
| Spring needle |
| Scissors |
| Hammer |

2 Place the springs in position on the webbing, facing the joints of the springs towards the centre. Put the front springs slightly wider apart to follow the contour of the seat. The two on the front outer edges, nearest the side and front rails, should be placed about 10 cm (4 in) away from the rails. Keep subsequent rows the same distance away from the side rails, following the frame contour. Leave a gap of about 15 cm (6 in) between the springs and the back rail to accommodate the stuffing on the inside back. Mark the spring positions with chalk so that you can remove them and sew them in individually.

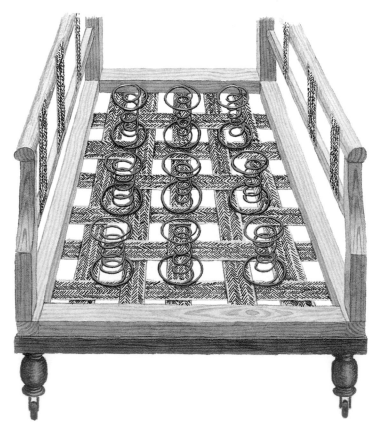

3 Stitch in the springs, starting with the front of the left back spring. Thread a spring needle with twine and, leaving a long end, push it from underneath the chair through the webbing. Take it around the bottom coil of the spring and back through the webbing again. Turn the chair over and make an upholsterer's slip knot. Then lock this knot off with a locking knot, which is simply a single knot, but used in conjunction with a slip or hitch knot to hold it secure. Turn the chair back the right way up.

4 Make a long stitch underneath the webbing and bring the needle back up through the webbing to the right side of the spring. Take the twine over the coil again and the needle back through the webbing. Make a single knot underneath, keeping a tight tension on the long stitch. The view in the next two illustrations shows the chair tipped up on its back legs.

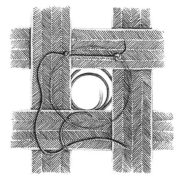

5 Continue the stitching and knotting process so there are four equally spaced knots to secure the first spring. Take the twine across to the middle spring on the back row. Repeat the process to secure this spring with only three equally spaced knots.

6 Continue this process, to finish the back row. Then work across the middle row and continue on to the front row. On every row, the side springs have

four knots and the middle springs just three knots. When you reach the last knot, tie it off underneath and secure with a locking knot. This method ensures that all the springs will remain securely held and will not slip out of position.

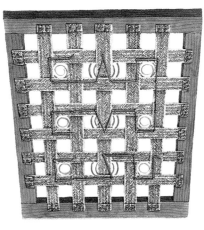

Lashing springs

1 Turn the chair onto its feet, ready to lash the springs down. Using a 16 mm (5/8 in) improved tack, place it at an angle, head facing out, in the centre of the back rail in line with the middle spring, and hammer it in halfway. Continue, placing a tack in line with each outer spring, and then repeat along the side and front rails.

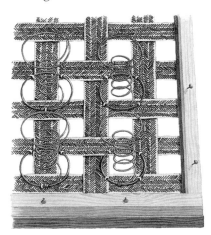

2 Measure off a length of laid cord to go from the front rail over the springs to the back rail, then double this length and cut. This allows enough cord to tie all the knots in this row.

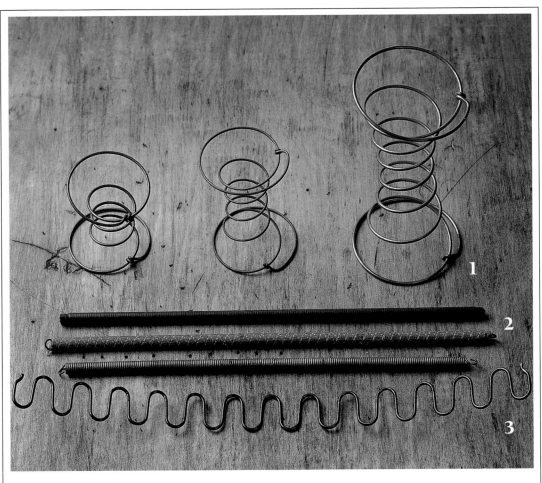

SPRINGS

Different types of springs are used for different types of chairs and sofas. Replace them with the same sort that were used in the original upholstery.

1. DOUBLE-CONE SPRINGS (waisted springs) These are available in various sizes, from 10 cm (4 in) to 32.5 cm (13 in) high and various gauges, depending on where the springs are to be used. Use the thickest, gauge 8 or 9, for seats, and a medium, gauge 10, for backs or seats. The thinnest springs, gauge 12 or 13, are used for backs and arms. Double-cone springs are used in traditional upholstery.

2. TENSION SPRINGS These consist of a long coil with a hook at each end that is usually slotted into a spring plate fitted to the side rails. They are used in modern upholstery.

3. SERPENTINE SPRINGS (zigzag or sinuous springs) These are cut to length and fixed with clips to the seat or back frame. They are used in modern upholstery.

MESH TOP SPRING UNITS (not shown) These spring units are made in average seat sizes from 45 x 50 x 45 cm (18 x 20 x 18 in) to 155 x 62.5 x 110 cm (62 x 25 x 44 in), depths 11.25 to 13.75 cm (4 1/2 in to 5 1/2 in), or can be made to measure. They make a good seat or back and are used with traditional materials.

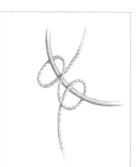

Hitch knot

Bring the cord over the top of the spring wire. Take it around underneath and back over the top of the wire. Wind it around underneath and over the wire again, taking the end through the second loop. Pull the knot tight. (See the photograph right.)

Half hitch knot

Bring the cord over the top of the spring wire. Take the end underneath the wire, over the cord and back under the wire. Pull the knot tight.

3 Starting at the back and working forward, tie a single knot around the tack on the centre back, leaving enough laid cord to return to the top of the spring later. Tie a locking knot at the tack, and then tack home.

4 Push the first spring down with your left hand until it feels firm when tested with the

other hand. Place the laid cord over the first coil, directly below the top of the spring, and tie a hitch knot. Release the spring and tie another hitch knot on the top coil on the opposite side of the spring.

5 Hold the centre spring down and, keeping it upright, tie the next hitch knot on the top coil. Take the cord across this spring and knot it on the other side.

6 Continue, lashing the cord to the front spring. Tie a hitch knot on the top coil and then tie one to the second coil on the opposite side.

7 Make sure the springs are upright, then tie a single knot around the tack already in place on the front of the frame and hammer it home. Return the

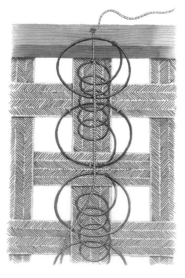

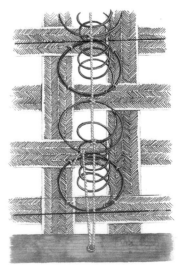

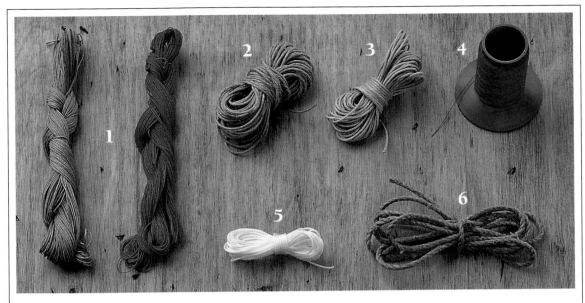

THREADS, TWINES AND CORDS

A variety of threads, twines and cords are used for stitching, making ties and lashing springs.

1. SLIPPING THREAD *Sold in skeins of 50 g (2 oz) in various colours. Used for hand sewing robust fabrics.*

2. UPHOLSTERY TWINE *Available in various thicknesses; no. 6, the thickest, and no. 3, a medium thickness, are most useful. This twine is used for bridle ties, stuffing ties and edge stitching. It is usually sold in 250 g (9 oz) balls. Choose a good-quality twine that runs smoothly.*

3. FLAX LINE TWINE *Not of such good quality, but is widely used for stitching. Sold in 250 g (9 oz) balls.*

4. BLENDED POLYESTER COTTON *Used mostly for machine sewing, but also for hand sewing fine fabrics. A medium-gauge strong thread is available in many colours, in 700 m (750 yd) and 4000 m (4375 yd) spools.*

5. NYLON BUTTONING TWINE *A very strong white twisted twine most suitable for buttoning, but sometimes used for stitching.*

6. LAID CORD (lacing cord) *Used for lashing down the double-cone springs in traditional upholstery. It is very strong and is sold in balls of 500 g (18 oz).*

CLEAR NYLON MACHINE SEWING THREAD *(not shown) This is used as an 'invisible' thread. Natural-coloured thread can also be used on lighter work.*

Locking or single knot

Take the end of the twine and loop it over itself at the base of the previous knot. Take the end through the loop and pull the knot tight.

cord to the top coil of the spring and, pulling the spring down a fraction, knot the cord off with a half hitch and a locking knot. Repeat this technique on the back spring.

8 Repeat this process on the other two rows, back to front, then lash from side to side. Where the laid cords cross each other on the top of the spring, twist the cord over the existing cord to hold it.

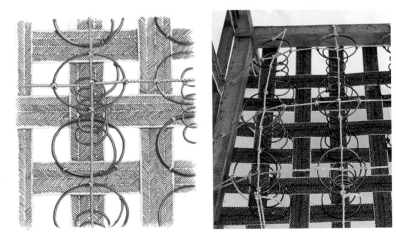

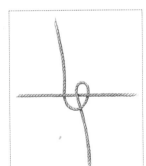

Holding twist

To hold one cord in position as it crosses another (see step 8), take it over and around the existing cord, pull tight and continue lashing.

HESSIAN

Hessian is the covering cloth that holds the stuffings in place and it is part of the foundation of every piece of upholstery. Without it, the stuffing on this chair would fall into the springs.

Hessian also holds the stuffings in position where no springs are required on a chair, either on a wooden base or over webbing.

Always use a good-quality hessian. One of poor quality will tend to be weak and is nearly always the reason for the collapse of the upholstery.

TOOLS

Scissors
Magnetic hammer
Circular needle
Spring needle

Seat

1 Measure and note down the measurements from the back to the front rail over the springs, adding 10 cm (4 in) extra for turnings. Then measure from one side rail to the other, again over the springs and adding the allowance for turnings.

2 Cut a piece of heavy hessian, of at least 340 g (12 oz) in weight, to size. Place the hessian over the springs. Making sure that the grain lines, or warp and weft threads, are square to the seat frame, temporary tack the hessian at the centre point of the back, front and side rails.

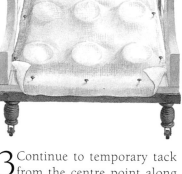

3 Continue to temporary tack from the centre point along each of the rails. When the hessian is square and taut, tack home. When you reach a corner, fold the hessian back from the upright symmetrically across the corner. Cut into the hessian from the corner of the cloth to the inner corner of the upright. Trim off the excess, leaving a 2 cm (3/4 in) turning allowance. Repeat at each corner.

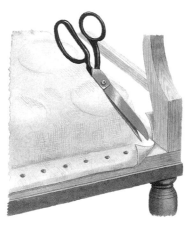

4 Fold the raw edges of the hessian back over themselves along each rail and tack down between the first tacks. Leave the raw edges showing. At the corners, fold the allowance away from the upright and tack down.

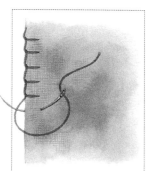

Blanket stitch

Secure the twine and bring it out on the edge of the fabric. Make a 1 cm (1/2 in) stitch, 1 cm (1/2 in) to the left. Take the thread around the back of the needle. Pull the needle through and proceed to the next stitch.

HESSIAN

Hessian is a loosely woven cloth that looks like sacking and is made from jute. It is used for the foundations of upholstery, holding the stuffings in place. The most frequently used weights are 285 g (10 oz) and 340 g (12 oz), in widths of 90 cm (36 in) and 180 cm (72 in). A heavier-weight tarpaulin (usually called 'tarp' by upholsterers and also known as spring canvas) is used over the springs.

Arms

1 The hessian covers the gap between the top and bottom arm rails, providing support over the webbing for the stuffing. Note the measurements for the inside arms from the top to bottom arm rail, adding 10 cm (4 in) for turnings. Measure from the folded webbing at the back to the front upright rail, adding a turning allowance.

2 Temporary tack the hessian at the centre of each rail and upright. Continue to temporary tack in place, leaving the back edge along the half webbing unsecured. When the hessian is positioned squarely, tack home.

3 Turn the edges over as on the seat and tack to each rail. On the back edge, pin the hessian to the folded edge of webbing. Using a circular needle and twine, blanket stitch the hessian along the edge of the webbing. Repeat on the other arm.

Back

1 Here the hessian supports the stuffing on the inside back. Note down the measurements from the back of the head rail to the inside back rail, adding 10 cm (4 in) extra for turnings. Then measure from one back upright to the other, adding an allowance for turnings. Tack the hessian to

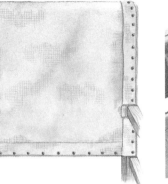

the inside back using exactly the same method as for the seat and cutting around the top arm rails.

Stitching in springs

Stitch the springs in place through the hessian, using a spring needle and twine. Use the same method and pattern as when the springs were stitched to the webbing.

BRIDLE TIES

These ties are now stitched into the hessian to form overlapping loops that hold the fibre as a continuous mass without leaving any gaps. They can also be adjusted to vary the depth of stuffing as required.

Bridle ties are now sewn into the inside arms, inside back and seat. A border of scrim panels is constructed around the inside back, also in preparation for the first stuffing. Bridle ties are also sewn into the centre panel of the inside back while this is accessible, but these are not used until later for the second stuffing.

TOOLS

Double-ended needle
Circular needle
Scissors
Magnetic hammer
Skewers
Marking pen

SCRIM

Scrim is a similar material to hessian, but has a finer thread and a looser weave and is made from linen thread or jute. Used to mould the first stuffing and stitched edges on traditional upholstery, it is much stronger than it looks. It is available in a width of 180 cm (72 in).

Arms

1 Thread a spring needle with a length of twine long enough to complete all the ties on one of the arms. Start at the top of the inside arm, close to the folded webbing, with an upholsterer's slip knot and a locking knot. Working from left to right, push the needle through the hessian 10–15 cm (4–6 in) to the right of the start to make a long loop on the inside arm. Bring the needle back out 2.5–5 cm (1–2 in) to the left, making a short backstitch. Leave some slack in the long stitch to allow for the stuffing later.

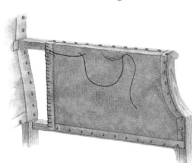

2 Continue in this way to the end of the top row, take one long stitch straight downwards and sew a second row midway along the arm. Take another stitch down and make a final

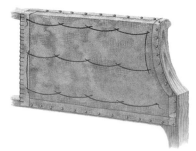

row of ties. Finish securely at the front upright end with two locking knots. Repeat on the other arm, starting from the front upright end.

3 Make a series of tack ties (bridle ties secured with tacks) along the top arm rail. Place pairs of 10 mm (3/8 in) improved tacks along the top of the rail, so each pair is on a slight diagonal. Place the tacks at similar intervals as the ties on the inside arm. Secure the first end of twine to the second tack from the back with a single knot and tack home. Repeat on the tack behind. Bring the twine to the next pair of tacks and tie it to the front one, leaving enough slack to stuff later. Tack home. Tie the twine to the tack behind as before. Continue to the end of the rail, then repeat on the second arm.

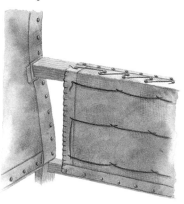

4 Place tack ties along the front upright rail, with the loops closer together. Start under the outside edge of the scroll and work down to the bottom of the front edge. Repeat the process on the second upright.

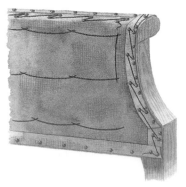

Inside back

1 Mark a central box on the hessian on the inside back. First, draw a horizontal line across the width of the inside back immediately below the curve of the back scrolls. Draw a horizontal line across the top of the lumbar region, about 5 cm (2 in) below the frame line of the arms. Then draw a vertical line down each side, a quarter of the way in from each edge, thus completing the central box and creating a border of panels around it.

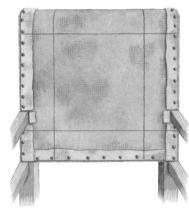

2 Measure for two lengths of scrim for the side panels, from the top line to the bottom line, adding turning allowances. Measure for the top panel of scrim from the top line over the back to the head rail and from one side to the other, around the edges to the back of the uprights. Measure for the bottom panel of scrim from the bottom line to the base of the back rail and then from side to side as before.

3 Cut four pieces of scrim, allowing for double the width measured on each panel. This allows enough to cover the first stuffing and turn under on the edges, ready to tack off.

4 Fold over the long edge of a side piece of scrim about 4 cm (1½ in), and lay the folded edge of the scrim on one of the vertical lines on the hessian with the main

bulk of the scrim temporarily over the central panel.

5 Backstitch the scrim to the hessian, from the top to the bottom corners of the box, using twine in a circular needle. Start by securing the twine and making the first stitch. Take the needle through to the back and bring it out again one stitch length ahead of the previous one. Take the needle through to the back at the end of the previous stitch. Repeat this process so that the stitches form a continuous straight line. Fold the scrim back over the side panel.

6 Repeat this process on the other side panel. Then repeat on the top and bottom panels, sewing through the hessian from one corner of the box to the other and then continuing to backstitch them to the loose ends of the side panels.

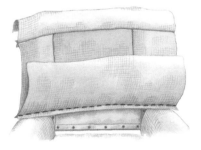

7 Pin the scrim panels into the middle of the centre box with a skewer to keep them out of the way and leave at this stage.

8 Make a series of bridle ties in the hessian on the top, side and bottom panels in the same manner as for the arms. Start at the top and work across the back, inserting rows of bridle ties approximately 15 cm (6 in) apart. Then work down each side and across the bottom panel in the same way. If you have to join the twine, do this by finishing off and restarting, but make sure the loops overlap.

9 Take out the skewer and fold the scrim back over the outer edges of the chair. Now work on the centre panel and stitch in four rows of bridle ties with continuous twine, starting at the top left corner.

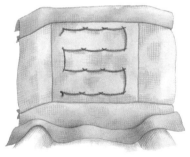

10 Skewer the scrim out of the way again and work on the back uprights. Place tack ties along one upright, starting under the back edge of the scroll and working down to where the upright meets the bottom arm rail, in the same way as for the front uprights. Repeat on the other side.

Seat

Stitch bridle ties through the hessian. Start at the front edge and work towards the back, using continuous twine and spacing the ties as on other sections.

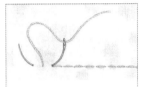

Backstitch

Working from right to left, make a stitch, pulling the needle through. Make the next stitch twice as long, starting at the end of the previous one. Repeat to produce a continuous row of stitches.

EXPERT TIP

Make sure you have cut the scrim to the thread, that is, between two threads along the warp. This makes it much easier to keep your sewing lines straight and the tension correct.

SECURING THE FIRST STUFFING

The first stuffing is the main padding, giving shape and comfort to the chair. Fibre is used to provide this firm base and the strands need to be teased and separated to take out knots and tangles so the fibre can be stuffed under the bridle ties to give it an even density.

If the first stuffing is done well, the next stage of covering in scrim will be more successful. Stuffing ties are then stitched in to hold the stuffing and scrim in place.

TOOLS
Hammer
Scissors
Double-ended needle
Regulator

Inside arms

1 Start with the arms as these are more accessible before the back or seat are padded. Weigh out two equal amounts of fibre into bags and use one for each arm. This should help you to keep both arms the same size.

2 Start stuffing fibre under the bridle ties on the inside arms

from the bottom arm rail upwards. Tease the fibre with your fingers so that any knots or lumps can be discarded. Taking a handful of fibre at a time, push it under the ties and tease it out. Stuff the fibre across in rows, making sure there are no gaps.

3 Start on the second row and tease the fibre down to the row below as well as making sure there are no gaps between them.

4 Bring the second arm up to the same level and then continue to fill both inside arms, working them in tandem to make sure they match.

5 Stuff the fibre under the tack ties along the top of the arm and around the front edge of the arm. When the stuffing has been completed, it should look much too bulky to fit because it will all be pulled in by the scrim and you may in fact have to add more before you are ready to stitch.

6 Take measurements for enough scrim to cover the inside arm, from the front to the back upright and from the bottom arm rail to the outside of the top arm rail. Then add an extra 15 cm (6 in) all around.

7 Cut two identical lengths of scrim and place a piece on one of the inside arms, making sure that the weave of the cloth runs straight to the frame.

8 Temporary tack the scrim on the outside of the bottom arm rail, then pull through the side

FIBRE AND COIR

Fibre and coir are used for the first stuffing and, when compacted, they make a thick padding.

FIBRE Black dyed fibre has long curly strands and is fairly coarse. It usually needs teasing out as it is inclined to have tangled lumps in it. Used mainly for first stuffing as it makes a very hard edge.

COIR Made from coconut husks, it is ginger in colour. Coir can also be used as a first stuffing.

gap to the inside arm. Ease the scrim up and around the stuffing over the top of the arm to the underside of the top arm rail.

Stuffing ties

1 Stitch stuffing ties right through the arm using upholsterer's twine and a double-ended needle. Start with an upholsterer's slip knot and a locking knot at the back of the arm nearest to the inside back. Working towards the front scroll, make a row of straight stitches approximately 3 cm (1¼ in) long on the outside arm and 15 cm (6 in) on the inside arm, stitching straight through the arm. Continue down and complete a second row below.

2 Pull the twine until the stuffing ties are holding the stuffing in place, but not too tight. Tie off with a temporary knot—instead of locking the knot, leave it as a loop so that it can be easily undone and tightened later.

3 Tuck the scrim under the fibre around the front scroll and down the front upright. Temporary tack all around.

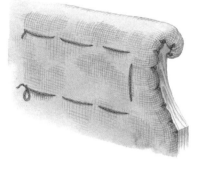

4 Ease the scrim towards the back of the arm. Cut into the scrim where it meets the top arm rail to allow it to be pulled through. Turn the edge under and stitch to the webbing.

5 Cut into the scrim again to allow it to spread around the back upright rail. Add more fibre under the scrim to keep a good shape here. Turn the edge of the scrim under so it does not fray, and tack down to the back upright rail using 10 mm (³⁄₈ in) improved tacks.

6 Take out the temporary tacks from the bottom arm rail. Turn the edge of the scrim under so it does not fray, and tack down.

7 Now start to work along underneath the top arm rail. As you take the temporary tacks out, add as much fibre as necessary to make a consistent and well-rounded shape, turn the edge of the scrim under and tack home new tacks along the rail as you work the stuffing in.

8 Smooth the scrim towards the front uprights and take out the temporary tacks. Add extra fibre to make the front of the arm firm. Check that the weave is running straight along the arm before continuing. Temporary tack back in place.

9 When you have fully stuffed the arms, stitch stuffing ties along the outside edge of the arm, pushing the needle in from the top and taking the stitches through the upholstery to the underside of the arm.

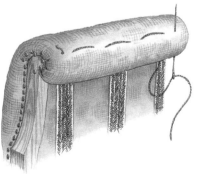

10 Now finish around the front upright. Starting at the centre top of the scroll and

EXPERT TIP
You may find it easier to alternate the stuffing so that you work on both arms at the same time. Make sure you use the same amount of stuffing for each arm, so if you run out of fibre, replenish with equal quantities.

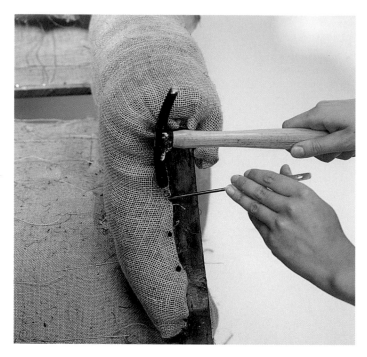

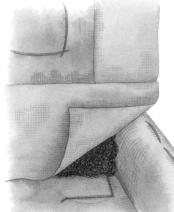

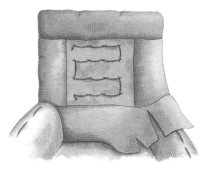

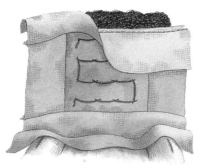

6 Stitch stuffing ties along the top edge of the back, as on the arms, to hold the fibre in place.

Seat

1 Return to the seat and stuff fibre under the bridle ties. Make sure that you use enough fibre to create a slight dome in the centre of the seat and to make a firm edge at the front. Cut a piece of scrim to cover right over the stuffing with enough to tack down along all the base rails.

2 Cover the seat with the scrim, ensuring that the weave of the cloth is straight to the frame. Cut the scrim in towards the upright rails, to allow it to be pulled down around the seat. Pull the scrim through and tack off on the side and back rails.

3 Pull the scrim over the front edge and, keeping the weave straight along the rail, tuck the raw edge under. Tack down all along the rail, keeping the tacks quite close together. The chair is now ready to have the stuffing moulded into firm stitched edges.

3 Pull the scrim on each side panel over the fibre. Tack off the scrim along each back upright in the same way as on the arm rails, adding extra fibre as necessary.

removing the temporary tacks as you work, pleat the scrim evenly around the scroll, using a regulator to hold it in place while tacking the edge under. Place the new tacks close together around the scroll and continue to secure the scrim down the upright.

11 Tack home all temporary tacks before going on.

Inside back

1 Stuff fibre under the bridle ties in the top panel on the inside back.

2 Stuff fibre under the bridle ties in each side panel and under tack ties around the scrolls and down the uprights. Stuff the bottom panel particularly well and firmly, to create a lumbar panel. Leave the centre panel empty.

4 Pull the top panel of scrim over the fibre and, adding more fibre to make a rounded contour, tack off across the head rail. Pleat the scrim around the top of the scrolls and tack off as on the front scrolls.

5 Make cuts in the bottom panel of scrim and the top and base of the arms, matching the cuts previously made in the scrim on the arms. Pull the scrim through the gap at each side, and tack home on the back upright rails. Check that there is enough stuffing in the lumbar panel and then pull the scrim through to the back and tack home on the top of the inside back rail.

STITCHED EDGES

Stitching edges is one area of upholstery that takes a bit of practice to achieve a good result. It is one of the most important techniques because it moulds and makes firm edges, improving wearability and defining the contours of the furniture.

After some experience, you will begin to feel if the edge is hard enough. First practise stitched edges on a small project, such as the Victorian dining chair (see page 174).

Two stitches are used to build up the edges. Blind stitching brings the stuffing towards the edge to make a firm wall. Top stitching pulls the stuffing right into the top edge to make a hard

TOOLS
Double-ended needle
Regulator
Scissors

roll. The amount of stitching used depends on the depth or width you wish to create. A seat, being quite deep, usually takes two or three rows of blind stitch and two rows of top stitch. Back scrolls are usually quite small across with one row of blind stitch and one row of top stitch, whereas wider front scrolls would have two rows of blind stitch and one row of top stitch.

Blind stitching

1 Before beginning to stitch, regulate the stuffing so that it is evenly distributed along the edge. Hold the scrim on the top and halfway down the side, between the thumb and fingers, and feel the regulator pulling the stuffing towards the edge. The edge should feel solidly packed and the stuffing evenly distributed.

2 Thread a double-ended needle with twine. Start at the left end just above the tack line. Push the needle upwards at an angle so the point comes out on the top surface, 10 cm (4 in) from the front edge. Pull the needle through until the threaded end is 13 mm (1/2 in) below the surface.

3 Return the needle so the threaded end comes out just above the tack line, 2 cm (3/4 in) to the left. Pull the needle right out and push

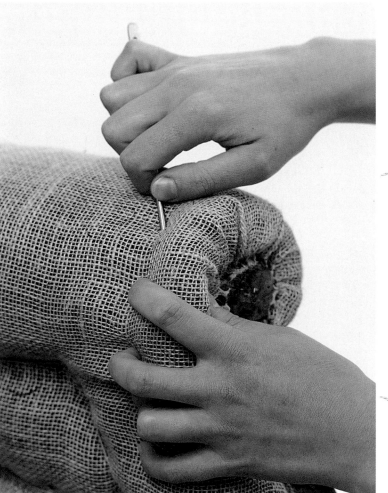

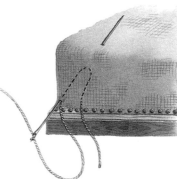

EXPERT TIP

Before you start stitching an edge, you must be sure there is enough stuffing in it. Your hand makes the perfect gauge. Make a right angle between your thumb and fingers. Run the flat of your hand along the top of the edge and your thumb along the front. If the stuffing sits hard into the right angle, there is enough. If not, more needs to be added or regulated to the front edge.

it temporarily into the top surface to keep it safe. Tie an upholsterer's slip knot with the two ends of twine and finish with a locking knot.

4 Now make a row of blind stitches. Move along 4 cm (1½ in) and push the needle in again, moving it slightly to the left so that it grabs the fibre. As before, do not pull the needle right out.

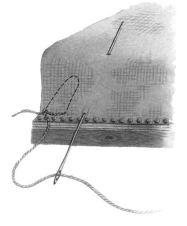

5 Push the threaded end of the needle back down to come out just above the tack line in the centre of the last stitch. Pull the needle halfway out and lay the twine over the needle with the right hand. Turn the twine around the needle three times.

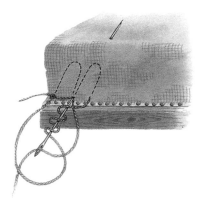

6 Now pull the needle right out and the twine through the loops. Push the needle into the top surface for safety. Wind the twine firmly around your hand. Pull it first to the left and then to

the right until the knot tightens, the stitch locks and the fibre is pulled down.

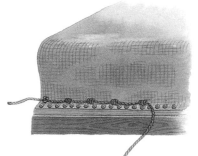

7 Continue stitching until you have worked along the whole edge. Fasten off by turning one end of the loop of twine once around the needle as normal, once in the opposite direction with the other end of the twine, then once again as normal. Pull the twine tight and lock off.

Top stitching

1 Make the top stitches as for blind stitch, but when the needle is pushed up from the front wall pull it right out at the top surface.

2 Make a visible stitch on the top surface by taking the threaded end of the needle back down about 2 cm (¾ in) to the left, and bringing it out on the front wall in the centre of the stitch.

3 Proceed as for blind stitch, but continue to make a row of stitches on the top as well as the front wall.

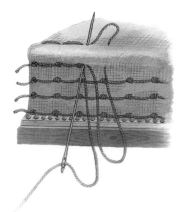

Seat

1 Regulate the stuffing in the front edge of the seat, keeping an even line.

2 Sew three rows of blind stitch along the front edge, starting just above the tack line on the front rail and spacing the rows evenly upwards to build up a firm wall.

3 Stitch a row of top stitches about 6 cm (2½ in) from the edge to form a hard roll.

Inside arms

1 Regulate the stuffing towards the front edge of the arm around the upright.

2 Stitch two rows of blind stitches around the front edge of the arm to form the scroll in the same manner as the front edge of the seat.

3 Stitch a row of top stitches about 6 cm (2½ in) from the edge to form a hard roll.

4 Repeat the processes on the second arm, checking as you stitch that the end is building up in the same way to create a shape identical to the first arm.

Inside back

Make stitched edges around the back uprights and scrolls in the same way as on the arms.

SECOND STUFFING

Hair is now used as the traditional second stuffing over the scrim on this chair, ready to create a soft and springy padding under the calico.

Hair stays in place well and is more springy and resilient than fibre. You must use skin wadding on top of the calico to prevent the hair working through. There are other materials that can be used instead of hair that are often well suited to other types of furniture, as you will see in the projects that follow.

3 Add extra hair in the places where you expect most wear. Now go to the next section of the book and fit the calico to the inside arms straight away so the hair is not displaced.

Inside arms

1 Place another set of bridle ties in the scrim on the arms, in rows across as before.

2 Tease the hair between your fingers and, working across the rows, place the hair under the bridle ties to form an even mat.

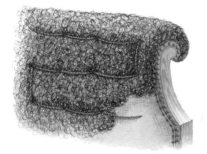

Inside back

1 Return to the inside back and stitch further bridle ties in the outer panels of scrim, in rows across as before.

2 Fill the whole inside back with hair, including the central panel. Stuff the central panel so it stands well forward in relation to the outer panels. Now go to the next section and fit the calico and prepare for the buttoning on the inside back.

Seat

Now return to work on the seat. Stitch further bridle ties in the scrim on the seat, in four rows, evenly spaced starting 5 cm (2 in) from the front edge. You are now ready to cover the chair in calico.

HAIR

Horsehair remains unsurpassed as a second stuffing for traditional upholstery, although it is rather expensive. Good-quality horsehair is long and curled specially, so it holds the stitches well and makes an excellent soft, but resilient, padding. You can reuse old horsehair if it is clean and in good condition, but it must be teased out well.

A mixture of other animal hairs is a modern alternative, but the hairs are short and tend to come up through the top cover more easily than horsehair.

Skin waddings must be used with all hair stuffings to prevent the strands coming up through to the top cover.

CALICO AND PLATFORM CLOTH

Calico is used over the second stuffing to hold it in place and platform cloth is used as a platform for a seat cushion, covering tension springs.

CALICO A cotton fabric, usually unbleached, available in various weights and in widths of 90 cm (36 in), 135 cm (54 in) and 180 cm (72 in). Used to cover and mould the stuffing to shape, prior to top covering. A good-quality heavy calico can also be used as a top cover under loose covers.

PLATFORM CLOTH A cotton made in plain colours. The best type is a twill weave as it is strong, but medium-weight cotton lining is mostly used. It is available in widths of 120 cm (48 in) and 135 cm (54 in). It is used as a platform under a seat cushion, over tension springs.

FITTING CALICO

The working of calico fabric over the stuffing is a very important technique in upholstery because it moulds the final shape. The calico is placed and fitted to each part of the chair as soon as the second stuffing is in place, so that the hair is not displaced.

The final shape of the chair is moulded at this stage, and extra hair may be added to give the chair a good contour.

The arms are the first part of the chair to be ready to cover in calico as described in this section. When the arms are covered, return to the inside back to start its second stuffing. Then cover it in calico and start the buttoning process as explained in the next section. After that, the back may require additional stuffing with hair, especially where the arms come to meet it to ensure they fit snugly together. Finally, give the seat its second stuffing and then cover it in calico as described at the end of the next section.

Use a good-quality calico that is closely woven, but not too heavy. A thin calico will not hold the stuffing, and may tear.

Arms

1 Measure the calico for the arms, from underneath the top of the arm rail over the stuffed arm down to the bottom arm rail, and the length along the outside of the arm from the back upright rail over the front to the scroll. Add extra cloth for handling and then cut two identical pieces.

2 Temporary tack the calico in place to establish its basic position, starting with a few tacks along the back of the bottom arm rail. Pull the calico up over the inside arm towards

TOOLS
Hammer
Scissors
Skewers
Circular needle

the top arm rail, using one hand to pull and the other one to smooth and push. Make sure the weave of the calico is straight to the frame. Now temporary tack underneath the top arm rail, placing one tack in the centre and one at each end of the rail.

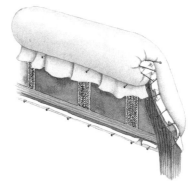

3 Pull the calico towards the back of the arm, push it through the gap between the arm and the inside back, and temporary tack it to the back upright rail. Then smooth the calico towards the front of the arm and secure it with skewers around the scroll to the stitched edge just under the roll made by the stitching.

4 Now the calico can be fitted more accurately. Release it from the back upright rail and return to temporary tacking along the bottom arm rail, starting at the front. When you reach the back upright rail, cut the calico in towards the rail with a 'Y'-shaped cut. Push the calico back through the gap between the inside back

and the arm. Finish temporary tacking to the bottom arm rail and skewer the calico temporarily to the folded webbing. Tack all the tacks home.

5 Return to temporary tacking all along the top arm rail, starting at the front. When you reach the back, make several straight cuts in towards the back upright rail. When you are satisfied the calico lies smoothly, tack home to the end of the arm rail and on to the back upright.

6 Return to the front of the arm. Pleat the calico around the front scroll and secure it with skewers again. (If you want a gathered rather than a pleated effect, run a line of straight stitches in slipping thread around the calico from where the scroll starts to curve on the inside arm to where the curve stops as it meets the outside arm. Place a temporary tack at each end and

gather the calico up between the two points.) Continue to secure the calico with skewers right down the stitched edge and temporary tack the bottom corner on the front upright.

7 Using a large circular needle, threaded with twine, stitch a row of blind stitch around the front edge of the arm, stitching through the calico along the line of the blind stitch in the scrim.

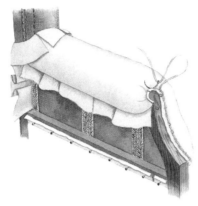

8 Trim the calico at the back of the arm, leaving a generous turning. Turn the calico under so it meets the inside back and then leave it so it can be adjusted after the back is stuffed.

9 Tack the calico securely to the front upright at the bottom of the stitched edge. Trim off the excess calico from all around the arm.

10 Repeat all these processes on the second arm, making sure its shape looks identical to the first arm.

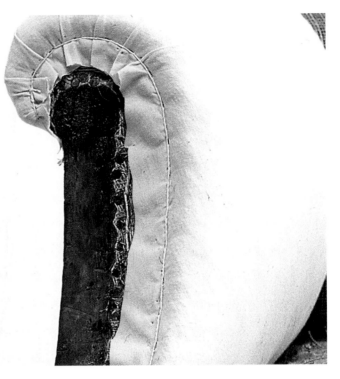

Straight cut

To allow cloth to go in different directions, such as around a side rail and a back upright, make a straight cut to the point where two rails meet.

'T' cut

To allow cloth to spread around two sides of a rail, fold it back on itself diagonally across the corner, lining the fold up close to the rail. Make a straight cut to the corner edge of the rail. Fold the cloth under or pull down around the rail.

'Y' cut

To fit cloth around three sides of a rail, fold it back on itself so the fold butts the rail. Make a straight cut towards the centre of the rail, stopping 2.5 cm (1 in) short. Cut to each side edge of the rail. Turn the centre flap of cloth under and take the two sides around the rail.

DEEP BUTTONING IN CALICO

Deep-buttoned backs are nearly always the first thing a student wants to do and it is one of the hardest techniques to learn, so if you wish to end up with a firm, evenly spaced deep-buttoned back on your favourite armchair, make sure you practise on a smaller and simpler project first.

The perfect button back is achieved by getting everything in place at the calico stage. You can make sure that the stuffing is firm and the buttons evenly spaced while still working in the cheap calico. Then the process of buttoning in the expensive top fabric will be much easier.

Inside back

1 Mark the button positions on the webbing on the outside back, which gives the button ties a firmer anchor. Mark a vertical line down the centre of the outside back and three lines on either side at equal intervals. Mark the first horizontal line just below the back scroll, and the bottom line just above the lumbar panel. Space another two at equal distances between them.

EXPERT TIP

If the diamond-shaped pad formed between the buttons is not very firm, add more hair before pulling the twine up tight.

TOOLS
Hammer
Scissors
Double-ended needle
Circular needle
Marking pen
Tape measure
Metre stick
Regulator

2 Mark the button positions in a diamond pattern, four on the top row, three on the second and so on.

3 Push a regulator from the back, through the marks and the stuffing. Part the stuffing around the point of the regulator to make a hole in the inside back.

4 Measure for the calico with a tape measure, from under the head rail, over the top of the stuffing into the first hole, then over the stuffing to the other holes, continuing on to measure over the lumbar panel and down underneath the back base rail. Measure across in the same manner, allowing extra to be sewn on the back scrolls.

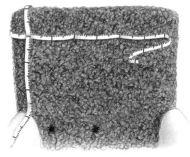

5 Cut a piece of calico to this basic size, allowing 10 cm (4 in) all around for handling.

6 Mark the button pattern on the calico. The basic pattern is as on the outside back, but extra calico needs to be allowed between the buttons to go over the stuffing. Take measurements for the distance between button holes by pushing a tape measure into the hole in the stuffing on the inside back until it reaches the back hessian and measuring down to the base of the next hole the same way. Take measurements between the button holes vertically and horizontally, and mark them out on the centre of the calico. Record the measurements to use on the top cover.

7 Place the calico over the inside back, matching up the marks and the holes. Thread a double-ended needle with button twine, and push it in through the mark for the bottom centre button on the outside back and out through the corresponding mark on the calico. Make a small stitch and take the needle back through to the outside back. Tuck a small roll of calico under the stitch on the inside back to prevent the stitch splitting the calico, pull the two ends of twine at the back and make an upholsterer's slip knot. Place a small roll of calico under this and pull the twine until it just holds the two rolls in place.

8 Repeat this process by working on the button position diagonally right on the next row up, then diagonally down to the right one on the bottom row, forming a half diamond shape.

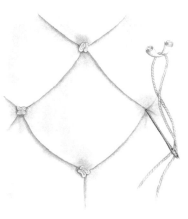

9 Work on the left side in the same manner, forming the first and second rows. Continue this process, row by row, until you reach the top.

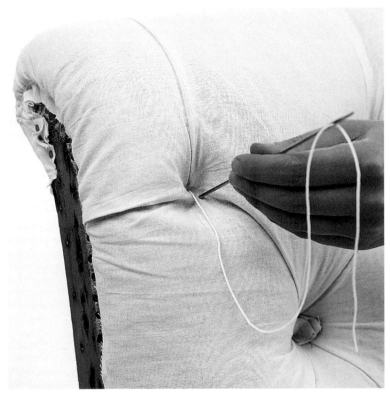

along each upright and around the scroll.

15 Cut the calico into the bottom arm rails where they meet the back upright rails. Push the rest of the bottom edge of the calico down behind the seat and finish temporary tacking along the inside back rail.

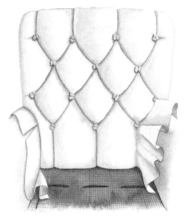

10 Using the blade of the regulator, ease in the folds formed in the calico between each button as you go. Arrange the folds so that they all face towards the seat.

16 Cut the calico into the top arm rails where they meet the back upright rails. Push the calico through to the back and temporary tack it to the back uprights.

17 Check if the buttoning is firm and all the pleats are straight, then tack off the calico all around.

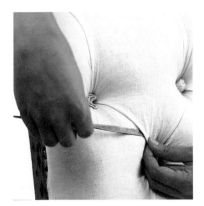

11 From the top button positions, fold the calico over the top of the back, forming four pleats, two facing left and two facing right. Temporary tack under the head rail.

12 Lift up the calico and part the stuffing in the lumbar panel in lines down from the bottom row of buttons.

13 Lay the calico back over the stuffing and pull the calico through under the inside back rail, and temporary tack as much as possible to the top of the rail, pleating the excess calico in a straight line from the button marks. Add more hair at this point to make the lumbar panel firm.

14 Fit the calico around the back scrolls in the same manner as the front scrolls, pleating it in a straight line from each button mark to the nearest scroll. Secure with skewers and stitch a row of blind stitch in place with a circular needle

Seat

1 Return to the seat to give it a second stuffing. Place the hair under the bridle ties after teasing it. Make a firm mat right across the seat, adding extra to the centre so that it is slightly domed. The hair should be high enough to meet the arms and back once the calico has been pulled down, so add enough hair to allow for this.

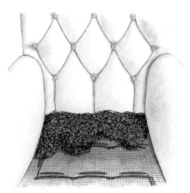

2 Measure and cut a piece of calico large enough to tack on to the back and side rails and over the front edge, allowing a handling allowance of 10 cm (4 in) all around. Place the calico over the seat, push under the back and temporary tack to the back rail, making cuts into the back corners to allow the calico to fit around the rails.

3 Push the calico through each side, cutting into the front corner to allow the calico to pass through. Temporary tack to the top of the bottom arm rails.

4 Pull the calico over the front edge of the seat, keeping the grain of the cloth straight. Skewer in place, keeping it taut from back to front and sideways along the front edge.

5 Stitch one row of blind stitch with twine under the front edge. Fold the calico under at each side to form a neat square corner, adding more hair to pad the corner firmly if necessary.

6 Start to tack home on the back rail. Then, working them in tandem, tack off on both bottom arm rails. Pull the calico taut as you work. Trim off all the excess calico.

ASSESSING YOUR UPHOLSTERY

Now the stuffing and stitching of the basic foundation of upholstery, moulded in place by the calico, is finished. If there are any problems with the upholstery, such as stuffing that is too soft or edges that are badly stitched, they will show up now. So this is the very best time to examine your work minutely and make any alterations necessary. It is better to do extra work now than to make expensive mistakes by cutting the top fabric too soon.

Most beginners to upholstery cannot wait to get to this stage because they think that all the hard work is over and they are anxious to start top covering. But stop, and take a good look at your piece of furniture when it is covered in calico to make sure everything is as it should be before rushing on to the top cover.

CHECK the following points and if any problems do show up, address them now. Either tighten up the calico or rectify the underlying upholstery, so that the top cover can be applied with ease and look professional.

• Is the upholstery comfortable? The best way to answer this is to sit down and test it out.

• Are the padded areas firm enough? Examine the seat when you get up again and look to see if the calico has stretched, leaving a dent in the middle.

• If you sit back in the chair and rest your arms, does this leave dents in the back or on the arms?

• Are the lines of the upholstery clean? Check that the shape is symmetrical and that the edges are firmly stuffed.

CHOOSING TOP FABRIC

Now that all the upholstery foundation is in place, you can start 'putting the icing on the cake' and choose the top cover. Most people find this is the most exciting part of upholstery as the finished piece of furniture emerges and you reap the reward for all your time and effort.

The colour, pattern and texture of the fabric you choose will give the furniture much of its character and influence the impact it has on its surroundings.

However, it is important to make the right choice of fabric if the project is to be successful and good value for money. So, it is worth investing some more time in making the following considerations. Remember, you will have to live with your choice.

What to look for

Make sure you buy a fabric that is of a suitable weight for upholstery. Look at the manufacturer's recommendations and do not be afraid to ask for advice if you are not sure of suitability. You will find that upholsterers and fabric retailers, through their experience, will know which fabrics wear well and which types of fabric are suitable for the sort of furniture you have.

Ultimately, the decision is yours, however, so do not commit yourself until you are sure.

Basic considerations

Consider the use and location of the upholstered item before you buy the fabric, and whether it will have light or heavy wear. For instance, it is certainly not a good idea to cover a chair in white cotton satin if it is intended for use in the children's room.

Fabrics are subject to safety standards, for example British regulations require that all top covers for upholstery must be fire retardant, unless the furniture pre-dates 1950. Furniture either made or reupholstered after this date has to comply with the regulations. This means that most of the exempt furniture is traditionally upholstered. A professional upholsterer will follow legal requirements, but, if you are upholstering the piece yourself, the onus is on you to use fire-retardant materials for your own safety.

Fabrics are available that have an inherent fire retardant. If you want to choose a fabric that does not meet the regulations, enquire about whether or not it can be treated. Fabrics can be back coated for a reasonable sum. Back coating has certainly improved since its inception, and is now easier to work with, but it still clogs up sewing machines and creates a great deal of dust when cut. Fabrics with an inherent fire retardancy medium, however, are more pliable and less stiff to work with, and so are more popular with upholsterers.

FABRIC CHOICES

The different types of fabrics available are as boundless as the ingenuity of manufacturers and the advances of technology. Whichever you choose, make sure it suits the purpose and is an upholstery weight.

BROCADE Made in silk originally, but now in cotton and man-made fibres. Usually floral patterned with a rich sheen on the surface. The back is striped across the weft. A strong warp thread gives it some strength, but the tendency of the satin threads on the front to tear makes it best suited for upholstering furniture subject to light wear.

BROCATELLE Similar to damask, but with a quilted look on the surface, it is made from cotton and rayon.

CHINTZ A heavy-glazed cotton. The glaze tends to wear off in time. The fabric can be patterned or plain. Not suitable for everyday wear, so generally used in bedroom upholstery.

COTTON A natural staple fibre, cotton is made into many different types of fabric. It is very versatile and can be woven or cut into a pile, plain-dyed or printed with patterns. It often produces a characteristically crisp effect. It is also used to back other fabrics.

DAMASK A self-patterned fabric with raised designs on a satin background. The light and shaded effect is achieved by a reversal of the weave on the back. Made in a variety of weights from silk, cotton, rayon and man-made fibres. Used for a variety of types of upholstery, depending on the weight of the fabric.

HIDE (LEATHER) Treated cow or buffalo hide is available dyed in many colours. Several layers, called skivers, are taken from a hide, ranging from thin, pliable ones to thick layers that are difficult to work with. Hide is rather wasteful as the main back is often marked with small cuts, and it thins out towards the edges. Careful planning before cutting will pay dividends. Rub-off hides imitate an antique surface. Suede, the inside of the hide, treated and shaved to an even surface, tends to age quickly.

LINEN Made from flax plant. It is often mixed with other fibres to give it additional strength and given the name 'linen union'. It is usually woven and can be plain-dyed or printed with patterns.

Wearability

General wearability is an important point to consider. If you are putting the item in a heavily used area, you will probably find that a patterned fabric is the most sensible choice. If you prefer plain materials, however, look at fabrics that can be washed or sponged. Many fabrics are pre-treated with a stain repellant or you can apply a spray stain repellant to the furniture after upholstering. These sprays do not cause any change of colour or texture and are recommended, especially on pale colours.

If the furniture is for light usage, you will have a choice of many fabrics and textures, but still make sure you use an upholstery-weight fabric (not a piece of dress fabric or soft furnishings fabric) or you will find the result disappointing. A light-weight fabric is much more difficult to work with and if you are a beginner you are much less likely to obtain a successful result.

Colour and pattern

Most people usually think of colour as the first requirement to consider. Again, however, you need to think in terms of practical usage and wearability. Bear in mind the room or setting where the furniture will be and consider the other colours that it will be near. Will it sit happily with them and even enhance them? If you have a show-wood chair, study the colour of the frame and pick up the shades in the wood so that your fabric complements the furniture.

Weigh up whether a plain or patterned fabric will be most suitable in terms of wearability and the type of usage to which the furniture will be put.

Pattern can add character to an item or follow through a particular style. It can also add a further visual dimension in enabling you to select fabrics that echo shapes or motifs on the frame of the furniture or complement other design details in the room. Make sure that the pattern you choose enhances and fits the item. For instance, do not overwhelm a small chair by using a pattern that is too large so that you have to spoil the design by cutting the fabric off at its head or tail in order to make it fit the seat.

Avoid choosing checks or stripes for rounded furniture until you have gained some experience. It can be difficult to get the lines to run evenly and great care is needed to match the pattern.

Value for money

Cost must come into the equation, but it is generally advisable to buy the best fabric that you can afford. Prices and standards of cloth differ, so check the quality of the fabric to see exactly what you are paying for.

Look at the weave to see that it is not loose, and examine the fabric carefully to make sure that no threads have come adrift and that there are no flaws.

If you are buying a bargain piece of fabric, look at the colour —check that the dye is even, and that the colour is not smudged. Make sure you have enough fabric if you are buying a discontinued line. It will not be a bargain if you find you do not have enough to cover the whole piece of furniture and have to buy a completely new length of different material.

Selecting in situ

Ask your local upholsterer if you may borrow pattern books, so that you can see the fabrics in both daylight and artificial light. Colours can change dramatically when you see them in a different setting and it is important to look at fabrics in the actual room or, if possible, in the position in which the furniture will be placed.

Many manufacturers offer the service of returnable samples. These are much larger than pattern-book samples and give you a better idea of how your fabric will look. Leave the sample draped over your furniture for a couple of days and you will soon know if you love it or hate it. Remember always to return the samples or you will have to pay for them.

It is not too early to consider the options for trimmings at this stage. Many of the same considerations are relevant, such as selecting colours and types that will suit both the fabric and the style of the furniture. Pattern books are available and you can order cuttings to place with the fabrics to obtain a good idea of how they will look together.

Weaves and fibres

Fabrics can be made of many different types of raw materials, all of which give them different qualities. Natural fibres include vegetable fibres, such as cotton and linen, and animal fibres, such as silk and wool. Rayon is also a natural fibre and is made from wood. Man-made fibres such as nylon, polyester and acrylic are made from petroleum products. Natural and man-made fibres can be mixed together and give the best of both worlds; for example, a linen and viscose mix will help the fabric to resist creasing.

The way the fibre is spun and woven determines the texture and handling of the fabric. When choosing your fabric, you need to consider how pliable it is, especially if your furniture has curves, so examine the weave carefully. Fabrics with a loose weave are not suitable as they tend to come apart when pulled or stretched. Handle the fabric to check its flexibility and its ability to keep its shape when applied to furniture.

EXPERT TIP

Take home samples of fabrics and trimmings to see how they look on the piece of furniture in situ and in different light conditions, before making your final decision.

FABRIC CHOICES

MATELASSE Is a very similar fabric to brocatelle, but it has a flatter weave.

MOQUETTE Has a looped pile that can be left uncut or cut, and designs are plain or patterned. It is a very hard-wearing fabric made in wool, cotton or synthetic fibres, and is often used in public areas with heavy use. Both cut and uncut fabrics were very popular in the 1950s and are now making a comeback.

PILE FABRICS Velvet, velour and chenille are still made in cotton or silk. Synthetic versions, however, tend to be more hard wearing and more easily cleaned. Natural or synthetic, these fabrics can be plain-dyed, patterned or embossed.

SILK Woven from silk fibres obtained from silkworms. The strands of silk are twisted to make a yarn that is then woven into a variety of finished fabrics, such as damasks, velours and brocades.

TAPESTRY Handmade tapestries on canvas can be used for simple upholstery, but fabric, designed for a similar effect, is also available and easier to handle. Made of cotton, linen or wool, the designs can be modern or traditional, and the fabric is very hard wearing.

TWEED Made from cotton, wool or a mixture of yarns. Can be woven in plain or twill weave structure. Tweed is hard wearing, warm looking, and a joy to work with, but tends to fray when cut, so leave extra allowance for turning and use a shorter stitch when machining.

VINYL A cloth that imitates the graining and colours of leather, but is also available in many designs and colours. It can be easily cleaned by wiping with a damp cloth. Used in cars and boats as well as domestic upholstery. Has a knitted backing to give extra flexibility.

WOOL Woven from the fleece of sheep and other animals, it can also be mixed with other fibres to give it more versatility. Wool tweed is often used in upholstery and can be plain-dyed or woven with different coloured threads.

ESTIMATING TOP FABRIC

Once you have chosen your top fabric, you need to calculate how much you will need. Take your measurements when the piece of furniture is in calico.

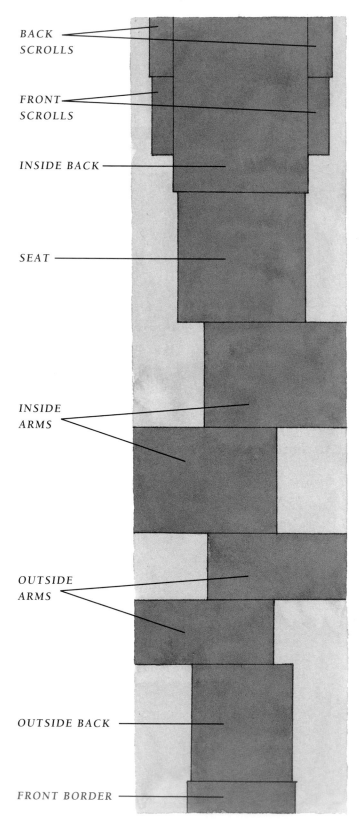

BACK SCROLLS

FRONT SCROLLS

INSIDE BACK

SEAT

INSIDE ARMS

OUTSIDE ARMS

OUTSIDE BACK

FRONT BORDER

Drawing up a cut sheet will help you visualize how the pieces for different sections can be cut from the fabric and to calculate the overall length needed. There are two types: an estimating sheet for plain fabric and a pattern sheet for patterned fabrics.

Measuring up

1 First make a rough sketch of your chair, marking the pieces to cut and the directions that the fabric and pattern will run. Take the measurements for each piece from the actual chair and note them on the sketch.

2 Always measure across the widest point and in the direction that the fabric will lie. Allow enough for turnings and at least 10 cm (4 in) extra so you can manoeuvre the fabric while covering. In particular, for the inside back, measure the length from the back of the head rail, right into the buttons and down to the base back rail, allowing

plenty of fabric to tack off. Then measure the width, including enough fabric to go into the buttons and around the side edges to sew under the scrolls. For the arms, measure from the top arm rail, over the top of the arm to the bottom arm rail.

3 Use your measurements to plan out an estimating sheet. Draw a long rectangle to represent the width of the fabric and draw on all the pieces as simple rectangles. Never cut a piece exactly to pattern or shape before you have tacked it temporarily in place on the chair. Make a list of the measured lengths along the side and the widths along the top of your sketch. Check that the widths fit the width of the fabric and add up the lengths to give the total length of fabric needed.

4 If you are using a plain fabric, you can use this sheet to cut out the fabric. If the fabric is patterned, do not start cutting yet.

Demonstration chair measurements
Width of fabric 137 cm (54 in)

	width cm (in)	length cm (in)
Inside back	85 (34)	109 (43)
Seat	81 (32)	81 (32)
Inside arms	91 (36)	66 (26)
Outside arms	89 (35)	41 (16)
Front border	66 (26)	20 (8)
Front scrolls	14 (6)	48 (19)
Back scrolls	15 (6)	38 (15)
Outside back	63 (25)	74 (29)
Piping *(fit into off-cuts and allow extra if required)*		

Positioning a pattern

1 If you have a patterned fabric, measure the pieces as before but plan the position of the pattern carefully and allow for extra fabric. The pattern must be centred down the centre of the chair, so that it runs vertically down the back, across the seat and down the front border. It must also run horizontally, for example across the lower inside back on to each inside arm, so that the pattern matches all around. You will need to allow for these extra considerations by creating a new pattern sheet.

2 Plan the inside back first. If the fabric has a large pattern, place it so that the main pattern does not disappear over the top of the back or the seat.

3 Line up the pattern for the seat with the pattern on the inside back and use the same principle if there is a seat cushion. Line up the pattern for the front border with the seat.

4 Line up the pattern for the inside arm with the inside back and the seat. The inside arms must also be cut as a symmetrical pair. The outside arms must also be cut as a pair, and match the inside arms.

5 Scrolls have to be paired, but they cannot always be symmetrical unless the pattern on the fabric is also symmetrical.

6 Plan out the pieces on a new pattern sheet, using the measurements and method for the estimating sheet, but positioning each piece according to where the pattern repeat falls. The larger the pattern, the more fabric you will need. A patterned fabric has an impact on the cost, but careful planning will minimise waste. Add the lengths to give the amount of fabric required.

Above: To join fabric for a wide section, find a distinctive part of the repeat and fold one piece of fabric under along that line. Put this piece of fabric on top of the other to match a whole pattern and pin along the new line. Place the fabric right-sides together and re-pin along the seam. Check the alignment before stitching.

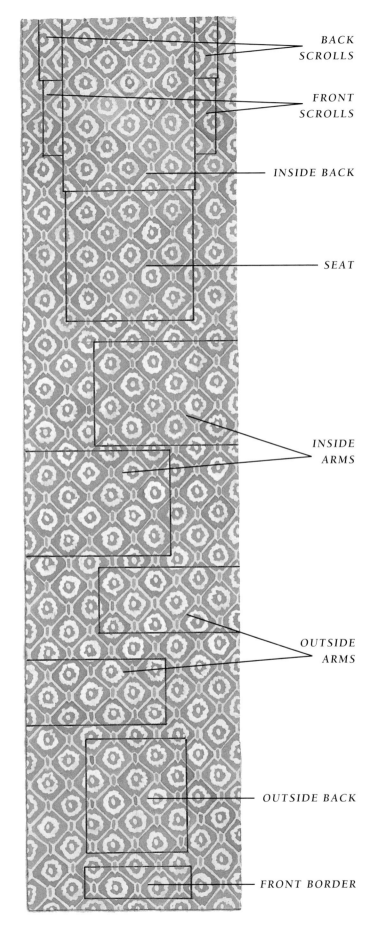

BACK SCROLLS

FRONT SCROLLS

INSIDE BACK

SEAT

INSIDE ARMS

OUTSIDE ARMS

OUTSIDE BACK

FRONT BORDER

STARTING TO TOP COVER

A beautiful rich fabric was chosen for this button-back armchair. Good positioning and matching of the fabric is essential to its success and here the pattern works particularly well with the buttoning pattern.

Once you are satisfied with the chair at calico stage, you can go on to the final layers of wadding and the top cover. Start with the insides of the chair so that you have access to the frame and then finish with the outsides. Plan the fabric pieces and the positioning of any pattern before you start cutting the fabric. Cut the pieces out as basic rectangles and do not cut any of them exactly to shape.

TOOLS
Cut sheet
Scissors
Tailor's chalk
Measuring tools
Skewers
Double-ended needle
Regulator
Hammer
Circular needle

Cutting out

1 Spread the top fabric out, right-side down, on a clean, flat surface. Use your pattern sheet and mark out all the pieces on the wrong side of the fabric with tailor's chalk. Mark the top of each piece with an arrow and label it as you cut it. This will save you hours of trying to recognize each piece later.

2 Cut the pieces out to the basic sizes on your guide. Do not cut them to shape now as you need the extra allowance to handle and fit the fabric to the frame. The surplus will be trimmed away later when it is securely in position on the chair. Do not cut from the old fabric pieces as they may have stretched or shrunk and certainly will not have the surplus needed for fitting.

3 Take all the fabric pieces for the insides of the chair and place them together. Fold the pieces for the outsides and leave them to one side.

Inside back

1 Lay the fabric for the inside back right-side down on a flat surface. Mark the two centre lines, one across the width and the other down the length. The vertical line will line up with the central line of buttons on the inside back, so make sure that the pattern aligns accordingly.

2 Lay the fabric on the inside back right-side up, lining up the pattern with the top centre button. Mark the position of that button on the back of the fabric.

3 Lay the fabric flat again and mark the positions for all the

other buttons with a cross on the back of the fabric. Refer to your notebook for the measurements between buttons.

4 Lay a length of sheet wadding, with the skin side uppermost, over the entire inside back, from the back of the head rail to the inside back rail, just tucked in between the arms and the back, and to each upright rail. Tear the wadding with your fingers to prevent a hard edge showing under the top fabric. If it just touches the rails, this reduces bulk on the tack line and protects the fabric on the frame edge.

5 Break open the wadding over the button positions by cutting a cross for each or pushing your fingers into each indentation.

6 Lay the top fabric over the inside back, centring the pattern as before. Align the marks on the top fabric with the buttoning pattern already in the calico. Take out and retain each

EXPERT TIP

Have your buttons made by your local upholsterer, or a sewing machine retailer will sometimes provide this service. The most useful sizes are 13 mm ($\frac{1}{2}$ in) and 20 mm ($\frac{3}{4}$ in).

SHEET WADDINGS

Various types of sheet wadding are used directly over some stuffing materials or over the calico to prevent the stuffings wearing up through the top fabric. They also add an extra layer of padding for comfort.

1. FLOCK *Made of cotton and animal fibre waste, this is usually multi-coloured. It is not recommended now, but is often found as padding over a solid surface on old furniture. It is inclined to go lumpy in use, usually falls apart when ripped out, and should be replaced.*

2. SKIN WADDING *(sheet wadding) This is made of cotton, with a fluffy layer between two skin-like layers that hold it together. It is most effecive when pulled apart and the inner, rougher layer is placed down on the calico so it does not slip. Skin wadding is available in different weights of 800 g (28 oz), 900 g (32 oz), 1200 g (42 oz) and, recommended as the best quality, 1700 g (48 oz), all in a width of 45 cm (18 in). Recommended for use over calico in traditional upholstery to prevent the hair penetrating the top fabric.*

3. POLYESTER WADDING *Available in different weights from 55 g to 500 g (2 oz to 18 oz) and in widths of 70 cm (27 in), 90 cm (36 in) and 1.4 m (54 in). It is often best to use the 55 g (2 oz) weight and build it up in layers to the required thickness to avoid hard edges. Polyester wadding is now often used between the calico and top fabric instead of cotton waddings where hair has not been used as a stuffing, especially on modern furniture. It is also used to wrap foam cushions.*

4. COTTON FELT *A thick sheet of cotton linters used for traditional upholstery, held together between sheets of paper removed before use. Tends to break up when working, but makes a good padding once in place.*

roll of calico covering the button positions and tighten the twine on the outside back.

7 Start with the bottom centre button position. Push a double-ended needle from the front through the corresponding mark on the wrong side of the fabric to the marker on the outside back. Do not pull the needle right through.

8 Thread a length of nylon button twine through the eye of the needle on the inside back, then through the button shank and then back through the eye of the needle.

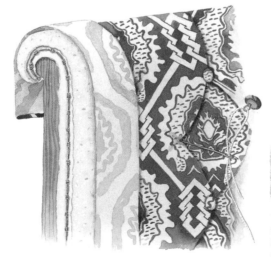

9 Push the needle right through to the outside back and remove the ends of the twine from the needle.

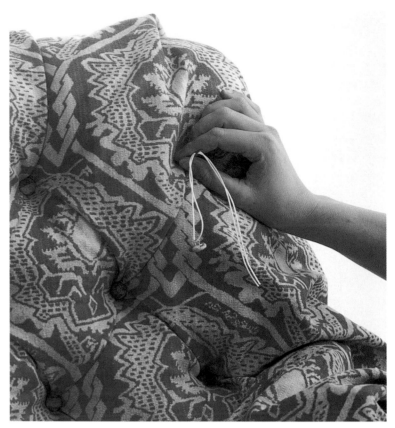

10 Position the button, pulling it and the fabric into the hole in the stuffing by gently pulling the twine from the outside back. Tie off the two ends of twine on the outside back, placing a calico roll under an upholsterer's slip knot. Do not lock off the knot at this stage.

11 Complete the buttoning in the same order as at the calico stage. Regulate the pleats between buttons as you work, making sure the open edge of each pleat faces downwards.

12 Arrange the pleats from the bottom row of buttons over the lumbar region so that the folds face outwards from the centre of the inside back. Push the fabric between the back and the seat and temporary tack it on the inside back rail. Use the regulator to arrange the pleats perfectly. Tack home as much as possible on the inside back rail.

13 Arrange the pleats from the top row of buttons with

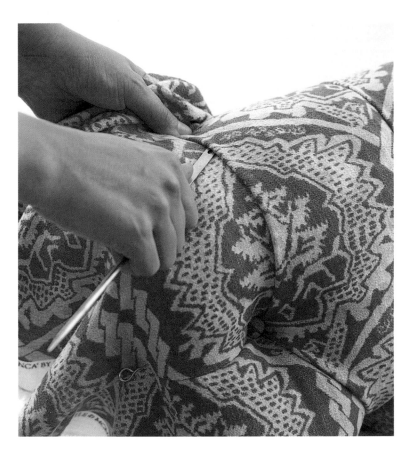

Seat

1 Place a layer of sheet wadding over the seat, to extend from the back rail to the blind stitch at the front, and to just tuck between the seat and inside arms. Tear the wadding to a feathered edge as for the inside back.

2 Lay the fabric over the seat so that the pattern is running in line with the pattern on the inside back and the grain lines run straight across at the front edge.

3 Skewer the fabric in place along the front edge under the row of blind stitch in the calico. Thread a circular needle with twine and backstitch the fabric in position under the front edge, pleating the front corners into neat folds.

the folds facing outwards, taking the fabric over the top of the back. Skewer the fabric in place under the head rail. Use the regulator to arrange the pleats. Tack the fabric down along the head rail. Trim off the excess fabric.

14 Return to the inside back. Cut the fabric into the bottom arm rail where it meets the back upright rail. Finish tacking down the bottom edge of fabric along the inside back rail.

15 Cut the fabric into the top arm rail where it meets back upright. Pull the fabric through to the back and tack to the back upright.

16 Arrange the pleats down each side of the inside back and skewer them underneath the stitched edge on each back scroll. Run a gathering thread around each edge and then secure the fabric with a blind stitch as at the calico stage.

4 Smooth the fabric over the seat towards the back and side rails. Cut the fabric in towards the front and back upright rails, taking care not to cut too far and risk creating a visible cut on the finished seat. Pull the fabric down to the base rails all around. Temporary tack it in place on the tops of the base rails. If the fabric looks slack in the corners, there is insufficient stuffing and this must be rectified at this stage. Tack home when satisfied.

5 On each rail, turn the excess fabric over and tack down. Trim off the excess fabric.

Inside arms

1 Place a layer of sheet wadding over one of the inside arms, so it extends from the top arm rail under the scroll to just tuck in around the seat, and from just short of the front of the arm to just tuck in where the arm meets the inside back.

2 Lay the fabric over the inside arm, taking care to keep the grain straight and line up the pattern with the inside back and seat. Temporary tack in position under the top arm rail.

3 Place a few temporary tacks around the arm scroll to prevent the fabric from moving. Cut in towards where the bottom arm rail meets the front upright to allow the fabric to wrap around to the front scroll.

4 Temporary tack the bottom edge of fabric, as far as is possible at this stage, along the side rail. Smooth the fabric towards the back of the arm, keeping the grain line straight.

5 Make a 'Y' cut in the fabric towards the bottom arm rail and a straight cut towards the top arm rail where they meet the back upright rail so it can be pulled through around the back of the arm.

6 Pull the centre section of fabric between the arm and the back to the outside. Secure it with skewers on the half webbing to which the calico is sewn.

7 Finish temporary tacking the bottom edge of the inside arm fabric to the side rail. Tack home and trim away any excess fabric at the bottom edge.

8 Make a further cut where the bottom of the back scroll on the inside back meets the top of the arm. Pull the fabric taut along the top of the arm towards the outside back. Temporary tack in place and make sure the fabric is lying smoothly. Leave this part of the inside arm for now. It will be finished later when the back scroll is fitted.

9 Return to the front of the arm. With a circular needle and twine, run a row of stitches around the front edge of fabric where it curves around the front scroll. Pull the stitching up tight

3 Now add the flange cord. Lay the scroll face down and position the flange around the front and top of it, finishing under the curve, so that the cord sits right on the edge. Staple the flange near to the edge of the scroll.

4 Line the scroll up so the back edge is level with the outside back. Place a piece of padding on a block of wood to shield the scroll, and, with a sharp tap, hammer the three nails home. Make sure the scroll is secure.

5 Tack the loose flap of fabric on to the outside of the back upright rail and trim off the excess fabric. Repeat these processes on the other scroll.

Finishing the arms

1 Remove the temporary tacks from the inside arm fabric tacked to the back upright. Turn the top edge of the fabric under and reposition it on top of the bottom edge of the back scroll fabric. Pull the fabric taut and tack home on the outside of the back upright rail.

and ease the gathers around the scroll. Trim away any excess fabric. Stitch a row of blind stitch under the front edge of the scroll.

10 Tack the fabric down around the front edge of the scroll and upright. Repeat the processes on the other arm, taking care to make it look like the first.

Back scrolls

1 Place three fine nails at intervals in the front of the wooden scroll shape, so that the nail heads are flush with the scroll face.

2 Cover the front of the scroll with a layer of sheet wadding, enough to wrap around the edges. Place the top fabric over the front of the scroll, taking care to position the fabric accurately, so that both scrolls eventually match. Make a cut in the fabric just under the back curve of the scroll. Turn the fabric over the top, front and bottom edges of the scroll. Use 8 mm ($^3/_8$ in) staples to secure, making sure they do not penetrate the fabric on the front. Leave the fabric on the back edge loose.

EXPERT TIP

Make a series of small cuts in the fabric towards the wood, but not right into it, on the curved part of the scroll. This will help the fabric to spread around the curve.

2 Take out the skewers holding the inside arm fabric on the webbing and reposition on the back upright rail. Tack home all tacks. Repeat on the other arm.

COVERING THE OUTSIDES

In these last stages, the details are still important. The gold cord and the outside panels will

all be on show and must be finished with care to repay the rest of your efforts.

Be sure to match the pattern and keep the fabric grain straight when covering the last sections of the chair.

Front border

1 Stitch bridle ties across the front border. Tease enough hair under the ties to cover the whole border.

2 Cover the border with calico and secure the top and side edges with skewers. Slip stitch the top edge in place under the front edge of top fabric. Make a cut on each side of the calico to allow the side edges on to the front uprights. Temporary tack these edges in position and the bottom edge of the calico to the front base rail.

3 Ensure the calico is neatly in place and tack home. Trim off the excess calico.

4 Place a length of sheet wadding over the calico, ensuring it comes to the bottom edge of the front base rail.

5 Position the top fabric over the border, and, turning the top edge under, match the pattern with the one on the seat. Secure the fabric with skewers. With a circular needle and a slipping thread that matches the top fabric, slip stitch the top edge of the border to the seat fabric under the front edge. Cut into the side edges and temporary tack them in position as with the calico. Temporary tack the bottom edge under the base rail. Tack home.

Front scrolls

1 Place three fine nails at intervals in the front of the wooden scroll shape, so that the nail heads are flush with the scroll face.

2 Cover the front of the scroll with a layer of sheet wadding, allowing enough to wrap around the edges and to eventually extend to the bottom of the front upright. Place the top fabric over the wadding on the front of the scroll, taking care to position the fabric accurately, so that both scrolls eventually match. Turn the fabric over the top and sides of the scroll. Use staples to secure, making sure they do not penetrate the fabric on the front. Leave the fabric on the bottom edge loose.

3 Now add the flange cord. Lay the scroll face down and position the flange around the inside edge and top of it, leaving a length hanging from just under the curve. Ensure the cord sits right on the edge and staple the flange down near to the edge of the scroll.

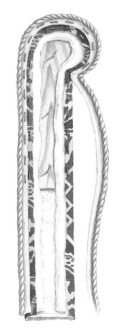

4 Line the scroll up so the outside edge is level with the outside arm. Place a piece of padding on a block of wood to shield the scroll, and, with a sharp tap, hammer the three nails right home. Make sure the scroll is secure.

5 Secure the loose cord by skewering the flange on the outside arm so the cord sits close to the edge of the scroll. Tack home. Repeat these processes on the other scroll.

Outside arms

1 Next, back up the outside arms. Temporary tack calico (hessian can be used instead) in place on the top arm and side base rails, turning the edges under. Keeping the calico taut, temporary tack it on the back and front upright rails. When it is evenly tensioned, tack home.

2 Lay one layer of sheet wadding over the calico and place the fabric for the outside arm over it. Make sure the grain line of the fabric is straight along the side base rail.

3 Trim the fabric on the front edge to allow for a turning. Remove the skewers holding the flange cord and turn the front edge of the outside arm fabric under so it meets the side of the front scroll. Replace the skewers to secure the fabric and the flange. With a circular needle and a matching thread, slip stitch the front edge of fabric in position through all the layers.

4 Fold the fabric under along the underside of the top arm rail and skewer it in place, ready to stitch later.

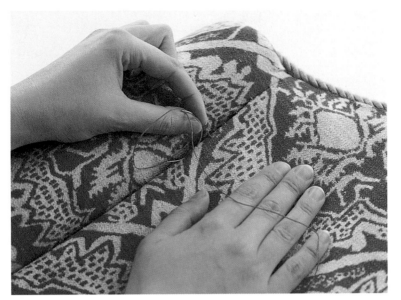

Pulling the fabric taut, temporary tack it to the outside of the back upright rail and under the side base rail. With a circular needle and a matching thread, slip stitch the top edge of fabric in position under the top arm rail.

5 Trim the excess fabric off the bottom and back edges. Tack home on the back and base rails. Cut in towards the front and back legs with a small series of cuts to allow the fabric to curve around them. Trim the fabric, allowing for a turning. Turn the fabric under and tack to the frame. Repeat these processes on the other arm.

Outside back

1 Back up the outside back with calico as for the outside arms. Place a length of sheet wadding over the calico. Tear the wadding with your fingers to just inside all the edges of the back.

2 Place the right side of the top edge of the top fabric just underneath the back of the head rail where the inside back is tacked off. Lay the rest of that piece of top fabric temporarily over the inside back. Make sure the pattern is centred and then put a temporary tack on each side of the head rail to hold the fabric in place.

3 Place a length of back tack strip under the head rail and temporary tack through the strip and the layers of fabric right along the head rail. When correctly positioned, tack home.

4 Fold the top fabric back over the wadding and down over the outside back. Make sure the pattern and the grain is hanging straight. Turn the fabric under all along each side and pin in place down the outside edge of each back upright.

BACKING-UP SUNDRIES

BOTTOMING CLOTH (black bottom) A slightly stretchy, finely woven black cloth used to cover the underside of furniture, to catch the dust and provide a neat finish.

BACK TACK STRIP (not shown) A strip of purpose-made card used to give a straight edge along the top fabric tack line.

5 With a circular needle and a matching thread, slip stitch the outside back fabric down both sides.

6 Turn the chair over on its knees. Cut the top fabric in towards the back legs. Trim the fabric around the legs to allow for a turning. Turn the fabric under and tack down. Tack home the rest of the bottom edge along the underside of the base rail.

7 Place a piece of black bottom on the base of the chair and fold under around all the edges. Fix the cloth with a temporary tack in the centre of each base rail, making sure that it is evenly tensioned and all raw edges of the top fabric are covered.

8 Cut the black bottom in around each leg. Trim the cloth back and turn under around each leg. Turn the long edges of the cloth under and tack it under all the way around.

9 Turn the chair over and enjoy a well-deserved sit down. Wonderful!

WINGS

There are many and various types of wings on chairs. They are there not only for decorative purposes, but to stop draughts, and they also make a good head rest.

Techniques for the most usual types of wings are described here. There is a wing chair in the projects section that demonstrates how a wing is incorporated into the complete chair.

Traditionally upholstered wings

This wing, with stitched edges, is best for a traditionally upholstered chair. It is stuffed and stitched to give it a firm edge around the contour. It is not traditionally piped, but single piping can be added for extra detail.

1 Stretch and secure a length of webbing, folded in half lengthways, from the top to the bottom at the back of the inside wing frame, leaving a gap between it and the chair inside back to pull the cover through.

2 Cover the inside of the wing with hessian, tacking securely all around the frame, then, with twine and a circular needle, blanket stitch the back edge down the length of the hessian.

3 Stitch bridle ties across the hessian on the inside wing. Wings vary in size, but three rows of ties would be needed on an average-sized wing. Tease the fibre and stuff it under the bridle ties.

4 Cover the wing in scrim, adding more fibre and pulling the scrim tight to form an even contour around the wing. Tack off around the back of the frame. Put in stuffing ties to hold the stuffing in place. Stitch one row of blind stitch around the outer edges.

5 Add a second stuffing of hair or cotton felt. Cover the inside of the wing in calico, pulling the excess on the back edge through between the inside back and the wing. Pleat the calico around the curved edge and temporary tack it to the back of the wing frame.

6 Cut the top fabric so that the pattern matches the inside back. Place skin wadding over the wing. Cover with top fabric, in the same manner as for calico. Back up the outside back and wings in the traditional way, slip stitching them in place.

Foam-upholstered wings

These wings are usually constructed of plywood or chipboard, which is covered with foam. Some are bolted or screwed on to the frame after the inside back has been covered.

1 Unbolt the wing from the chair, ready to cover it separately. After upholstering the inside back of the chair, hold the wing in its former position and mark on the inside wing where the padding on the inside back meets it.

2 Place the wing on a piece of thick 2.5 cm (1 in) foam and draw around it. Cut the foam

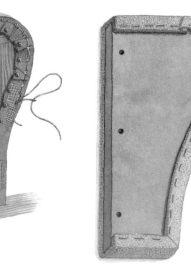

oversize by 2.5 cm (1 in) around the curved and bottom edges, and to the line on the vertical back edge. Spray glue onto the centre of the inside wing, and press the foam in position. Take the foam over the edge and secure with staples on the back of the frame.

3 Place a piece of skin or polyester wadding over the foam. Place the top fabric over the inside wing, matching the pattern with the inside back of the chair, and tack off or staple over the edge, making pleats if necessary to ease the fabric around the edge.

4 Upholster the second wing and bolt them both back on the chair frame. Tack a length of piping from the bottom edge of the outside wing, following the curved outline, around the top of the outside back and down to the bottom edge of the second wing. Place top fabric on the outside wing, lining up the pattern with the inside wing, and pin in place. Trim the fabric around the curved edge and back, leaving a turning of 2 cm (1 in). Turn the edge under and slip stitch in place, close to the piping. Temporary tack the other edges of excess fabric to the relevant rails. Continue to back up and cover the other outside sections of the chair as usual, slip stitching in place along the edges and covering all raw edges.

Capped-on wings

The top fabric for a wing can also be capped on, which means that the fabric sections are sewn on the machine and made up complete with the piping and outside back attached. It can then be pulled on to any type of wing and is added after the inside back and arms are covered. This method is mostly used on modern furniture during manufacture, but can be used in reupholstery.

1 Place the top fabric for both the inside and outside wing on the wing, right-sides out, matching the pattern with the inside back. Pin the two pieces together along a line that follows the outer edge of the wing. Trim and notch the seam from where it meets the outside back at the top to the arm at the bottom. Mark the frame to show the position of the seam between the outside back and the wing, and pin the seam position on the fabric. Take the fabric off the wing and on both pieces mark a seam line, allowing 1.5 cm (3/4 in) extra for the padding. Trim the fabric, allowing an additional seam allowance.

2 Pin the outside back fabric in place and pin along the seam line with the wing. Trim the fabric all around, leaving only seam allowances. Remove the fabric from the chair.

3 Sew the two outside wings to the outside back, making each seam 6 cm (2½ in) long from the top edge. Pipe the outside wings and back section as usual.

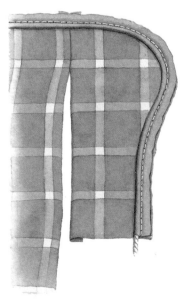

4 Place the inside wings on the outside wings, right-sides together, matching the notches. Sew together and trim the seam.

5 Place a piece of cotton felt on the inside of the wing and tear off the excess around the contour of the wing. Glue it in place with spray adhesive. Then place a layer of polyester wadding over the inside and outside wings. Pull the whole made-up section of top fabric on, keeping the seam on the piped edge flat.

6 Fit the bottom edge of the outside wing with temporary tacks to the top rail of the outside arm. Cut in towards the base of the inside wing, matching the cuts on the inside arm. Push the excess fabric through to the back upright and tack home. Tack home the temporary tacks on the arm.

7 The outside back is now in position, ready to slip stitch in place when the outside arms have been fitted.

EXPERT TIP

If the wing is very curved, make a series of cuts in the fabric to ease it around the curves before folding it under.

FLYS AND COLLARS

Flys are pieces of cloth that are used to extend the top fabric, either to save expense or to reduce bulk. Collars are extra pieces of top fabric sewn to main sections of top fabric to give a good line around curved sections.

Flys

Flys are made from lining cloth or calico and are attached in strips to the top fabric to extend it. The method here is to extend the fabric on the seat, but can be adapted to extend the bottom edge of the inside back or inside arm covers. Enough fabric is allowed to extend beyond the edges of the seat and the flys are tucked down, not visible once the chair is covered, and tacked to the rails.

1 Cut the top fabric for the seat, allowing enough fabric to extend beyond the inside back and bottom arm rails. Then measure from under the inside back rail to the back base rail, add a 1 cm (½ in) turning and a handling allowance and cut three strips of calico or lining to this width for the flys.

2 Cut one back fly as long as the width of the seat fabric and the two side flys as long as the sides of the seat fabric plus the width of the back fly.

3 Fold a turning of 2 cm (1 in) on one long side of each fly to give extra strength to the seams.

Attach the back fly to the seat fabric, and sew in a 1 cm (½ in) seam through the three layers of fabric. Repeat with each side fly.

4 Use this section just as you would a normal seat section.

Collars

Collars are made of top fabric and attached to the main section to allow the cover to sit smoothly around a curved shape. For example, where the inside back meets the inside arms, there is a tendency for drag lines to appear if the main section of fabric is not able to splay around the curve. A series of cuts to allow the fabric to spread would work around a slight curve, but these may tear with wear. A collar is a more satisfactory solution.

INSIDE BACK COLLAR

This collar allows the inside back fabric to sit around the arms, and the section is usually completed before the arms are top covered.

1 Place the inside back fabric in position on the chair, right-side up, and mark with a piece of chalk where the fabric goes over the curve of both arms. Cut into the fabric to allow it to spread.

2 Cut the fabric to the bottom of both back uprights to allow free passage around the bottom back rail and uprights, but do not trim off any fabric below this cut line. Trim the fabric around the curves marked with chalk, making enough cuts to ease the fabric, and leaving a seam allowance.

3 Cut a strip of top fabric on the straight grain about 15 cm (6 in) wide and sew this to one curved edge of the inside back. Cut in to the seam to match the cuts in the main piece of fabric. Cut a second strip and attach in the same way.

4 The collars are now an integral part of the inside back. Push them through to the back and temporary tack to the back of the uprights. Trim the excess fabric where the uprights meet the bottom back rail, allowing a small turning to fold the edges under. Push the fabric through between the seat and the inside back, and temporary tack to the outside of the back bottom rail. Upholster the rest of the chair as usual.

SEAT COLLAR

This type of collar is essential on a tub chair. Despite its name, it is actually attached to the inside back and arm sections once they have been sewn together, allowing the fabric to sit neatly around the seat. The whole section is usually constructed and attached to the chair after the seat has been covered.

1 Place the fabric for the inside back and arms, already sewn together, right-side out on the chair. On the bottom edge of this section, mark where the tuck-in starts, just below the inside back and arm rails where the top fabric goes out of sight.

2 Make cuts in the inside back, close to the marked line so that the fabric will spread. Trim, leaving a seam allowance.

3 Cut three pieces of top fabric to make the collar, wide enough to tuck down to the bottom back rail, to match the shaping at the bottom of the

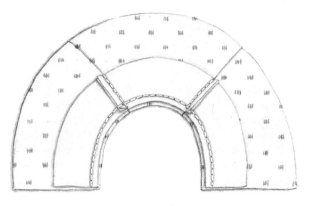

inside back and arms section. Sew the collar together and then sew in place on the bottom edge of the main section.

4 Reposition the whole section on the chair, and temporary

tack. Pull the collar through to the back and sides, cutting in to the uprights to allow clear passage. Tack home on the side and back base rails. Trim off the excess fabric, turn over the raw edges and tack down.

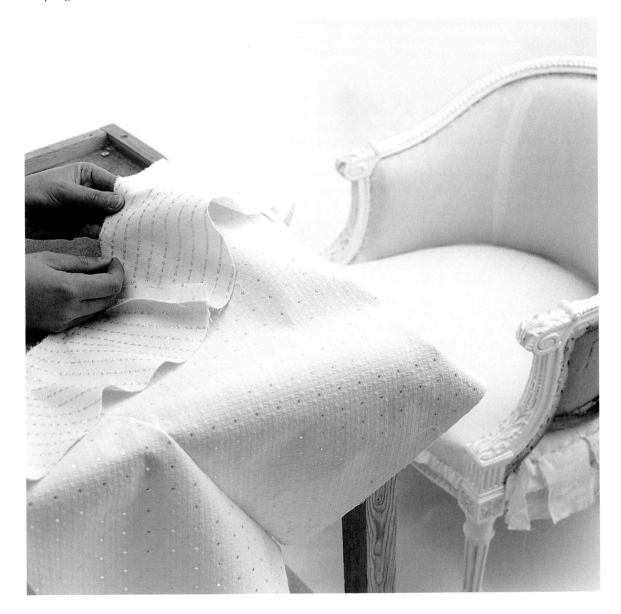

BORDERS

Borders are flat bands of fabric that join the inside and

outside sections on traditional and modern furniture.

There are borders that run up the front and along the arms of pieces of furniture, along the edge of the back and also along the front of the seat. They can be sewn with plain seams, but are often trimmed with piping, cord or ruche.

Arm borders

1 Cut the top fabric for the inside and outside arms. Measure for the length of fabric needed for the border from the bottom edge of the outside arm to the point where it meets the outside back. For the border width, measure across the width of the arm front and top, usually the same width all the way along. Cut the borders out.

2 Place the pieces of fabric on the arm, right-sides out, and pin together, following the contours of the arm. Trim the edges to a seam allowance and cut notches.

3 Sew the pieces together, matching the notches and starting from the back edge. Insert piping or other trimming at this stage if desired.

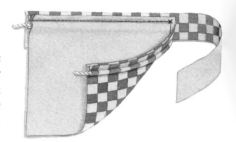

4 Turn the section right-sides out and cap or pull on over the stuffed arm. Tack the fabric in place on the appropriate rails, cutting into the uprights as necessary. Continue with upholstering the rest of the piece of furniture.

ARM BORDER

BACK BORDER

FRONT BORDER

KICK PLEAT

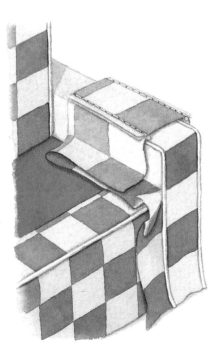

Back borders

1 Cut out the inside back. Measure for the length of the back border from where it meets the top of one arm, upwards across the back and down to the top of the other arm. Measure for its width from the depth of the back at its widest point, usually where it meets the arm. Cut the border out.

2 Place the pieces of fabric on the back, right-sides out, and pin together, following the contours. Trim the edges to a seam allowance and cut notches.

3 Sew the pieces together, matching the notches. Insert piping or other trimming, on the front edge only, at this stage.

4 Pull or cap the section on to the inside back. Temporary

tack the back edge of the border to the outside back uprights and head rail.

Front borders

1 Cut and construct the section for the top of the seat. Measure for the depth of the border from the top edge of the seat to either underneath the base rail or to where any base finish is to be attached. Measure for the width from one inside arm to the other, adding an allowance to tuck fabric around each side. Add seam allowances and cut out the top fabric for the border.

2 Position the pieces of fabric on the seat, right-sides out, and pin them together, following the contours. Trim the edges to a seam allowance and cut notches.

3 Sew the pieces together, matching the notches. Insert piping or other trimming, on the top edge only, at this stage.

4 Pull or cap the section on to the seat. Temporary tack in place.

BASE FINISHES

These fabric finishes around the base line most usually occur on modern furniture and replace the more traditional treatment of adding fringe.

Base finishes can be constructed with gathers, box pleats or kick pleats. Kick pleats give the most tailored, contemporary finish, with the pleats occuring on each corner. The method for constructing kick pleats is explained below.

Kick pleats

1 Mark a line all around the bottom of the chair or sofa 15 cm (6 in) from the floor.

2 Cut strips of top fabric measuring 15 cm (6 in), plus 6 cm (2½ in) turning, across the width of the fabric, allowing for pattern matching. Four strips are usually enough for a chair, six or eight for a sofa.

3 Position a strip of fabric on the front, sides and back of the chair in turn, matching the pattern with the sections of top fabric already in place and with the other pleat sections. Measure and mark with a pin the corners where the pleats meet and leave a set of corresponding pins on the chair. Cut each pleat section 15 cm (6 in) longer than the marks on each side to allow for turnings.

4 Cut four strips of lining the same width as the fabric, but only a total of 19 cm (8 in) deep.

5 Join the lining and the fabric along the bottom edge. Turn right-sides out and align the top edges, leaving 2 cm (1 in) of top fabric showing on the wrong side. Press the seam turnings towards the bottom to give more weight.

6 Cut four pieces of stiff upholstery liner to the exact length between the pin marks for each pleat section and place them in between the lining and the fabric. This step is not essential on a heavy fabric, but it will make a lighter fabric hang better.

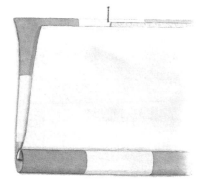

7 Hold the pleat sections up to the marks on the chair, and check that the corner marking pins are exactly in place. Turn the ends of the sections in and slip stitch or machine stitch across. Double stitch or overlock along the top edge. Put these sections to one side.

8 Make four corner pieces of fabric and lining in a similar way, to finished measurements of 15 cm (6 in) wide and 16 cm (6½ in) deep. Use the pieces of fabric left over from the main kick pleats.

9 Tack or staple a length of piping into the frame along the marked line. Join the ends of the piping at the back. Tack the corner pieces in place on each corner of the chair just below the piping, so that they will hang slightly shorter than the main kick pleats.

10 Position one main kick pleat, right side to the chair, and temporary tack. Position a length of back tack strip on top of the wrong side of the pleat close to the piping, and tack or staple home. Lay the kick pleat down. Repeat on the other pleat sections.

EXPERT TIP

Gently hammer the top edge of the pleat to make it lie flat. Cover your hammer with a piece of cloth to prevent damage to the fabric.

TRIMMINGS

Not all upholstery needs embellishment, but well-chosen

trimmings can enhance the outline or give an extra

dimension to some pieces of furniture.

Choose your type of trimming with care—too much could look ridiculous, while to understate and use too little trimming or none at all could make the piece look very dull.

There are many exciting types of trimming that you can make up yourself, buy ready made or have made up specially. Single piping, ruche and flange cord are all types of trimming that are machine stitched between two pieces of fabric. Double piping, cord, gimp, braid and fringe are all attached after the furniture has been finished, with adhesive, staples, gimp pins or decorative nails. Even more exuberant trimmings such as tassels, rosettes and embellished fringes can be used to attract attention, and these are often slip stitched in place.

Single piping

One of the most popular trimmings consists of cord sewn into the centre of a length of matching or contrasting folded fabric. The fabric is usually cut and joined on the bias, but to avoid too many joins it can also be cut up the warp (the length of the fabric). Piping is used for edging cushions and to outline furniture. It can be inserted between two pieces of fabric and fitted on to the furniture or can be machine stitched on to one piece of fabric that is then tacked or hand sewn into place.

1 Cut strips of fabric about 4 cm (1½ in) wide on the bias. Then join the strips into a long length with bias seams, matching the pattern if it is striped, checked or similar.

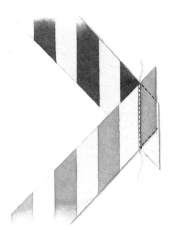

2 Place a length of piping cord along the centre of the wrong side of the fabric, and fold the fabric over so that it encases the cord. Keep the two edges together and use a piping foot to machine sew a line of stitching close to the cord.

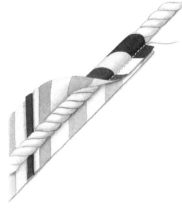

3 Lay the length of piping on the right side of the main fabric with the raw edges level and machine sew together over the same line of stitches as before. Then lay the second

section of fabric underneath, right-sides together with the raw edges level, and stitch inside the original stitch line as close as possible to the cord.

EXPERT TIP

A grooved foot will allow you to stitch closer when enclosing piping between two sections of fabric.

4 Open the two sections of fabric to reveal the piping inserted between the two pieces like a small roll.

TURNING PIPED CORNERS

1 Machine stitch the piping up to the corner point of the main fabric where the turning allowance of both edges is an equal distance from the machine needle.

2 Leave the needle in the fabric and make a cut in the raw

edge of the piping case, close in to the needle, allowing the piping to turn the corner.

3 Lift the presser foot and turn both the fabric and the piping, ready to stitch down the next edge. Lower the presser foot and continue stitching the piping to the fabric. Repeat on all corners.

JOINING SINGLE PIPING

Always make a long enough length of piping so that, wherever possible, it does not need to be joined on the piece of furniture. Sometimes this is unavoidable, for example where the piping starts and finishes at the same place, as on a cushion. The join must then be made as neatly and

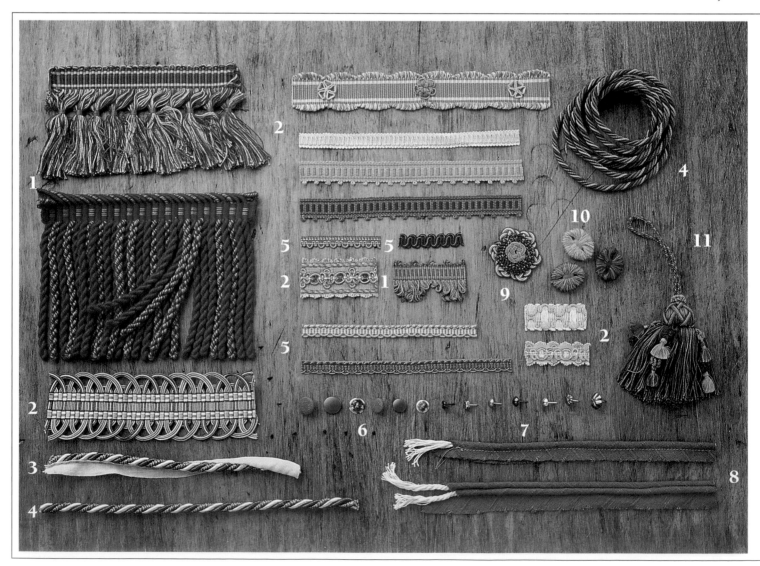

securely as possible using the method given here.

1 Machine stitch the piping in position around the main section of fabric, starting a few centimetres (about an inch) in from the end of the length of piping. Finish stitching when the piping has been attached right around and nearly returned to the starting point.

2 Pin the ends of fabric together to create a bias seam and trim, leaving enough for the turning. Check that the seam is slightly tensioned across the fabric. Machine stitch the seam, trim the turnings and open the seam.

3 Lay the two ends of the cord side by side and cut across the centre point so that they can then be butted together. Lay the fabric back around the cord and machine stitch the piping to the main section of fabric as before.

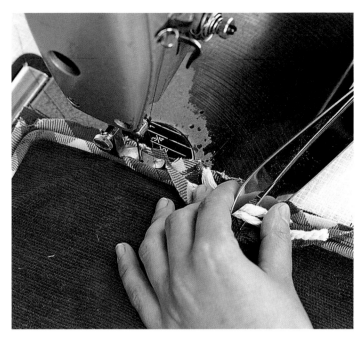

TRIMMINGS

The variety of trimmings in different designs and colours available to the upholsterer is quite breathtaking. They often have to be specially ordered and can also be custom made, but chosen well, they can make precisely the right finishing touch.

1. FRINGE Consists of a heading like gimp or braid with a hanging fringed edge, which can be cut or uncut, plain or decorated with embellishments such as tassels. As well as many colours and designs, there are a variety of fringe lengths and weights to suit many types of furniture, a typical fringe for the base of a chair being 10 or 15 cm (4 or 6 in) deep.

2. BRAID Similar to gimp, braid is usually flatter in appearance, with the threads woven rather than overlaid. There are many widths, colours and designs available.

3. FLANGE CORD Usually a three-stranded cord stitched to a cotton tape or flange. It is available in a variety of thicknesses, of which 1 cm (1/2 in) is perhaps the most useful, and an infinite variety of colours and designs.

4. CORD It is available in a variety of thicknesses, 3 mm (1/8 in) to 4 cm (1 1/2 in), all being suitable for upholstery and in a wealth of colours and designs.

5. GIMP This is made in many widths, but is typically 1.5 cm (3/4 in) wide and is sold by the metre (yard). It can be single- or multi-coloured and designs are many and varied. The strands are usually overlaid, giving quite a heavy appearance.

6. BUTTON FORMS Metal button forms are available in many sizes, 13 mm (1/2 in) and 20 mm (3/4 in) being most used for upholstery. These are covered in top fabric to give matching or contrasting effects.

7. DECORATIVE NAILS These are available in a number of sizes, the most frequently used for close nailing are 9 mm (3/8 in) wide. They are also available in a number of finishes of which antique or domed-head brass or bronzed nails are popular.

8. PIPING CORD The most usual is twisted unbleached cotton cord, available in a variety of thicknesses suitable for upholstery, ranging from size 6 (thin) to size 10 (thick) and sold by the roll. A soft cotton piping cord, available on 500 m (550 yd) reels, that is preshrunk and covered in stockinette to give a smooth surface makes an alternative, although it is not as strong. A soft paper piping cord is also available by the roll in sizes 4 to 8 and gives a smooth finish for use with thin fabric.

9. ROSETTES As varied as tassels, rosettes can be used on their own or with matching tassels.

10. TUFTS Styles of tufts are very varied, from flat pieces of leather to cut or looped hanks of thread pulled in around the middle.

11. TASSELS Many designs, colours and sizes are available. Key tassels can be attractive on cushions and scrolls, whereas much larger tassels used with cord are the right size to hold the arms on a Knole settee.

fabric, encasing the cord and allowing for a turning. Sew down the length with a double piping foot.

3 Position the second piece of cord on the wrong side of the fabric so that the two cords lie side by side. Fold the first cord, in its casing, over the second cord so that they again lie side by side, and sew down the middle between the two cords on top of the first line.

4 To use the double piping as a top finish, trim the surplus fabric underneath the cords, close to the stitching trim.

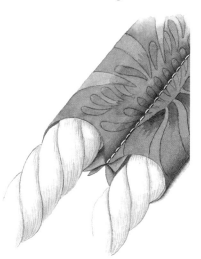

5 Glue the piping in position for a smooth finish. The piping can also be stapled on if there is no risk of the staples showing on the finished piece.

6 If you want to use the double piping along the bottom edge of a frame, trim back the raw edge of fabric along the length of piping to leave an excess that will act as a flange. Position the double piping along the bottom edge of the frame and glue it in place, leaving the flange hanging free. Then tack or staple the flange securely underneath the frame.

JOINING DOUBLE PIPING

It is best to make enough double piping to avoid joining it, but it may be necessary to do this *in situ* when the piping starts and finishes in the same place.

1 Mark the position of the join on both ends of piping. Cut across the piping, including seam allowances. Unpick the stitching in the fabric sufficiently to flatten the fabric out, and, matching the marks, machine stitch a seam straight across. Cut the exposed cords so they butt neatly. Wrap the fabric back around both cords as before and stitch down the centre gully.

2 If double piping is being used as a top trimming, cut the piping, leaving enough to turn under. Trim the cord to the exact length required and turn the excess fabric neatly under. Butt the two ends of the piping together and staple or glue securely in place.

Double piping

A very popular trimming that can be made in matching or contrasting fabric, double piping turns well around curves and gives a very neat finish. It is made in a similar manner to single piping, but has two lengths of cord side by side with a machine stitch down the middle. It is applied directly on to the furniture and not sewn to sections of fabric first.

1 Cut strips of fabric 5.5 cm (2¼ in) wide on the bias. Join them together in a long length with bias seams, matching any pattern, and trim the seam turnings to minimize bulk.

2 Lay the first length of cord on the wrong side of the

EXPERT TIP

With practice, you will be able to roll the fabric around both cords for double piping and machine stitch just once, thus taking half the time. Practise on short lengths first.

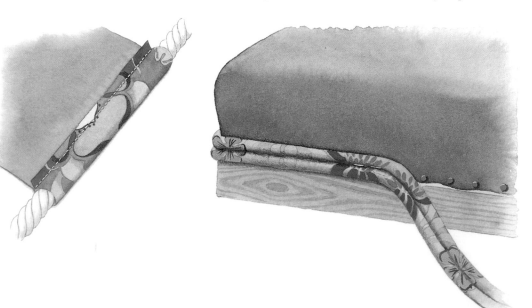

Ruche

Ruche is available ready made in several types, cut or uncut, in many colours, and looks like a miniature fringe. It is inserted between fabric sections using the same method as for piping.

1 Lay the length of ruche on the right side of the main fabric with its heading level with the raw edge of the fabric. Machine stitch the two together. Turn this section over.

2 Lay the second section of fabric underneath, right-sides together, and stitch just inside the first stitch line.

3 For uncut ruche, pull away the holding threads on the bottom edge and fluff the threads up to look attractive.

FABRIC RUCHE

You can also make a different style of ruche using fabric. This is heavier and more bulky, and usually matches the main fabric.

1 Cut straight lengths of fabric approximately 5 cm (2 in) in width.

2 Fold the fabric over lengthways, wrong-sides together, inserting piping cord in the centre. Fasten the end of the cord to the fabric with a pin.

3 Pleat or gather the edges as you machine stitch the fabric

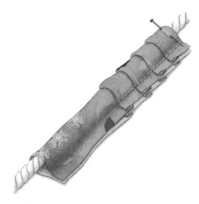

close to the cord, pulling the cord just enough to make the fabric gather.

4 Make enough ruche for your needs and attach in exactly the same way as described for single piping.

Flange cord

Flange cord consists of strands of cord twisted to make a rope, attached to a length of tape called a flange. There are usually three strands twisted together, in the same or different colours, but variations are available. The flange allows this type of cord to be inserted between two pieces of fabric in the same manner as shown for piping.

STITCHING IN FLANGE CORD

1 Lay the length of flange cord on the right side of the main fabric, aligning the flange edge along the raw edges, and, using a piping or grooved foot, machine stitch together.

2 Lay the section with the cord on top of the next section of fabric, right-sides together and with the raw edges aligned. Machine stitch the two sections together. Use a grooved foot on the sewing machine to stitch inside the original stitch line and as close as possible to the cord.

Cord

Cord consists of three or more lengths of cord twisted to make a rope effect. Traditionally, cord has always been hand sewn on to an edge, to accentuate an outline or cover a seam, using a circular needle and linen thread. This is very time consuming, but is still worthwhile because this achieves the best results.

1 Cut the cord a little longer than needed and unravel some of the covering thread. Cut the inner cord again to the desired length, leaving the unravelled thread attached, and use it to bind the cut end of cord. Fasten off securely.

2 Tuck the cut end under the cord or into a seam and stitch in position. Working towards you, take a stitch through the main fabric and pull the thread through.

3 Push the cord towards the needle until the individual

EXPERT TIP

Use a grooved foot on the sewing machine as it holds the flange cord firmer while sewing, making the process easier.

strands open out. Take the needle through a gap between the strands and then take a stitch through the main fabric again, twisting the cord to close it up and lay it back in position.

4 Take the next stitch in the main fabric, pulling the thread up tight and securing the cord into position.

5 Repeat this procedure until the end and then cut the cord and bind it. Tuck the end under and sew securely in place.

Gimp

Gimp is made in a variety of widths, typically 1.5 cm (³/₄ in), and sold by the metre (yard). It can be plain or multicoloured and designs are many and varied. The strands are usually overlaid, giving quite a heavy appearance. Gimp is mainly used for covering raw edges where the fabric meets the show wood, and it is usually glued on. Scroll gimps, with a scalloped finish along one edge, are particularly suitable for curves.

FIXING GIMP WITH HOT ADHESIVE

1 Before attaching the gimp, make sure that all the top fabric is trimmed back neatly, so that the gimp will lay flat.

2 Before starting, make sure the glue gun is very hot so that

the adhesive runs freely. Starting at a corner if possible, place a dot of adhesive on the end of the gimp and fold under to seal the end. Use a gimp pin if necessary to temporarily hold the gimp in place. Spread the adhesive 15 cm (6 in) along the back of the gimp and then lay it in place. Continue in short sections to avoid the adhesive drying and stiffening before you have time to position the gimp.

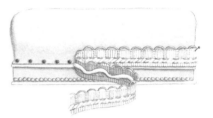

3 To turn a corner, put adhesive on the gimp to take it past the corner, then attach the outside corner of the gimp to the frame with a temporary gimp pin. Fold the gimp under on the diagonal to create a mitre with the fold flattening out on the outside corner. Place a dot of adhesive on the gimp and press it in place so that the inside corners meet exactly.

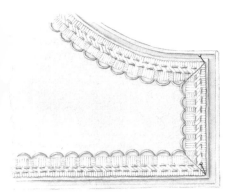

4 Continue to glue the gimp down until within 4 cm (1³/₄ in) of the end. Cut the gimp, allowing a turning. Place a dot of adhesive on the end and turn the gimp under. Glue the end in place. Hold in place until the adhesive dries, with a temporary gimp pin if necessary.

5 If the gimp needs to be joined, butt the folded ends together. Temporarily place a gimp pin in the two ends until the adhesive is hard, then remove.

FIXING GIMP WITH FABRIC ADHESIVE

1 Position the end of gimp on the furniture, turning a small amount underneath. Tack down just the turning with one or two gimp pins, depending on the width of the gimp. Squeeze a line of fabric adhesive from the tube down the centre of the main length of gimp and a small amount on the top fabric. Work on a relatively short length of gimp at a time and continue in the same way as for hot adhesive.

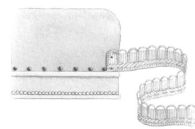

2 Gently hammer along the gimp to make sure it adheres to the fabric when using adhesive.

USING GIMP PINS

Gimp pins are sometimes used to secure gimp without the need to use adhesive.

1 Place the gimp in position, turning the end under. Place a gimp pin in the centre and tack it nearly home. Lift the top threads of the gimp with the point of a skewer and tack the gimp pin home underneath them. Lay the threads back over the pin.

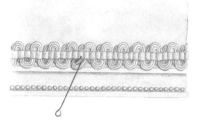

2 Continue to place pins at intervals of approximately 4 cm (1³/₄ in). Place them closer together round curves.

Braid

Braid is similar in structure to gimp, but made in many widths. It is generally flatter in appearance and woven rather than overlaid. Many designs and colours are available. Braid can be used as a feature to outline shapes or cover raw edges. It can be machined on to the fabric before covering, hand sewn on after covering, or glued in the same manner as gimp.

Fringe

Fringe usually has a heading like a gimp or braid incorporated into the top edge. The fringed edge can be cut or uncut, plain, tassled or bobbled. Made in many colours and designs, fringes are available in a variety of weights and lengths to suit many types of furniture. One of the most typically used types of fringe is 10 or 15 cm (4 or 6 in) deep and is put around the base of chairs as a luxurious embellishment. Fringe is usually hand stitched in place, but may be glued like gimp.

1 Fold the end of the fringe under and secure it in place with skewers, pulling the fringe slightly to keep it taut.

2 Backstitch the fringe in position along the top edge of the heading, using a fine slipping thread and a circular needle. Stitch two rows if the heading is deep. Finish the ends by folding under and sewing off securely.

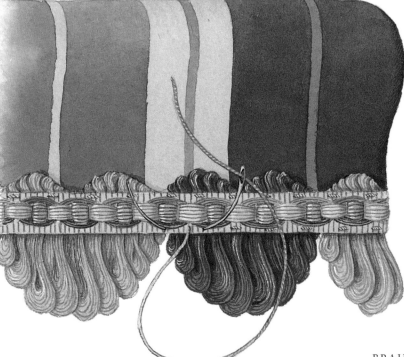

1 Using a double-ended needle and length of twine, thread the twine through the button or the loop on the tuft.

2 Then, with both ends of thread in the needle, push the needle, eye end first, right through from the top to the underside of the cushion.

3 Take one end of the twine out of the needle and thread the other end through the second button or tuft. Take that twine out of the needle and tie off the two ends of twine with a slip knot and a locking knot.

4 Trim off the ends of twine and tuck under the button or tuft. Trim tufts if they are uneven and fluff up to look attractive.

Buttons and tufts

Buttons and tufts can be used to hold stuffing in place, as with the deep buttoning already explained on the button-back armchair, or floating as pure decoration. Button forms come in various sizes, 13 mm (1/2 in) and 20 mm (3/4 in) being most used for upholstery, and they can be covered in the main or contrasting fabric. Tufts come in a variety of designs, from flat pieces of leather to cut or looped threads tied in the centre.

Deep buttoning using calico as anchor plugs on the back of the furniture is described for the button-back armchair (see page 70). Float buttons or tufts remain nearer the surface, indenting the fabric less, and the techniques used are described on the child's headboard (see page 114).

Buttons and tufts can also be sewn in pairs; for example, with one on the top and one on the bottom of a seat cushion.

Tassels and rosettes

Many designs, colours and sizes of tassels and rosettes are available and they can be made to order to match other trimmings. Tassels used with a cord can be a practical means of holding or tying arms in place, such as on a Knole settee. Both tassels and rosettes can also be used as decoration on scrolls, the bases of chairs and cushions. Most of these trimmings are sewn on by hand.

1 Thread the tassel cord from the front through the centre of the rosette and secure it at the back with a knot or by stitching it down. Trim the cord.

2 Sew the tassel and rosette on to the furniture with a slip stitch, using a circular needle and slipping thread.

3 To make a bolster decorated with a rosette, follow the method for bolster cushions (see page 110).

Nailing

Close nailing is a neat and decorative traditional method of finishing edges, where the nails are placed in a continuous row, each touching the next. Nails can also be spaced at intervals on their own or over braid or leather banding, or placed in patterns. Nails are available in several sizes, and a variety of colours and head shapes, although the most frequently used are 9 mm (³⁄₈ in) antique or domed-head brass or bronzed nails. It takes a great deal of skill to nail them evenly and needs practice as well as careful planning if a pattern is used. It is possible to buy strips of nails that give a similar effect to close nailing. These are fixed by nailing every few centimetres or so in a pre-cut hole. The effect looks the same from a distance, but does not pass close scrutiny.

1 Use a cabriole hammer to minimize damage to the nail heads. Pad the end with a small pad of wadding and cover the end of the hammer head with a circle of leather tied on with a length of twine.

2 It is advisable to use either a bought or home-made gauge for close nailing. Nails can also be spaced decoratively at intervals of approximately 7.5 cm (3 in) along a straight line.

3 Cut a piece of card 10 cm (4 in) wide and 2.5 cm (1 in) deep. Measure the radius of the decorative nails and draw a line to this depth along the long top edge. Push a row of nails into the card along this line and draw around the outline of the nails.

4 Remove the nails and mark along the edge at an equal distance between the nail holes. Draw a zigzag line joining the points along the edge to the nail holes and cut out this line.

5 Hold the gauge up to the edge to be nailed, starting in the centre of the furniture and working outwards. Hammer the nails partly in at the lower points on the zigzags. Leave one nail space free on the gauge so that you are able to continue with the next batch.

6 Remove the gauge and hammer all but the last nail home. Hold the gauge up to the work again, using the last nail to register the gauge, and repeat until the process is finished.

CUSHIONS

There are many types and shapes of cushions that can enhance a piece of furniture as well as provide extra comfort. Some cushions are an integral part of certain types of furniture, and methods for making them are given here.

Bordered cushions are essential to the design of furniture such as modern sofas, where the seat and back cushions provide the main padding and source of comfort. Most smaller cushions can be a matter of choice and their construction is not described here. However, the bolster can also be regarded as a vital part of some period pieces, as well as being decorative, and the method for making one is given at the end of this section.

Bordered cushions

In upholstery, the most common type of cushions are bordered back and seat cushions. They have a zip along the centre of the back border or they can be slip stitched to close them. The pads are made in a variety of materials. Feather pads are still available and for a seat or back bordered cushion are best bought ready made and specially to size because they need partitioned interiors to keep the feathers in place. Your local upholsterer should be able to order these for you if you provide the finished size. Allow for a pad slightly bigger than the space so that it looks generous when stuffed into the cushion cover. Many types of foam, latex and man-made fillings in various densities are also available and are used for different purposes. So take note of the upholsterer's advice, and then sit on the cushion to make sure it suits your needs before purchasing it.

When cutting fabric for an arm cushion or any shaped cushion, the procedure is exactly the same as for seat and back cushions. Make sure that you draw around the shape accurately, using the old cushion as a guide only to make your template.

MAKING A TEMPLATE

1 Make templates for bordered cushions after the upholstery of the main frame is finished. For a seat cushion, place the original cushion pad on the seat. Make sure it is still a good fit and the right depth, and use it as a guide for the template. For an arm or back cushion, make sure you allow for the seat cushion being in place.

2 Lay the top fabric on top of the cushion and pin it to each corner. Make sure the fabric is central and the pattern lines up on the inside back and front border.

3 With a piece of tailor's chalk, mark the outline of the seat cushion, allowing for any shaping around the inside back and arms. Mark the front edge of the cushion, keeping the lines straight, rather than following the lines of the old cushion, which will probably be out of shape.

4 Remove the fabric from the cushion and cut around the shape, leaving a seam allowance of 1.5 cm (½ in) all around. On the wrong side of the fabric, mark either the top for a back cushion or the front for a seat cushion. Now use this piece as your template. Lay the template on the rest of the fabric, wrong-sides together, matching the pattern, and cut out an identical second piece for the bottom of the cushion.

EXPERT TIP

If the cushion pad is very firm, make the zip border long enough to go around the sides. This will make it much easier to fit the cover on.

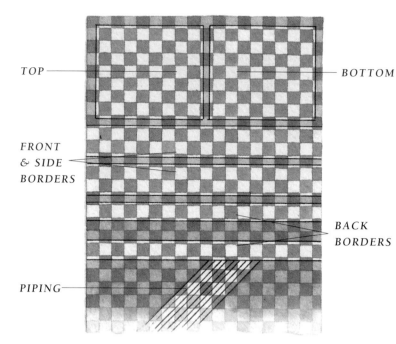

TOP — BOTTOM

FRONT
& SIDE
BORDERS

BACK
BORDERS

PIPING —

MAKING THE COVER

1 Overlock the inside edges of both back border sections. Fold over a 1.5 cm (½ in) turning along one of the edges and lay the zip just under it so that the zip teeth are covered. Pin in place.

2 Using a zip foot, machine stitch the zip in place as close to the zip teeth as the foot allows. Repeat the process to attach the second section of border on the other side of the zip, matching the pattern.

3 Make enough piping to go around the top and bottom of the cushion. Stitch this in place on the top and bottom sections, joining the piping at the back. Sew the border pieces together in the correct sequence, planning the positioning of the seams so that they will be least visible on the finished cushion. Do not cut the final side border to length until later.

4 Place the top of the cushion right-sides together with the top of the border, making sure the pattern lines up, and, starting with the back border, sew with a zip foot or grooved foot inside the first row of stitching. Before

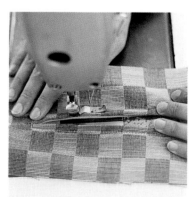

5 Check the depth of the border on the old cushion and add a seam allowance to this measurement. Cut lengths of fabric to the required width to make the borders to go around the two sides and front of the cushion. Cut a length of border for the back of the cushion, allowing for matching the pattern and twice the seam allowance. Cut the back border in half lengthways, so the zip can be inserted. Cut and make up enough piping to go around the top and base of the cushion.

CUTTING THE FOAM

1 Choose foam the correct depth for the cushion. This should be the same as the cover to avoid a ridge showing.

2 Lay the cover template on the foam and mark around it, thus including the turning allowances and making the foam at least 2 cm (1 in) larger than the cover, so that it fills out the cover well.

3 Using a foam cutter or a serrated bread knife, cut the foam while holding the knife absolutely straight, so that the cushion foam is the same size at the top and bottom.

4 Cut enough polyester wadding to wrap around the cushion. Spray adhesive on the top and base of the foam and lay the wadding on, butting the wadding on the back. Wrap the wadding over the ends.

5 Cut a length of stockinette and pull it over the cushion from one side to the other. Trim the excess stockinette off, tuck in the edges and hand sew using large oversewing stitches.

EXPERT TIP

An electric carving knife is very useful for cutting foam, but it may not be much use afterwards in the kitchen.

CUSHION FILLINGS & OTHER PADDINGS

A variety of materials are used to provide comfortable padding for modern furniture, either as part of the fixed upholstery or in the seat and back cushions.

1. RUBBERIZED HAIR A mixture of animal hair bonded in a rubber solution and made into sheets 2.5 cm or 5 cm (1 in or 2 in) thick. A good base for arms, backs and small seats on modern furniture.

2. POLYESTER WADDING Available in weights from 55 g to 500 g (2 oz to 18 oz) and in widths of 70 cm (27 in), 90 cm (36 in) and 1.4 m (54 in). Often used as padding over calico, but also to cover foam in cushions.

3. POLYURETHANE FOAM Available in different densities and thicknesses of 6 mm to 15 cm (1/4 in to 6 in), and sold in single cushions or in sheets. Use the densest for a firm seat to the least dense for inside backs.

4. PINCORE LATEX FOAM Available in soft, medium and firm densities. Made in large sheets or available in cut sizes 2.5 cm to 15 cm (1 in to 6 in) thick. It is heavy to handle but makes a firm, comfortable seat.

5. CHIP FOAM A very hard and dense, reconstituted foam made from foam offcuts and waste into sheets of up to 12 cm (5 in) thick. Used extensively in manufactured furniture.

6. STOCKINETTE A stretchy, loosely woven cotton or polyester mix fabric, of tubular construction, used to cover foam cushions. Available off the roll in widths of 30 cm (12 in) and 37.5 cm (15 in).

7. CUSHION PADS Pads of natural or synthetic fillings, available either ready made or made to measure. Bordered cushions often have interior walling to keep the filling evenly distributed.

the last side border is in position, check the exact length now needed to meet up with the back border. Pin the two borders together, trim the edges, and sew a seam. Finish stitching the border in place.

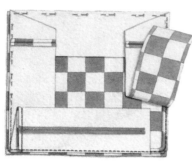

5 Now place the bottom piece of the cushion and the border right-sides together. Stitch in place.

EXPERT TIP
Undo the zip before sewing the bottom piece because you will have difficulty undoing it afterwards.

6 Turn the cover right-sides out. To fit the cover on the cushion, fold the pad in half lengthways. Put your knee on it if it is very resistant. Open the cover and push the pad well into the front corners. Turn all the pipings one way so that they lie flat. Tuck the back end of the pad in well and zip up.

Bolsters

Bolsters are often used as a feature on the end of couches, but, of course, they can be used on many pieces of furniture. This particular bolster has a pleated end and is decorated with a contrasting button for an added touch of style.

1 Decide on the size of the circular end of the bolster and make a paper or calico pattern that size. Draw around a plate if you have one the same size. If not, use a piece of twine the length of the radius, with one end knotted around a skewer and the other around a pencil, to use like a pair of compasses to draw a circle. Keep the pattern for future use.

2 For the length of fabric required to go around the main section of the bolster, measure around the outside circumference of the circular pattern and add seam allowances, plus extra for a zip if required. Decide how wide the bolster should be and add two seam allowances.

3 For the length of fabric needed to make the pleated ends, take the pattern circumference and add only the seam allowance. For the width of this piece of fabric, measure the radius of the pattern and add two seam allowances.

4 Transfer the measurements for one main section and two pleated ends of the bolster to the fabric, making sure the pattern on the end sections matches. Check all turnings have been

MAIN BOLSTER PANEL

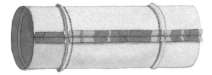

END PANELS

Make the stitches 2.5 cm (1 in) on the right side and 3 mm (¹/₈ in) on the wrong side of the fabric. Pull the stitching up very tightly, tucking the turnings in towards the cushion pad. Fasten off securely. Pleat the fabric neatly around the circular shape.

9 Thread the buttonless end of the loose twine through a second button and make an upholsterer's slip knot. Pull this end of twine tight until both ends are indented. Finish by locking off the knot securely, cutting off the ends of the twine and tucking them in behind the button.

allowed and cut out the pieces. Also cut out bias strips for piping if required.

5 Sew the two short ends of the main section together to form a tube and press the seam open. Put a zip in now if you wish, although this is not necessary for a buttoned-ended bolster. Join the two short sides of each end section together in the same manner. Pipe around both ends of the main section at this stage if desired, joining the piping at the back seam, or insert flange cord.

6 Join the two end pieces to the main section, matching the seams, and stitching inside the piping line.

Leave the twine dangling at both ends. Push the pad into the outside case, until it fits snugly into the main section of fabric.

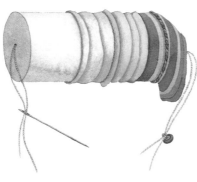

8 With a circular needle and a strong twine, sew a series of running stitches just inside the turning allowance around the edge of one of the end sections.

7 Thread a double-ended needle with one end of nylon twine and pass it through the shank of a button. Then thread the other end of the twine through the needle as well and take the needle through the bolster pad from the centre of one end to the centre of the other.

THE PROJECTS

Headboards

Two styles of headboard are shown here, both using the same basic upholstery materials and techniques. They are made from new plywood, but if you already have a headboard you can easily adapt the method to suit a different size or shape.

Dimensions (single bed)

height: 68 cm (27 in)
width: 76 cm (30 in)
depth: 2.5 cm (1 in)

Materials

- plywood 10 mm (³/8 in) thick
- foam 2.5 cm (1 in) thick, 80 x 85 cm (32 x 34 in)
- spray adhesive
- polyester wadding 56 g (2 oz), 1 m (1¹/4 yd)
- top cover fabric 1 m (1¹/4 yd)
- nylon twine
- 8 button forms 30 mm (1¹/4 in)
- fine tacks 13 mm (¹/2 in)
- staples 10 mm (³/8 in)
- lining 1 m (1¹/4 yd)
- slipping thread
- 2 lengths of wood for legs 50 mm x 12 mm x 30 cm (2 x ¹/2 x 12 in)
- 4 wood screws

❦ Quick Reference

Starting to top cover, positioning the buttons, page 80

Child's headboard

THE FABRIC FOR the child's headboard was chosen for the characters on it, which are bound to appeal to girls or boys. The broad spectrum of colours will blend with many bedroom schemes and, because the fabric is a cotton pocket weave, it is practical, too. You could pick out any of the colours in your fabric to accent with the buttons. Yellow worked well here and the rectangular shapes provided the perfect spacing for the float buttoning.

1 Measure the width of the bed to give the width of the board. Decide the height and shape of the board by drawing it on paper and checking the effect *in situ*. Mark out the shape on the plywood, including 15 cm (6 in) for the base section, and cut out with a saw. Alternatively, have the board cut at a local hardware store. Draw a line across the board 15 cm (6 in) from the bottom. The lower base section will be covered, but will not need buttoning as it will sit behind the mattress and pillows.

2 Decide on the positions for the buttons, bearing in mind the dimensions of the board and the pattern on the fabric. Do not place the buttons too near the edges of the board, but leave a minimum of 7.5 cm (3 in) all around and make sure they are positioned above the line already drawn. Work out the placement on the fabric first and transfer the measurements to the board.

3 When you are sure that the button marks are in the correct position, drill holes right through the board. Remember that you need a drill hole large enough for the needle and two widths of twine to pass through.

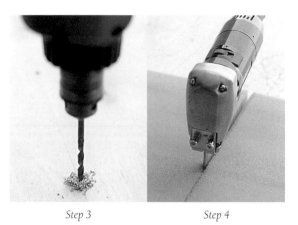

Step 3   *Step 4*

4 Lay the board on a piece of the foam and then draw around the shape. Mark another outline 2.5 cm (1 in) outside the first one. Use a foam cutter or a bread knife to cut around the larger outline. Chamfer the foam from the inner line to the outer edges.

5 Spray adhesive on to the centre of the board and lay it on the foam, keeping the inner marked line level with the board edges. Turn the

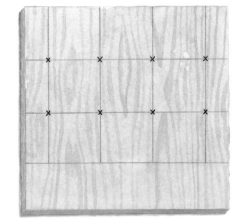

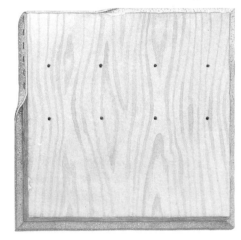

Experiment by drawing on paper first and tacking the design to the board. Look at the fabric to see if the pattern has a repeat that you can use to advantage. On this board, the rectangles on the fabric govern where the buttons are placed. They must be of equal distance from the centre.

Below: The yellow buttons on the brightly coloured fabric give the headboard a soft, rounded finish.

chamfered edges of foam over the edges of the board and staple all around, giving the edges a rounded appearance.

6 Push a double-ended needle through each drilled hole from the back, until it pierces the foam on the front. Using a craft knife, cut a tiny cross where the needle comes through. Cut a length of the wadding slightly larger than the front of the board and place it over the foam. Break the wadding open with your fingers where the button holes are marked.

7 Cut the top fabric to fit the board, allowing an extra 5 cm (2 in) all around. Mark the back of the fabric to correspond with the marks on the board and lay the fabric over the wadding.

8 Push the needle from the back of the board to the front through the marks on the fabric, with the eye of the needle going through first. Thread one end of the nylon twine through the button and then both ends through the needle. Pull the twine through until the button meets the board and the ends are on the back.

9 Place a temporary tack on the back of the board either side of the drilled hole. Wind one end of the twine twice around the tack and tack home, trapping the twine. Place a second tack near the first, and secure the other end of the twine around it, making sure that the button is tight to the board. Tack home. Repeat until all the buttons are in place, then trim off any long lengths of twine.

10 Pull the fabric over the edges of the board to the back. Secure with staples 2.5 cm (1 in) from the edge. Trim off any excess fabric.

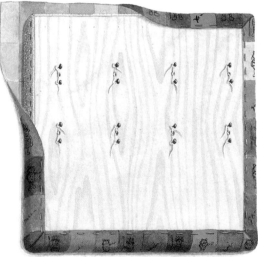

11 Place a piece of wadding over the back of the board, just in from the edge. Cut a piece of lining to fit the back of the board with a 1.25 cm (½ in) turning allowance all around. Turn the edges under and pin the lining in place close to the edge. Slip stitch the lining to the back all around.

12 Mark positions for the legs, screw in place on the back of the board and attach to the bed.

Dimensions
(single bed)

height: 65 cm (26 in)
width: 75 cm (30 in)
depth: 5 cm (2 in)

Materials

- plywood 10 mm (3/8 in) thick
- foam 5 cm (2 in) thick, 80 x 100 cm (32 x 40 in)
- spray adhesive
- staples 10 mm (3/8 in)
- polyester wadding 56 g (2 oz), 1.5 m (1 3/4 yd)
- top cover fabric 1.5 m (1 3/4 yd)
- fine tacks 13 mm (1/2 in)
- flange cord 4 m (4 1/2 yd)
- staples 14 mm (5/8 in)
- back tack strip 75 cm (30 in)
- lining 1 m (1 1/4 yd)
- slipping thread
- 2 picture plates

Romantic headboard

SOFT, ROUNDED CONTOURS and pleating give this headboard a feminine look. The fabric used for this project is a subtle cream-coloured silk damask. The central pattern has been carefully positioned to create a main feature and the light and shade in the fabric design give it many varied facets, depending on the angle from which it is viewed.

1 Decide on the shape and size of your headboard by drawing it on paper and checking the effect *in situ*. For the shape shown here, a height of approximately twice the distance from the floor to the top of the mattress gives pleasing proportions. Mark out the shape on the plywood, including 15 cm (6 in) for the base section, and cut out with a jigsaw. Alternatively, have the board cut at your local hardware store.

2 Draw a line across the board 15 cm (6 in) from the bottom. The lower base section will be covered, but will sit behind the mattress. Draw another line for the pleated border section, around the sides and top, 12.5 cm (5 in) from the edges. Adjust this line to create a pleasing contour and make sure the design is perfectly symmetrical.

3 Cut a piece of the foam to fit the exact size of the board down to the line for the base section. Carefully mark and cut the foam following the border contour, and retain both the centre and border sections of foam.

4 Spray adhesive on to the centre of the board and glue the centre section of foam to it. Staple 10 mm (3/8 in) staples all around the foam just inside the edges of the board. Place a layer of wadding over the foam and tear it just inside the line.

5 Plan the positioning of the top fabric so a motif falls centrally, and cut the fabric to cover the centre panel with at least 5 cm (2 in) extra all around. Temporary tack the fabric in position.

✖ *Quick Reference*

Covering the outsides, attaching flange cord, page 86

117

SILK

*Silk fibre has an
incomparable sheen.
Even when woven into a
heavy gauge, slub fabric,
it produces a surface
that reflects the light in
a unique and magical
way. Some examples are
quite extreme. Shot silk,
for example, appears to
be different colours
when viewed from
different viewpoints.
Between the heavy,
almost matt slubs and
the butterfly iridescence
of shot silk lies a broad
spectrum of silk and
silk-mix fabrics, which
have been used in
upholstery for centuries
to produce furnishings of
splendour. Woven into
damasks and brocades,
alone, or mixed with
other fibres such as
cotton and jute for
durability, silk is the
ultimate in glamourous
top coverings.*

6 When the fabric on the centre panel is smooth, use 10 mm (3/8 in) staples to secure it all around the marked line. Remove the temporary tacks.

7 Place the flange cord on the line, with the cord side tight against the padded centre section. Staple the cord along the sides and top of the centre section with 14 mm (5/8 in) staples.

8 Cut strips for the pleated border across the width of the remaining fabric, each strip deep enough to cover the foam and wadding and to pull over the outer edge with a turning of 7.5 cm (3 in). Join the strips, matching the pattern, to make one length. Starting at the centre top, pleat the border into place so the turning allowance lies just outside the cord line and the bulk of the fabric lies, right-sides together, on top of the centre section. Work out from the top and down both sides so the pleats fold out from the centre. Ease extra fabric into the pleats on the corners to allow for the extra width of the border at these points. Staple back tack strip over the turning allowance, tight against the cord underneath.

9 Push the border section of foam in place to meet the centre section, so that it fits snugly, and cover with wadding. Pull the pleated fabric over the border and arrange the pleats over the outer edge. Staple the fabric to the back of the board 2 cm (1 in) from the edge with 10 mm (3/8 in) staples. Measure a length of flange cord long enough to take it from one bottom edge of the board, along the top and down the other side. Fit it along the back edge of the padded border and staple tight against the pleating, leaving enough cord at each end to attach to the base board.

10 Position a length of fabric along the marked line of the base section, right-side down over the padded section, matching the pattern to the centre panel. Temporary tack from one edge to the other using a back tack strip. Staple in place with 10 mm (3/8 in) staples and remove the tacks.

11 Pad the base section with wadding and pull the fabric down over it. Secure the fabric at the back of the board with 10 mm (3/8 in) staples.

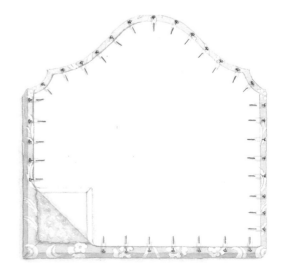

Cut off all excess fabric on the back of the board. Secure the remaining lengths of flange cord along the edges. Cut a piece of wadding a little smaller than the board and lay in position on the back. Cut a piece of lining slightly larger than the board, turn the edges under and pin in place on the back, just inside the outer edge. Slip stitch in position.

12 Fit picture plates to the back of the board so that it can be fixed to the wall, holding it rigidly in position. Alternatively, you may wish to fix the board to the bed rather than the wall. In this case, screw two legs in position on the back of the board, as for the child's headboard, and then attach them to the bed.

Above: Co-ordinating bed linen has been chosen to carry the soft, romantic theme of the headboard.

TRIMMINGS *decorative disguise*

There are many interesting trimmings available. Even if the trimming is to be a functional one, there is no need for it to be boring. Decorative nails can be particularly surprising as they range through different shapes and antique finishes, and can be applied in elaborate patterns, as on the stool here.

THIS LOOK AT trimmings encompasses what can be described as the nuts and bolts of the trimmings world—those that are so much a part of the upholstery that they perform constructional roles as well as provide decorative interest.

Effective cover up

Many trimmings have developed out of sheer necessity. Early looms were not wide enough to produce cloth to span wide backs and seats, so braids were devised to conceal the seams and by the eighteenth century were in regular use. The practical need to conceal a raw edge and a line of

tacks where upholstery meets show wood can be dealt with simply and decoratively by choosing to add braid, gimp, piping or close nailing. A line of double piping can easily be as wide as braid and has an understated, refined appeal. Gimp, though often more expensive than braid, makes a good choice because its scrolled structure gives it the flexibility to go smoothly around curves and mitre neatly at corners.

Decorative nailing, closely butted or spaced imaginatively, applied directly on to the top cover or through a band of leather, braid or fringe, has been popular for centuries. It requires great

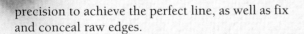

precision to achieve the perfect line, as well as fix and conceal raw edges.

Defining shapes

Piping is a particularly versatile trimming. As it is tough and pliable, it is indispensable where wearability is of prime importance. Relatively inexpensive, it can be made from bias strips of the top cover, matching the rest of the upholstery precisely. It really comes into its own when used to define the contours of a piece of furniture, equally capable of giving a distinctive character to the slick, straight lines of a modern sofa or the soft shapes of an antique tub chair. Different effects can be further enhanced by choosing matching or toning fabric, or a wild contrast for your piping.

Enjoy experimenting with these unsung heroes of the trimmings department. Although their use may be essential to the functionality of your upholstery, used creatively they can also enhance the shape of the furniture and the choice of top fabric. The right trimming on a carefully executed piece of upholstery can produce a finish that brings out all the care and discipline that went into its making.

Trimmings can be useful for hiding unsightly joins, or for covering up tacks and staples. The double piping on this button-back chair neatly covers the raw edge of fabric around the chair frame, particularly on the arm pads. On such a traditional chair, conventional trimmings are often the most appropriate choice.

121

Four-fold Screen

Two different fabrics were chosen to give the two sides of this screen a complete contrast that would suit different moods. The braid trimming complements and blends with the fabrics on both sides of the screen.

Dimensions

height: 1.7 m (72 in)
width: 1.6 m (63 in)
depth: 2 cm (1 in)

Materials

- brown parcel paper to cover both sides
- spray adhesive
- wallpaper size (small packet) or water
- main top cover fabric 4 m (4½ yd)
- contrast top cover fabric 3.5 m (4 yd)
- bump interlining 7 m (7½ yd)
- fine tacks 13 mm (½ in)
- staples 10 mm (³/₈ in)
- 6 hinges and screws
- hot adhesive sticks
- braid 17.5 m (19½ yd)
- cotton webbing 1.75 m (2 yd)
- 8 large antique nails

THIS SCREEN WAS found covered in a cotton curtain fabric, which was in poor condition, although this was obviously not the original covering. The frame is a bit warped, but still sturdy, so the screen was well worth re-covering.

A cotton fabric with fresh meadow flowers gives a crisp, clean look to one side, and is well worth the extra fabric needed for matching the pattern. A printed cotton with classic gold and cream stripes lends a sophisticated and smart appearance to the reverse.

There is a revival in the popularity of screens. They provide a flexible division of areas throughout the home and a re-covered screen makes a very useful accessory.

1 Strip all the old cover from the frame. Remove the old tacks and paper and scrape the edges of the frame so that they are free from adhesive. Remove the screws from the hinges and store in a safe place if you wish to reuse them, although usually it is better to renew them.

2 Cut eight lengths of brown parcel paper to fit both sides of the panels. Spray adhesive on the flat surface of the first panel frame. Place the paper on the frame, pulling it taut as you position it on the adhesive. Paper all the panels in this manner on both sides, and allow the adhesive to dry.

3 Trim the edges of the paper with a craft knife, so that the paper does not overlap. Using a brush, paint the screen with wallpaper size or water across the centre hollow on each side of each panel, taking care not to wet the glued edge. As the paper dries, it shrinks so that it is drum tight.

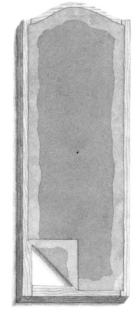

4 Measure the first panel for the main top fabric, making an allowance to cover the edges of the frame all around. Position the fabric so that the pattern is central and, if possible, so that you do not cut through a pattern repeat at the top or the bottom of the panel. Mark your measurements on the fabric on the wrong side, and cut out the first section. Measure and cut the other three sections in exactly the same way.

5 Using the contrast fabric, measure and cut out the four sections for the reverse of the screen, repeating the process used for cutting out the fabric for the front.

EXPERT TIP

Covering the panel with bump interlining will give a padded look, but if you prefer a sharper edge you can use curtain lining instead.

Below: The cream and gold stripes not only give a sophisticated look, they also create an illusion of height.

Step 6   Step 7

6 Cut eight lengths of bump interlining, enough to cover each panel with an allowance all around. Place the first panel on a firm surface, then place the bump on top. Stretching the bump as you work, temporary tack it around the edges of the frame. Staple the bump around the edges of the frame, then remove the temporary tacks and trim off the excess. Repeat this process on both sides of all the panels.

7 Using the same method, cover the panels with the fabric. Slightly overlap the front and back fabrics along the centre line on the sides of the frames. Staple in place and trim off the excess.

8 Place the first and second panels together with the contrast fabric sides facing each other. Cut a strip of contrast fabric wide enough to cover both side edges of the two panels and long enough to cover both edges from top to bottom plus a 4 cm (1½ in) turning at each end. Place the strip right-side down and staple it in place along both edges of each frame to join the panels and stop the gap. Trim the strip, leaving a raw edge down each side. Turn over the top and bottom of the strip and staple down. Repeat this process to join all the panels, matching the fabric on the strips and the panels to the inner folds of the screen.

9 Mark the strip where the hinges will be fitted to the frame, and drill pilot holes for the screws.

Left: Continuity is achieved by matching the fabric used on the panels to that used to line the inner folds of the screen.

Fit the hinges carefully, making sure that they are level along the edges.

10 Glue the braid along all the side and top edges of each panel, covering the hinges and taking care to keep the lines very straight.

11 Staple cotton webbing to the bottom edge of the screen. Place an antique nail on the bottom edge of each panel to prevent the fabric from wearing and to help slide the screen across the floor.

Quick Reference
Trimmings, fixing gimp with hot adhesive, page 102

Circular Stool

The Jacquard weave fabric with its free-flowing geometric design complements the simple lines of this stool. Stripes are an unusual choice for a round shape but, by taking care to centre the pattern, this type of fabric can be made to work successfully.

Dimensions

height: 14 cm (6 in)
width: 38 cm (15 in)
depth: 38 cm (15 in)

Materials

- foam 2.5 cm (1 in) thick, 46 x 46 cm (18 x 18 in)
- spray adhesive
- staples 14 mm (⁵/₈ in)
- polyester wadding 56 g (2 oz), 50 cm (20 in)
- top cover fabric 50 cm (20 in)
- fine tacks 13 mm (¹/₂ in)
- black bottom 50 cm (20 in)
- staples 10 mm (³/₈ in)

A SMALL CIRCULAR STOOL makes a useful piece of furniture for resting your feet or for a child to perch on, as well as making an attractive accessory. Small stools can be bought ready for covering in your own choice of fabric or you may be lucky enough to find an old one in an antique shop. The stool that is refurbished here is very well made, with a removable centre section that is ready for upholstery. The joins in the base give an interesting contrast in the grain of the wood.

The fabric colours blend very well with the tones and grain of the wood and together make this a lively little stool.

1 Remove the screws holding the centre board in place and remove the feet. Lay the centre board on the foam and draw around it with a marking pen. Mark another line 2.5 cm (1 in) outside the first line. Cut around the outer circle on the marked line with a foam cutter or a bread knife. Chamfer the foam from the inner line to the outer edge.

2 Spray a circle of adhesive onto the board and place the foam on it centrally so that the top edge overhangs the board. Fold the top edge of the foam down to the board, and staple it around the top of the board close to the edge with 14 mm (⁵/₈ in) staples. Do not go over the edge or the board will not fit in the frame. Always check the gap before proceeding.

3 Cut a circle of polyester wadding and place this over the foam, tearing off the edge just short of the foam edge.

4 Cut the top fabric into a square and place it, with the pattern central, on top of the wadding. Place four temporary tacks at equal intervals apart, on the underside of the board, making sure the fabric has not moved. Place temporary tacks at 2.5 cm (1 in) intervals, working across from opposite sides, and pulling the fabric tight as you work. Ease the excess fabric on the underside of the board until the sides and top are smooth. Staple 2.5 cm (1 in) from the outer edge. Remove the tacks and trim off the excess fabric.

with 10 mm (3/8 in) staples. Locate the screw holes in the base and pierce the fabric with a regulator.

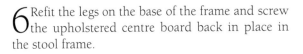

5 Cut a circle of black bottom for the base, allowing a 1.5 cm (1/2 in) turning. Place on the base, turn under just inside the edge of the stool and secure

6 Refit the legs on the base of the frame and screw the upholstered centre board back in place in the stool frame.

STRIPES

Stripes are typically associated with straight, even lines, but there is actually a wide variety to choose from when it comes to selecting fabrics and trimmings. A shaded striped ribbon might be a better choice for trimming a softly contoured piece covered in a pale fabric than a crisp, bright, candy-pole stripe.

STRIPES HAVE ENJOYED popularity throughout decorating history. Their crisp regularity combines well with both patterned and plain fabrics to add a touch of order to a scheme without being intrusive.

The overall effect achieved depends on the sort of stripe you use. Whether they are evenly spaced or in random widths, rigidly straight or waywardly wavy, with a plain texture or with patterning in the weave, stripes are available in every variant imaginable, from workaday cottons to the most luxurious damasks, brocades and silks.

Crisp stripes

The fashion for natural fibres and the wider acceptance of fabrics that in the past were thought of as utilitarian has meant that cotton stripes are now produced in a wide array of sophisticated colours far beyond the classic navy and white. Not only the stripe, but the starchy, crisp handle of the fabric adds to the brisk, well-pressed and invigorating look. No wonder stripes remind us of deck chairs at the seaside and stimulate a happy, holiday feel.

With careful choice it is possible to play off stripes on an unpretentious fabric against an intricate piece of furniture to produce a pared-down, sophisticated effect. Even an elegant, antique gilded chair dressed in modest cotton or linen stripes acquires a clean, cool look.

Elegant stripes
Of course, stripes can also look supremely luxurious. Throughout history, designers have borrowed stripes from the military to give an air of confident elegance to décor. Stripes in sumptuous fabrics spell success and classic luxury. Think of Cecil Beaton's designs for *My Fair Lady*—broad stripes in black and white silk turned flower girl Eliza into a society darling.

For dramatic effect, use wide stripes on a pale background. For a more subtle finish that still exudes quality, choose closely related colours, such as bottle green and cobalt blue.

Wavy stripes
Stripes are not necessarily in straight lines, but can follow a linear design more loosely and still retain their graphic quality. Undulating stripes filled with diamonds on a richly coloured fabric combine the best of both worlds, with a jolly abandon that is sumptuous at the same time.

The loose stripes of the fabric on this little round stool may be a surprising choice, tightly contained as they are by the circle of the wooden frame. But the combination works well and, in such warm colours, offers a welcome invitation to weary feet.

129

Drop-in Seat

The base on this seat is plywood, so with minimal upholstery the finished seat would be quite hard. Adding a small amount of fibre under the cotton felt gives the seat a lift, with a more rounded appearance and some extra comfort for the sitter.

Dimensions

height: 95 cm (38 in)
width: 41 cm (16 in)
depth: 41 cm (16 in)

Materials

- hessian 50 cm (20 in)
- fine tacks 13 mm (1/2 in)
- twine
- fibre (two handfuls)
- cotton felt 50 cm (20 in)
- calico 50 cm (20 in)
- gimp pins 13 mm (1/2 in)
- fine tacks 10 mm (3/8 in)
- skin wadding 1700 g (48 oz), 50 cm (20 in)
- top cover fabric 50 cm (20 in)
- black bottom 50 cm (20 in)

◯ *Quick Reference*
Bridle ties, page 60

THIS TYPE OF drop-in seat has the front corners cut out to accommodate the frame. It is therefore slightly more fiddly to upholster than the type with all-square corners, but as a result it is a more interesting piece to work on.

The fabric chosen as a top cover is a strong, hard-wearing woven check suitable for the amount of wear and tear often given to these sturdy chairs. The colouring and repeated woven motif is reminiscent of a gingham, but is subtle enough to suit either a country or town scheme. This chair was painted to match the fabric and distressed to give it a well-loved look.

1 Remove the drop-in seat from the chair frame. Cut a piece of hessian large enough to cover the seat to the edge with a turning allowance. Place the hessian on the seat, covering the plywood. Stretch it from side to side and back to front, securing it in the centre of each section of the seat with a 13 mm (1/2 in) temporary tack. Continue to stretch the hessian over the plywood, temporary tacking all around at 5 cm (2 in) intervals just inside the edge of the seat.

2 Tack home all the tacks and fold the excess hessian in towards the centre of the seat. Place another row of tacks all around, in the spaces between the first row, to secure the folded hessian in place. Fold the hessian at the corners, first one edge down, then the other over the top, and tack home. Neatly trim off any excess hessian.

3 Stitch three rows of bridle ties across the hessian, then tease a few handfuls of fibre under the ties until the centre of the seat is covered. Place two layers of cotton felt over the fibre and trim off the excess just inside the seat edge.

4 Cut a piece of calico 5 cm (2 in) larger than the seat size all around. Secure the calico under the centre front of the seat with a temporary tack, pull it over the seat and temporary tack under the centre back of the seat. Repeat from side to side, placing a temporary tack in the centre of each side. Working from the centres to the corners, push the calico over the edge of the seat with one hand while pulling with the other, and secure with temporary tacks around the underside as you work.

5 Fold the two back corners under and tack home. At the front corners, pull the excess calico down into each shaped front corner and

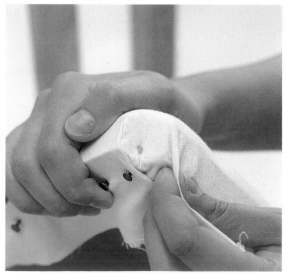

place one gimp pin right in the centre to secure it. Cut away the excess calico and make a fold on each of the outer edges of both corners. Secure the calico under the seat with 10 mm (3/8 in) tacks.

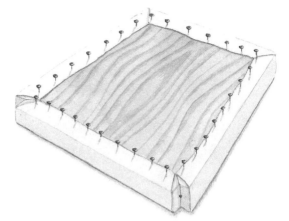

6 When the calico is tight and the edges look sharp with no bumps, tack home. Lay a piece of wadding over the calico, and tear the edge so that it just meets the top edge of the stuffing. Do not let the wadding go over the edge or the seat will not fit back into the chair frame.

7 Cut the top fabric, centring the pattern and allowing an extra 5 cm (2 in) beyond the lower edge. Cover the seat with the fabric in the same way as with the calico, temporary tacking with 13 mm (1/2 in) tacks to keep the pattern in line.

8 Tack home the fabric underneath the bottom of the seat. Trim off the excess, leaving a raw edge. Place a piece of black bottom over the underside of the seat, and cut it to fit the actual seat size. Turn the edges under and tack all around the seat with 10 mm (3/8 in) tacks at 5 cm (2 in) intervals just in from the edge. Push the finished seat into the chair frame, easing the back in first.

Metal Chair

The chair is covered in a crisp white cotton fabric that features lemons so vibrant that they are almost edible. The sharp outlines of the citrus fruit design work well with the clean, modern lines of the metal frame.

THIS TYPE OF metal-legged chair is fairly inexpensive to buy. Although already upholstered, it is quick and easy to re-upholster a whole set of chairs to co-ordinate with other furnishings.

With a random pattern such as this, experiment before cutting the fabric. Position the pattern so that it looks pleasing and well balanced. Pale-coloured fabrics can be sprayed with a protector before use so that any spills can be wiped off without staining.

1 First remove the screws securing the seat from the underside of the frame. Strip the old cover off carefully without damaging the calico or the foam under it. The foam is fire retardant, and, as it is already moulded to shape, it would be a shame to waste it. Leave the foam and calico in place.

2 Cover the seat with a piece of polyester wadding and cut it a little oversize so that it can be turned under the seat to give a soft edge. Do not cut it more than 1.25 cm (¹/₂ in) oversize, so that later the top fabric can be turned under with minimum bulk and stapled down between the edge and the chair legs.

3 Mark the centre of the front, back and sides of the seat frame on the fabric. Place the top fabric over the seat, carefully positioning the pattern, and put a fine pin into the fabric to align with each of the four marks on the frame.

4 Turn the seat over and, keeping the pins lined up with the marks, start temporary tacking at these points first. Temporary tack around the underside of the seat, working out from each centre point towards the corners and easing the fabric around the corners. When the fabric is taut and evenly distributed, staple it all around just under the bottom edge. Remove the temporary tacks.

5 Place the black bottom on the underside of the seat. Turn the raw edges under and staple in place, neatly covering the first row of staples holding the fabric. To complete the chair, screw the seat back on to the metal frame.

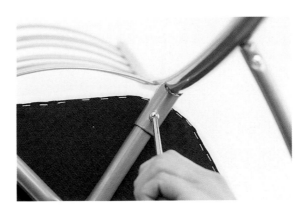

Dimensions
height: 105 cm (42 in)
width: 45 cm (18 in)
depth: 45 cm (18 in)

Materials
- polyester wadding 56 g (2 oz), 50 cm (20 in)
- top cover fabric 68.5 cm (27 in)
- fine tacks 13 mm (¹/₂ in)
- staples 10 mm (³/₈ in)
- black bottom 50 cm (20 in)

∞ *Quick Reference*
Estimating top fabric, positioning a pattern, page 79

YELLOWS

Yellow looks equally at home in a traditional or modern setting. The strong, smooth lines of this metal chair provide a perfect frame for the simple citrus pattern. A crisp cotton fabric such as this is an ideal choice for a chrome or steel frame, both contributing to the freshness of a modern style.

YELLOW IS SYNONYMOUS with sunshine, streaming in through the window to gladden the heart and light everything in its path with a golden glow.

Of all the colours, yellow is the best able to create an uplifting and cheerful mood, without the risk of giving offence. It has the power to add warmth to the dullest corner and, not being overbearing, is perfect for multipurpose rooms. A soft yellow dining room, for example, is enlivening at breakfast, but not overwhelming enough to distract the student who needs the dining table later.

Classic combinations
Yellow combines happily with other colours to create many different effects. It can be very sophisticated, whether it plays a subdued part with neutrals or spells opulence when presented in deep rich golds. Soft buttery yellows woven with creams into luxurious fabrics such as silks and damasks will highlight the beauty of classically shaped furniture. On the other hand, mixed with white, black and silver, yellow will look much sharper and suit contemporary, urban-style interiors furnished with glass, steel and chrome.

Idyllic country cottage warmth is another look that can be created with yellows, whether in a farmhouse or a townhouse kitchen. Generous layering of shades from the warmer end of the spectrum, using natural fabrics such as sturdy cottons and crunchy linens, will create just the appropriate homely air.

The fresh alternative

In contrast, yellow can also be contemporary and fun. Taken towards the green end of the colour spectrum, citrus shades produce schemes that are lively and dynamic. Bright, acid colours can become exhausting over time, so limit them to small accent pieces of furniture or use them on larger ones with more care. A grapefruit-coloured sofa bed, for example, with the added zing of lime-coloured cushions or trimmings, would make a focal point in a teenager's room but would certainly not be the best choice for a relaxing study.

There is a yellow to suit every style of furniture, antique or modern. Just remember the mood you wish to create, choose your yellows from the appropriate end of the spectrum and have fun combining them with other colours.

The fabric chosen for this settle creates an elegant, yet quite formal look, particularly when trimmed with the elegant gold gimp. The golden yellow floral pattern, along with the dark wood of the frame, would give a room a warm, inviting feel.

135

Campaign Chair

The combination of warm colours and the glow of the orange in the check cotton fabric complement the wooden frame of this campaign chair well. The straight lines of the pattern and bronzed decorative nails echo its military heritage.

Dimensions

height: 100 cm (40 in)
width: 50 cm (20 in)
depth: 50 cm (20 in)

Materials

- top cover fabric 1.5 m (1³/4 yd)
- platform cloth 50 cm (20 in)
- machine thread
- webbing 3 m (3¹/2 yd)
- cotton felt 50 cm (20 in)
- skin wadding 1700 g (48 oz), 1 m (1¹/4 yd)
- fine tacks 13 mm (¹/2 in)
- 25 antique nails
- staples 14 mm (⁵/8 in)

✇ Quick Reference

Estimating top fabric, page 78

Machine stitching, page 30

Trimmings, nailing, page 106

THE CAMPAIGN CHAIR originated when armies were on the move from camp to camp. It is rather like a sophisticated deck chair, making a comfortable seat, yet is reasonably light and compact to carry around. Campaign chairs can still be found, but they are not likely to be in mint condition.

The chair shown here has been in our family for a long time. My father re-covered it once, but it was now due for complete refurbishment, so it is a matter of starting from scratch. Look at your own project and decide if the upholstery is going to last as long as the new cover. On a chair of this size, it is generally a false economy to renew just the cover.

1 Remove the old cover, complete with the original padding, by carefully taking out all the old tacks using a mallet and ripping chisel.

2 To estimate the amount of top fabric you will need, make a note of the following measurements. Measure across the width of the top and bottom rails of the inside back. Next measure from under the top rail, allowing for the fabric to wrap around the rail and finish flush at the base of the bottom rail. Repeat the steps above on the seat, allowing for wrapping the fabric over the front and back rails. Transfer all of these measurements to a cut sheet, allowing turnings of 1.25 cm (¹/2 in) on all sides. You will need two pieces of fabric for the back, and one piece of fabric for the top of the seat. For the underside of the seat, you will need two strips of fabric, each 10 cm (4 in) wide and the same length as the other seat section.

3 Mark the measurements on the wrong side of the top fabric, taking care to match the pattern on all of the sections, particularly so that it runs down the back and seat along the centre line. Cut out the fabric.

4 Platform cloth is used with the top fabric panels underneath the seat to give a firm foundation. Cut a piece of platform cloth the same size as the top seat section. Mark a line 9 cm (3¹/2 in) in from both long sides of the cloth.

5 Pin one strip of fabric for the underside of the seat to each line on the platform cloth, right-sides together and allowing a 1 cm (¹/2 in) seam allowance on the top cover. Machine stitch the fabric along each line, and fold it back so that it is level with the outer edge of the platform cloth. Press the seams and pin the outer edges together. Now treat this as one piece of fabric.

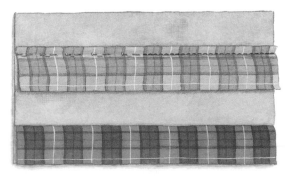

NAILS

Since the earliest upholstery, nails have been not only an integral part of upholstery manufacture, but a decorative feature in their own right. In the seventeenth century, every available form of decoration was employed, including high-domed nails that seem, to modern tastes, quite inappropriately scaled. Some of these nails were at least four times larger than the nails that are in use today, and were arranged in elaborate patterns for even greater visual impact. Today, we still have a vast array of decorative nails with which to add interest to a piece, whether by elaborate double nailing or as a discreet close-nailed accent offering practical protection to the bottom edge or corner of a seat, but the emphasis is on subtlety, not brashness.

6 Place the top and the underneath sections of the seat right-sides together. Pin and machine stitch a 1 cm (½ in) seam down each side. Turn the fabric right-sides out.

7 Place the top and bottom pieces of the back section right-sides together, and machine stitch down both sides. Turn the back section of fabric right sides out.

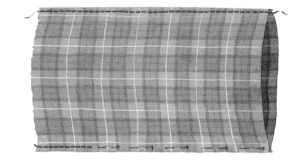

8 Cut two pieces of webbing 10 cm (4 in) longer than the seat section, and two pieces 10 cm (4 in) longer than the back section. Place two pieces of webbing inside each section, the same distance from the seams and from each other. Secure the webbing with upholstery pins at each end to hold in place temporarily. This webbing will hold the main weight when the chair is sat on, and prevent the fabric from splitting.

9 Make a padding of cotton felt wrapped in a layer of wadding approximately 3 cm (1½ in) thick, to fit inside both the seat and back sections. Carefully place the padding inside each section, keeping the webbing on the underside. Pin across each end of the two sections and then machine stitch across the ends to secure the padding to the sections.

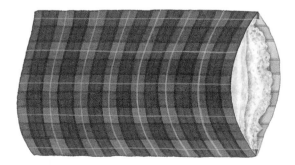

10 Position the top end of the back pad 2.5 cm (1 in) up from the bottom edge of the front of the head rail. Tack along this rail, keeping the fabric level. Fold the back pad under the head rail and pull it over the top of the rail to the front.

11 Turn the raw edges at the bottom end of the back section to make a neat closure. Place this end on the bottom edge of the inside back rail and tack in place, with one tack at each edge and one in the centre.

12 Removing the temporary tacks as you work, place antique nails at measured intervals along the front side of the head rail and along the bottom of the inside back rail, to hold the fabric in position.

13 Secure the back edge of the seat section to the front of the bottom back rail with staples. Fold over the top of the rail, across the seat area, and secure to the underside of the front rail with staples. Fold the chair into a flat position in order to gain access to the underside of the rails.

Chippendale-style Stool

This stool has a tack roll, an alternative to the stitched edge. Fibre is rolled in hessian and tacked down to make a hard edge, which gives a good line to the finished stool. A stool of this size is a good introduction to upholstery.

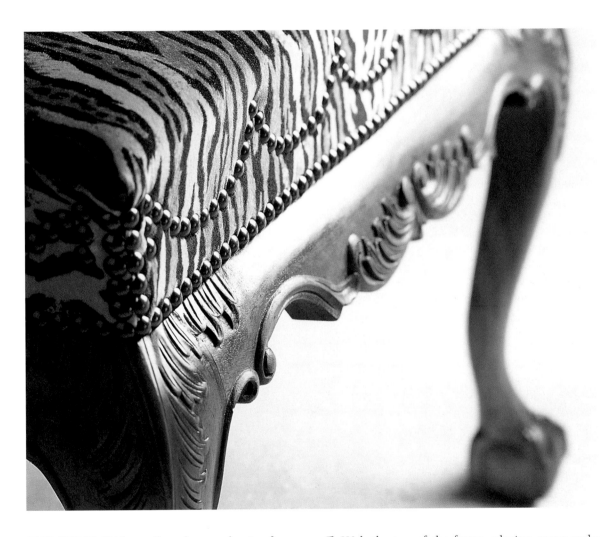

Dimensions

height: 49 cm (20 in)
width: 67 cm (27 in)
depth: 48 cm (19 in)

Materials

- English webbing 6.5 m (7 yd)
- improved tacks 13 mm (1/2 in)
- hessian 1 m (1 1/4 yd)
- fine tacks 13 mm (1/2 in)
- fibre 1.4 kg (3 lb)
- improved tacks 10 mm (3/8 in)
- twine
- cotton felt 1 m (1 1/4 yd)
- calico 75 cm (30 in)
- staples 10 mm (3/8 in)
- skin wadding 1700 g (48 oz), 1 m (1 1/4 yd)
- top cover fabric 75 cm (30 in)
- antique nails

THIS STOOL HAS a well-made reproduction frame, stained to complement the colour of the animal print fabric. Animal patterns are often revived from time to time and give an opulent elegance to a piece of furniture, a theme carried through here with the ball and claw leg on the frame. The pattern of antique nailing also adds a unique touch.

This frame was originally intended to have a drop-in seat, but, as it is quite sturdy, it is possible to take the fabric over the edges to form a padded border. A newly polished or waxed stool could receive damage during upholstery, so wrap the legs in calico while working on it.

1 Web the top of the frame, placing seven webs across the width and weaving four webs across the length. Use improved 13 mm (1/2 in) tacks on this type of stool.

2 Cut a piece of hessian large enough to cover to the top edge plus 15 cm (6 in) extra all around. Place the hessian over the webbing and temporary tack, one 13 mm (1/2 in) fine tack in the centre of each side and one on the front and back, to keep the grain straight. Stretch the hessian on tight, securing with temporary tacks at 2.5 cm (1 in) intervals all around the edge of the frame. Tack home.

⚬ Quick Reference

Webbing, page 51

Hessian, page 58

Bridle ties, page 60

Trimmings, nailing, page 106

3 To make the tack roll, turn back the raw edge of hessian on one side and, starting in the centre, stuff it tightly with fibre to form a firm rolled edge. Turn the hessian under the fibre and push the roll down tight towards the outer edge, placing 10 mm (3/8 in) tacks at 1.25 cm (1/2 in) intervals along the inner edge and working towards the corners. Repeat on the other sides. Fold the excess hessian under at each corner, trim off if necessary and add enough fibre to make the corner hard. Fold the hessian into a mitre on each corner, making sure the corners are all of equal density.

EXPERT TIP

Draw the nail design on paper first. Pin the paper on the chair and mark with a pin or chalk where the nails will go. Do not try nailing into the fabric until you are sure of the design, since you may damage the fabric.

4 Stitch three rows of bridle ties into the centre hessian. Tease fibre under the ties until the centre is evenly filled and tightly packed. Fill to a level just above the tack roll. Place two layers of cotton felt on top of the fibre, trimming it level with the outside edge by tearing it with your fingers.

5 Place a piece of calico over the whole seat area with enough to secure the sides. Work the calico over the padding to make a clean sharp edge and temporary tack in place with fine 13 mm (1/2 in) tacks as you work. Fold the corners under and cut off the excess calico on each corner. Staple, trim away any excess calico, and remove the temporary tacks.

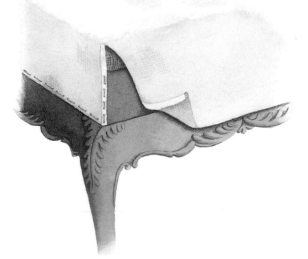

Right: The chair has been decorated with a complex nailing pattern, but you could also design your own.

6 Place a piece of wadding over the calico, covering the top and sides. Cut the top fabric to fit over the top and down each side to meet the edge of the show wood, adding an allowance of 1.2 cm (1/2 in).

7 Keeping the fabric straight and taut, temporary tack all around with fine 13 mm (1/2 in) tacks, turning the bottom edge under. Cut away excess fabric on the corners and turn in, working them in pairs so the folds on the short sides are facing. Staple close to the edge. Remove the temporary tacks.

8 Close nail evenly all around the bottom edge and up the corner seams, using a padding on your hammer to avoid damaging the show wood.

9 If you choose a more complex pattern for the decorative nails, work it out carefully on paper first, checking the fit before nailing. Nail the base line first using a nail gauge to keep the line straight. Transfer the design for the more intricate shapes onto a piece of cardboard. Pin the cardboard to the sides of the stool and nail following your design.

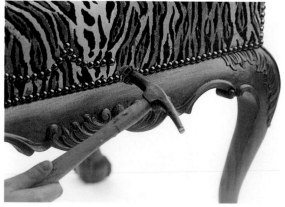

TEXTURE

Texture is always an important factor to consider when choosing fabric, but also when choosing trimmings. A short, smart fringe may be more in character with a piece of furniture than a long, silky one and could be much more practical, too.

COLOURS SEND OUT such quick, powerful messages to the eye and mind that they can overwhelm the senses, leaving the matter of texture quite neglected until you get a fabric home and feel disappointed that it does not look the same as it did on the bolt.

Texture matters

Before you fall in love with a fabric, make sure that the texture, as well as the colour, is right for the job. Colour behaves quite variably depending on the texture. The same rich red will look quite different on a filmy red gauze across a window and a heavy floor-length red velvet curtain. The two fabrics might technically be identically pigmented, but the light passing through the gauze looks fresh and youthful, while the velvet absorbs light and mutes sound, giving a hushed, reverent quality perfect for a cosy living room.

As the opacity and weight of a fabric affects colour, so the surface and depth of the fabric play crucial roles in defining the mood of a piece of furniture. Light travels differently over different surfaces. Flat, shiny fabrics reflect light with an attention-grabbing, dynamic sheen. Another impact altogether would be created by using a

figured fabric with a complex weave of various textures, exciting the sense of touch as well as making a dramatic visual statement. This may be what is needed to bring a faded sofa back into the limelight, but if you want to create a subtle, intimate mood, try the deep inviting pile of a plain cotton velvet.

Making the most of light

The amount of light available also plays a part in the decision-making process. A chunky, heavily ribbed orange cotton might look bright and breezy under the artificial lights of the shop, but if

it is destined for a chair in a dark corner at home, the light falling across those ribs will form shadows. A better choice might be a fabric in the same colour, but with the slight sheen of silk or a glazed cotton to reflect any available light.

If you are not constrained by the demands of low light conditions, you can use texture to create dramatically different effects. Layering textures can result in deeply satisfying combinations that look and feel stimulating and sensuous.

The intrigue of textured fabrics has recently been rediscovered and there are many available, so experiment and create a unique style.

It is wise to consider the texture of a fabric not only in terms of appearance and style, but also in terms of its feel and practicality. A beautiful silk fabric and glitzy cord will certainly create a conversation piece, but, if the cover of a footstool is not comfortable, it will not be the favourite place for a well-earned rest.

143

Georgian Drop-on Seat

Unlike most chairs with loose seats, this frame does not hold the seat in at the front.

To stop the seat moving forward, a peg in the centre front of the frame slots into a

hole under the seat. The front of the seat has a rolled edge that is stuffed and stitched.

Dimensions

height: 95 cm (38 in)
width: 53 cm (21 in)
depth: 48 cm (19 in)

Materials

- English webbing 3 m (3¹/₂ yd)
- hessian 50 cm (20 in)
- fine tacks 13 mm (¹/₂ in)
- scrim 50 cm (20 in)
- twine
- fibre 1 kg (2 lb)
- improved tacks 10 mm (³/₈ in)
- hair 500 g (1 lb)
- cotton felt 75 cm (30 in)
- calico 75 cm (30 in)
- skin wadding 1700 g (48 oz), 1 m (1¹/₄ yd)
- top cover fabric 75 cm (30 in)
- black bottom 50 cm (20 in)
- gimp pins 13 mm (¹/₂ in)

THIS CHAIR HAS been used for a number of years by Fred, a good friend and Master Upholsterer, when he sits at the sewing machine in his workshop. It looked as if it could do with refurbishing, and now that it is so smart, it will be promoted to a more worthy position.

To complement the deep mahogany show wood of the frame, the drop-on seat is covered in a rich red silk damask fabric. The colour suits the warmth of a traditional dining-room setting, and the pattern of the fabric fits snugly over the seat and front edge. The reupholstered chair now looks very grand.

1 Lift the seat frame off the chair and carefully strip off the old cover and stuffing.

2 Web the frame using three webs each way, weaving them basket fashion. Cut a piece of hessian to fit the frame, with a turning allowance, and place it over the top of the webbing. Temporary tack the hessian in place with 13 mm (¹/₂ in) tacks just inside the edge of the frame, pulling it taut. Tack home. Turn the raw edges towards the middle of the seat and tack all around. Draw a line 12.5 cm (5 in) from the front edge across the seat.

3 Cut a piece of scrim 20 cm (8 in) wide and 38 cm (15 in) long. Make a 1.25 cm (¹/₂ in) turning along one long edge and lay the fold on the

line, leaving an equal length overhanging on each side. Backstitch along the line through the scrim and the hessian. Stitch bridle ties in the area in front of the line and tease fibre under these until the stuffing is firm.

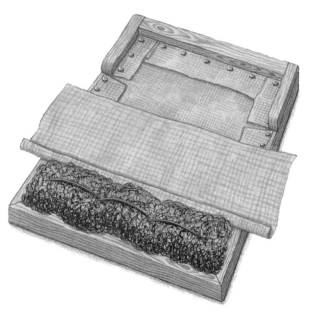

4 Pull the scrim over the fibre towards the front edge. Tuck the scrim under the fibre and tack with 10 mm (³/₈ in) tacks along the front edge and sides of the frame, thus forming a wide roll. Regulate the stuffing towards the front edge.

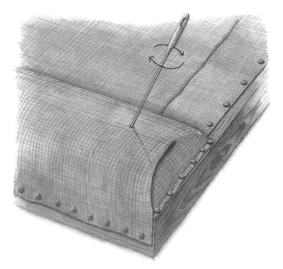

5 Make a row of blind stitches along the base of the front edge. Regulate again and top stitch along the roll, forming a firm edge.

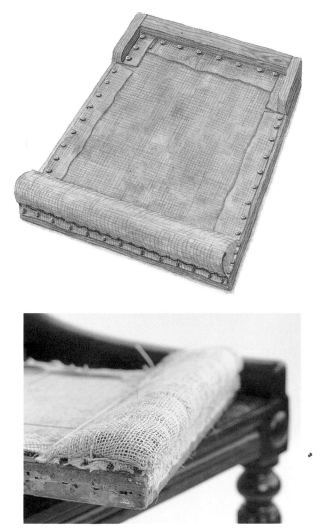

6 Stitch bridle ties over the whole seat area, including the front roll. Tease hair under the ties until a firm mat is achieved. Place a layer of cotton felt to cover the whole top area and over the front, but be careful not to take it down the sides or the seat will not go back into the frame.

7 Cover the seat in calico, tacking with 13 mm (1/2 in) tacks around the underneath of the frame. Trim the calico and place wadding on the top and front area, but do not take it down the sides.

8 Cut the top fabric, centring the pattern on the top of the seat, and allowing about 5 cm (2 in) extra to pull under the seat all around. Position the fabric on the seat and temporary tack it underneath the frame, keeping the pattern straight. Fold the fabric in neatly down the front corners. Tack home when you are satisfied that the cover is firm.

9 Trim off the excess fabric and place a piece of black bottom over the base. Turn the raw edges in, set in place with temporary tacks, then tack home all around. Cut across the peg hole and turn the edges under. Place gimp pins in a circle around the hole.

10 Place on the chair frame, lining up the peg and hole. Then push down, keeping the seat level.

🐚 *Quick Reference*

Ripping out, page 50

Webbing, page 51

Bridle ties, page 60

Modern Dining Chair

Here is a simple project for starting upholstery. This style of chair is often available covered only in calico and just needs a top cover. It is therefore easy and relatively inexpensive to reupholster a set of chairs to match a newly decorated room.

Dimensions

height: 97 cm (38 in)
width: 47 cm (19 in)
depth: 46 cm (18 in)

Materials

- top cover fabric 2 m (2¼ yd)
- polyester wadding 56 g (2 oz), 1.5 m (1¾ yd)
- fine tacks 13 mm (½ in)
- gimp pins 13 mm (½ in)
- staples 10 mm (⅜ in)
- back tack strip 46 cm (18 in)
- slipping thread
- black bottom 50 cm (20 in)
- 32 antique nails

❧ Quick Reference

Estimating top fabric, page 78

Covering the outsides, page 86

Trimmings, nailing, page 106

ALTHOUGH THIS CHAIR only needs re-covering, some of the calico must be removed in order to gain access to secure the upholstery to the frame.

The fabric chosen for this chair is pure cotton. It is therefore very practical and would take hard wear in a family home. The small repeat pattern, very easy to position, also gives the chair an elegance that would suit a more refined environment. The colours work well with the tone of the wood and a set of chairs like this would look harmonious in any setting.

1 With a mallet and ripping chisel, take off the black bottom, and then remove the outside back calico so that you will be able to reach the frame. Save the piece of calico as it can be used to back up the outside back later.

2 Measure for the top fabric, and make a cut sheet. Measure the length and width of the inside and outside back. Measure the seat from under one side, over the seat, to under the other side, and then from the underside of the front, over the seat, down to the bottom rail where the fabric tucks in between the seat and the inside back. Plan these measurements on your cut sheet. Do not forget to add an allowance for turnings and for handling the fabric, allowing at least 5 cm (2 in) all around. Label the pieces on the back of the fabric with a marking chalk. Cut out all the pieces.

3 Place a piece of wadding over the seat to cover just short of the frame edge, and tear it all around to feather the edge. Lay the seat top fabric over the wadding and put a temporary tack under the frame at the front and on each side to keep the pattern correctly positioned. Push the fabric over the back of the seat and make a cut in to the inside of each back upright to allow the fabric through to the back and down to the bottom back rail. Pull the fabric down, and temporary tack on to the top of the bottom back rail.

4 Smooth the fabric forward over the front edge and continue temporary tacking underneath. Cut into the fabric to allow it around the legs. Trim and turn the edges under where the legs meet the underside of the frame. Cut away the excess fabric on the front corners and fold in neatly by mitring the fabric, creating a vertical seam down each corner edge. Turn the fabric under to make a straight edge across the top of each leg and secure

COTTON

Cotton is an economical and versatile fibre. It is available in a wide variety of weights and textures, and is resilient, tough, and practical. Cotton possesses a crispness and durability that has made it a popular upholstery fabric for centuries. Cotton also takes dye particularly well. Whether mixed with more luxurious fibres, such as silk or linen, into sophisticated fabrics such as velvet or damask, or woven alone into sturdy materials such as denim, repp or cretonne, cotton prevails as an affordable, multiple-use fibre.

with gimp pins, ready to close nail later. Tack home or staple the cover underneath the seat and remove the temporary tacks.

5 Cut into the corner where the back meets the seat and allow the fabric to spread around to the back. Staple on to the bottom back rail and then staple on to the outside back upright rail. Remove the temporary tacks. Trim away excess fabric.

6 Place wadding and then the top fabric on the inside back, lining up the pattern with the seat. Take the fabric around the edges of the back and temporary tack to the back of the upright rails, and over the top onto the head rail. Make a fold on the top back corners in the same manner as the front of the seat.

7 Cut into the corners where the back meets the seat to allow the fabric to be tucked down between the seat and the inside back. Push the fabric through the gap. Pull the fabric tight and staple to the top of the bottom back rail. Trim away

excess fabric. Remove the temporary tacks on the back of the upright rails and staple home. Trim away excess fabric.

8 Replace the calico to back up the outside back and place a piece of wadding over the calico.

9 Place the right side of the top edge of the top cover just under the top edge with the bulk of the fabric over the inside back. Staple a length of back tack strip along the fabric to just inside the side edges. Fold the fabric back over the outside back and turn the side edges in. Pin the sides in position and then cut around the legs at the back, turning the fabric under neatly. Temporary tack the fabric under the seat. Slip stitch the fabric down the sides and finish by stapling the fabric under the seat.

10 Fit a piece of black bottom to the underside of the seat, cutting around the legs and folding the cloth neatly under. Finish with staples. Place antique nails around the front and side of the seat at the top of the front legs. Repeat on the back legs.

Pin-cushion Settle

This charming settle has been given a new top cover that complements the delicate design of the frame and the colour of the wood. The fabric chosen is a dainty repetitive Jacquard weave with a floral pattern in light gold on a cream background.

Dimensions

height: 74 cm (29 in)
width: 1.25 m (50 in)
depth: 48 cm (19 in)

Materials

- English webbing 10 m (11 yd)
- staples 14 mm (5/8 in)
- fine tacks 13 mm (1/2 in)
- hessian 50 cm (20 in)
- staples 10 mm (3/8 in)
- cotton felt 2.5 m (2 3/4 yd)
- calico 65 cm (24 in)
- skin wadding 1700 g (48 oz), 1.25 m (1 1/3 yd)
- top cover fabric 60 cm (24 in)
- gimp 3.5 m (4 yd)
- gimp pins 13 mm (1/2 in)
- hot adhesive sticks

EXPERT TIP
Hold a block of wood under the section you are tacking to absorb the shock and prevent you from chopping the furniture in half.

THE SETTLE IS a good example of how sensitive upholstering can rejuvenate a damaged piece of furniture. The show wood on the seat had been damaged when very large tacks had been used in previous upholstery. With a delicate frame such as this, it is more advisable to use staples, small fine tacks or gimp pins. The new fabric is taken just over the rebate at the back and sides to hide the damage, but without spoiling the line of the show wood. Fortunately, the front wood is in fairly good condition and the finished settle looks exquisite.

The reupholstered settle will enhance any room without dominating neighbouring furniture, or make quite a showpiece standing on its own.

❦ *Quick Reference*

Ripping out, page 50

Webbing, page 51

Trimmings, fixing gimp
with hot adhesive,
page 102

EXPERT TIP

*If the fabric is likely
to fray easily, trim back
to 1.25 cm (¹/₂ in) and
turn it under before
securing it to the rebate
with staples.*

1 Remove all fabric and stuffing from the seat and carefully remove the webbing using a tack lifter or mallet and ripping chisel.

2 Web the seat from back to front at 7.5 cm (3 in) intervals, folding the webbing at an angle to follow the curve of the frame. The rebate is very narrow on a settle of this style, so it is advisable to use 14 mm (⁵/₈ in) staples. Alternatively, use 13 mm (¹/₂ in) fine tacks. Weave webbing across from side to side.

3 Cut a piece of hessian to fit over the webbing plus 5 cm (2 in) all around. Staple the hessian in place. Fold the turning upwards and staple all around just inside the webbing, pulling the hessian taut as you work.

4 Place two layers of cotton felt on the hessian. The first layer should be 15 cm (3 in) short of the edge all around to create a slight dome in the centre. The second layer should cover the first and finish just short of the hessian. Tear the cotton felt with your fingers to feather the edge and prevent a hard line under the cover.

5 Cut a piece of calico the shape of the seat plus 7.5 cm (3 in) all around. Place it over the cotton felt and temporary tack it all around the rebate. Pull the calico tight and staple it in position. Trim off the excess calico, leaving a raw edge. Place a piece of wadding over the calico and tear to feather the edges just inside the rebate.

6 Measure the top fabric to fit the seat, making sure that the pattern is centred and allowing an extra 5 cm (2 in) all around to work with. Temporary tack the fabric in place, working evenly from front to back and side to side until the cover is tight.

7 Staple the fabric all around just inside the rebate. On this particular settle, the fabric was stapled inside the rebate along the front edge, but, because the back and sides were damaged, the fabric was stapled just beyond the rebate around those

WEBBING

Webbing was used from the fourteenth century to secure horse blankets and saddles. Gradually, webbing specifically for upholstery was developed and has changed surprisingly little since its fifteenth and sixteenth century origins. Its development has been for practical improvements, mainly in the fibres used. Early webbing was made of flax, perfect for its elasticity, smoothness and strength. Economy has forced changes since then and led to the use of hemp, then jute and cotton. To strengthen these more brittle fibres, cotton selvedges and twill weaves were introduced. Manufacturers throughout history have marked the origin and grade of their webbing with unique stripes or their company name.

edges to cover the holes in the show wood. You may have to make similar decisions with furniture that has previously been badly upholstered. Finish by trimming off the excess fabric.

8 Trim the seat with gimp, starting with a gimp pin under the first end. Continue to position the gimp using hot adhesive in a glue gun, tapping gently with a hammer to help it adhere to the fabric. Mitre the corners so the folds face each other. At the end, fold the gimp under, butting it to the starting fold to give a neat finish. Place a temporary gimp pin in the end and remove when the adhesive is dry.

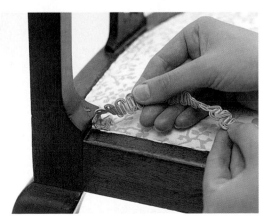

Above: The gimp hides the raw edges of fabric around the show wood.

SMALL REPEAT PATTERNS

Small repeat patterns can be either irregular patterns, such as floral designs, or geometrical designs, such as the purple and cream fabric chosen for this dining chair. Because small repeat patterns are subtle and not as overwhelming as larger ones, they are the perfect choice for upholstering a whole set of chairs.

CERTAIN MOTIFS RECUR over and over again in small-scale patterns. Although the religious and historical connotations of their original applications have been muted with time, we are still subconsciously tapping into centuries of visual association when we choose to use these fabrics. For example, fleur-de-lys motifs confer a traditional, slightly majestic feel that stems from their origins in medieval pageantry. On the other hand, the refreshingly simple polka dot reminds us of the bright and breezy clothing of the 1950s or of feminine innocence, an image enhanced by the muslin dresses of a Jane Austin heroine.

Using small patterns

Small repeats are ideally suited to smaller pieces of furniture that would be overwhelmed by large-scale designs, but which demand something more interesting than a plain fabric. They can also be used with equal success to visually diminish a large piece of furniture that would look oppressive in a flat, solid colour or a large attention-seeking pattern.

On a practical level, small patterns will conceal wear and tear most obligingly, any marks simply being overlooked as being part of the overall pattern. This is particularly true if a slightly irregular pattern, rather than a very precise and rigid geometric one, is used.

Perfect partners

Small repeat patterns are the good neighbours of the decorator's palette. They partner large-scale patterns well, adding another level of interest to a scheme. Try using them as scatter cushions on a sofa or as a lining fabric in an Ottoman. They can intensify and add liveliness, providing a quiet hum of background activity that would be missed if not there. For example, the colours and shapes of a paisley design used to cover a chair can be

brought out by a cushion in a quietly coloured matt fabric that repeats the same motif on a simpler and smaller scale.

If mixing scales and patterns seems too daunting, combining small repeats of different types can be a good way to begin experimenting with pattern mixing. Checks and florals, spots and stripes all live in perfect harmony as long as the colours and textures relate. However, you can overdo it and too many small scale designs can look mean and sparce, rather than effective.

No matter what period or mood you choose, there is a small repeat to answer your needs.

This delicate antique settle was the perfect piece of furniture for a fabric with a small free-flowing pattern. The daintiness of the floral tendrils echoes the spirit of the settle and yet the golden pattern and the gimp on the plain cream background look particularly effective against the dark wood.

153

Blanket Box

Successful use of a large pattern requires careful planning when cutting and placing the cover, but the result is well worth the extra time taken. This dramatic design is positioned so that the fish do not lose their heads or tails when the lid is closed.

THIS BLANKET BOX was made by my son Matthew, following an old design. It was originally covered in damask, but this had begun to look rather shabby. The new fabric chosen is a striking cotton with a matt finish, which makes it practical enough to sit on as well as to use for storage.

The colours in the fabric are an unusual blend of warm and cool hues, which is complemented by the understated, but effective, striped cotton lining. The vibrant colours and pattern of the fish design give the box a real presence, making it a piece as much for decorative display as for functional use.

1 Using your mallet, ripping chisel and a craft knife, remove all the old fabric. Dismantle the box by removing the base from the main box and unscrewing the hinges to take off the lid.

2 Plan the pattern layout by making a cut sheet. Measure the height and width of each of the four panels, and measure the width and length of the lid, allowing turnings and enough fabric to go over all the edges of the panels. Transfer the measurements to a cut sheet. Plan the positioning of the pattern so that it matches when the lid is closed, allowing for the extra fabric that is unseen

under the lid and on the top edge of the box. Also plan the sections for lining the box, making a cut sheet in the same manner as for the top cover.

3 Line the front and back panels first. Spray some adhesive in the centre of each panel and lay a piece of wadding on it, tearing the edges level with the top edge of the box. Lay the section of lining fabric over the wadding and staple it on to the top edge of the box. Pull the fabric down to the bottom of the box below the position of the base board and secure with staples. Smooth the excess fabric out to the sides and secure the fabric on the end panels just in from the corner. Trim off the excess fabric.

4 Line the two end panels of the box in the same manner at the top and bottom, but at the sides trim back to 1.25 cm (¹/₂ in) and fold the edges under so that the fold fits right into the corner. Pull tight between the top and bottom on each corner and staple to secure.

5 Cover the base of the box with wadding as far as the edge and then cover with lining fabric. Pull the lining tight over the edge and staple 1.25 cm (¹/₂ in) in from the edge on the underside. Push the

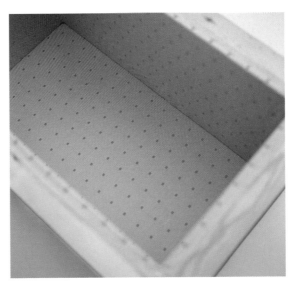

Dimensions

height: 43 cm (17 in)
width: 97 cm (38 in)
depth: 52 cm (21 in)

Materials

- top cover fabric 3 m (3¹/₂ yd)
- lining fabric 2.25 m (2¹/₂ yd)
- spray adhesive
- polyester wadding 56 g (2 oz), 7.5 m (8¹/₂ yd)
- staples 10 mm (³/₈ in)
- back tack strip 3 m (3¹/₂ yd)
- fine tacks 13 mm (¹/₂ in)
- slipping thread
- gimp 3.5 m (4 yd)
- hot adhesive sticks
- black bottom 55 cm (24 in)
- machine thread
- cord 75 cm (30 in)
- 2 antique nails

155

lined board into the base of the box from underneath to check the fit. Remove and put to one side, leaving the final fixing of this until the top cover is finished.

6 To cover the outside of the box, start by gluing a piece of wadding on one of the end panels, taking it just over the top edge. Take a section of top fabric, position the pattern, and place the turning allowance on the top edge down on the inside edge of the top of the box, with the bulk of the fabric in the box. Lay a length of back tack strip along the fabric, and staple in position so that the fabric is secured to the inside edge. The fabric should be secured just short of the inside corners and the back tack strip cut off there.

7 Take the fabric back over the wadding on the outside of the box. Temporary tack the side edges of the fabric to the side panels, starting at the top and working from side to side towards the base to ensure that the fabric stays straight and follows the contours of the box. Then tack home when the whole panel is in position. Tack the bottom edge of the fabric just above the top of the plinth that surrounds the base of the box. Repeat the same process with the other end panel.

Below: The padded lid gives another soft contour to the box and makes it a comfortable seat.

8 Pad the front panel, including the top edge, with wadding. Line the pattern up so that it is correctly positioned and attach with back tack strip in the same manner as for the end panels. Fold the fabric to the outside of the box. Cut the excess away at an angle on the top corners and fold the fabric under to form a mitre, overlapping the fabric from the side panels. Trim the sides of the fabric, turn them under and pin in place, following

Left: The fabric must be carefully planned before cutting so that the pattern matches up.

the contour of the box down the edges. Slip stitch the fabric down the edges.

9 Tack the fabric just above the top of the plinth as for the end panels. Repeat the same process on the back panel.

10 Spray adhesive on the wooden plinth and cover with a thin layer of wadding. Spray adhesive on the wadding and cover with top fabric, pushing the fabric into the contour of the plinth. Mitre the fabric at the corners. Tack the fabric underneath the base. Trim off the excess fabric along the top edge of the plinth.

11 Trim along the top of the plinth with a length of gimp. Turn the box over and screw the lined base in. Finish the underside with a piece of black bottom, turned under and stapled all around.

12 Place a piece of wadding over the top and sides of the lid, and trim the corners. Put the lid on the box and position the top fabric so that the pattern lines up on the front edge when the box is closed. Mark the edge on the wrong side. Remove the lid from the box and temporary tack the fabric underneath the lid just in from the edge, lining up the mark in the correct position.

13 Pull the fabric over to the back edge and temporary tack just under the lid. Repeat with both sides. Turn the fabric in on the corners to make a fold and mitre the excess on the underside of the lid. Staple all around and remove the temporary tacks. Fit the hinges back on the lid and box at this stage.

14 Make a tab from a length of fabric 15 cm (6 in) long and 10 cm (4 in) wide. Fold the fabric lengthways, right-sides together. Machine stitch a seam lengthways. Turn right-side out and press.

15 Fold the tab in half and place it in the centre of the lid under the front edge with two-thirds protruding. Temporary tack the raw ends to the lid. Secure with staples and remove the temporary tacks.

16 Lay a thin layer of wadding on the underside of the lid. Place a piece of lining on top. Turn the edges under and slip stitch all around, covering the tab ends and edges of the top cover. Fit a length of cord, one end along the inside edge of the side and the other on the lid. Cover with antique nails.

Quick Reference

Ripping out, page 50

Estimating top fabric, page 78

Trimmings, nailing, page 106

LARGE PATTERNS

Careful consideration of the placement of any pattern is important, but particularly one like the fish pattern used to cover the blanket box. The continuity of this piece is achieved by placing the pattern so that none of the fish are cut off, creating the impression that the box was designed to fit the fabric, rather than the other way round.

WE SEEM TO like to decorate our homes with large patterns, especially of the floral variety—perhaps the entwining tendrils, leaves, fronds and flowers fulfil a romantic yearning for a deeper connection with the natural world.

One of the great masters of large-scale design was William Morris, who was responsible for a prodigious collection of large printed patterns based on sweeping, naturalistic forms. In fact, many of his original designs are still available.

Pattern is not always printed on to the fabric, but can also be intrinsic to the weave. Large floral images on damasks and brocades give a rich, embroidered quality. Where large printed patterns can be very dominant, these more restrained patterns allow fabrics to add interest without taking over.

Careful planning

Using large patterns effectively takes a degree of skill and judgment if a cluttered effect is to be avoided. What may appear striking on a scatter cushion may be completely overwhelming on a large piece of furniture. Patterns, even in quite subdued deep colours, do tend to dominate a room, which is fine if you wish a piece of furniture to make a statement, but not if you would rather it blend quietly into the background.

Large-scale patterns can be successfully mixed in one room if their colours, motifs and textures complement each other. To play safe, however, they are best offset with plain fabrics or patterns of a different scale or type to avoid visual chaos.

Some pattern pairings work very well together, each adding to the impact of the other. Curtains in toile de jouy, that most romantic and pretty of figurative designs, would acquire a fresh vivacity when teamed with chairs upholstered in checks of similarly clear, clean colours.

Practical considerations

The type and shape of your piece of furniture will affect your choice of patterned fabric. Free, painterly styles with an exuberant feel might suit modern pieces best, while finely drawn, detailed patterns are more traditional and sit well on classic, period pieces. You also need to consider the placement of dominant motifs. Large patterns often look best flat, unimpeded by pleats and folds, so look at how buttoning and other shaping will affect the design.

Choose large patterns for your upholstery with care and you can create a masterpiece.

Large patterns are usually best suited to large pieces such as a screen or sofa. However, with careful planning, a large pattern can be used effectively as a feature of a piece, for example by placing it centrally on a seat.

Tapestry Fireside Stool

Chip foam was chosen to form the basic shape of this stool as it is substantial and produces firm corners. This base was covered in thinner foam and a layer of wadding to give a softer look and prevent the chip foam wearing the tapestry from underneath.

Dimensions

height: 56 cm (22 in)
width: 1.41 m (54 in)
depth: 87 cm (34 in)

Materials

• English webbing 21 m (23 yd)
• improved tacks 13 mm (½ in)
• hessian 1.5 m (1¾ yd)
• fine tacks 13 mm (½ in)
• chip foam 5 cm (2 in) thick, 150 x 100 cm (60 x 40 in)
• spray adhesive
• foam 1.25 cm (½ in) thick, 180 x 125 cm (70 x 50 in)
• polyester wadding 56 g (2 oz), 1.5 m (1¾ yd)
• tapestry cover with bordered edge
• slipping thread
• staples 10 mm (⅜ in)
• black bottom 1.5 m (1¾ yd)
• 4 brass casters

THE BEAUTIFUL TAPESTRY rug featured here seemed much too special to place on the floor, so it was decided to have a stool made to show it off to advantage. The rug is quite heavy and difficult to handle, and, as is the nature of tapestry, not very square. The upholstery therefore required careful consideration, but was successful because of the simple lines of the stool.

This piece will double as a stool or table, blends into any environment and makes a good focal point in a room. The colours are soft and muted on the main central section, and the dark background of the border provides a dramatic contrast.

1 This frame has a centre bearer, which gives extra strength in the middle of the frame. Web the frame on top of the rails with twelve webs across, and then weave six webs lengthways. The long webs are tacked down on to the centre bearer with improved tacks. Fold a piece of webbing in half lengthways and tack it down the bearer to hold all the lengths of webbing firmly in place.

2 Place hessian over the webbing and temporary tack all around with fine tacks until it is stretched tight across the webbing. Tack home and turn the edges over. Place another row of tacks around the edge. Trim off the excess hessian.

3 Place the stool upside down on top of the sheet of chip foam and draw around it. Cut the chip foam to the exact size with a foam cutter or a bread knife. Turn the stool over again. Spray adhesive on the hessian and place the chip foam on top, lining it up with the edges of the frame. Spray adhesive on the top of the chip foam and place a sheet of the thinner foam on the top and down the sides. Cut down the corners so that they butt on the sides.

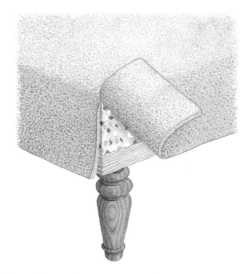

4 Place the wadding over the foam and tear away at the bottom edge. Position the tapestry on the

stool and temporary tack on the underside. Pin the corners to fit the sides and cut, leaving a 1.25 cm (½ in) turning. Tuck the turning in and slip stitch from the top corner to the bottom edge.

5 Turn the edges to the underside and staple to secure. Ideally the legs of the stool will be set in slightly so that the tapestry does not need to be cut to accommodate them. Place the black bottom on the underside of the stool and cut into the inside corners, so that it will fit around the legs. Turn the edges of the black bottom under and staple all around just inside the edge, covering the previous staples. Fit the casters to the legs.

🜂 *Quick Reference*
Webbing, page 51

161

Louis XVI Tub Chair

This antique tub chair is in the bergere style of Louis XVI and dates from circa 1785. It was probably a prototype that was used as a model to show styles of chair for future orders. Quite small in stature, its dainty lines would grace a bedroom very stylishly.

DESPITE ITS AGE, much of this chair was in good condition. Once the old cover was removed, the wood was repainted and gilded, and it was obvious that the original padding was worth retaining.

Only a new top cover and trimming were needed. A cotton and rayon mix with a Lurex thread, in a strong, hard-wearing weave, was chosen. The cream fabric with its tiny gold dots and the beautiful gimp chosen to match, all complement the gilded woodwork and enhance this delicate little chair.

1 If you are going to strip a chair like this down to the frame, follow the methods used for traditional upholstery, adapting the number of webs and springs required to suit the size of the chair. Otherwise, carefully remove the old calico, leaving the original upholstery in place. Cover the seat in new calico and staple all around.

2 Fit calico to the inside back and arms, and machine stitch the sections together. Fit the calico to the front and top rebates, and tack home. Cut into the bottom of the back uprights. Pull the calico through between the rails and temporary tack to the top of the bottom back rail.

3 Measure all the chair sections, allowing 5 cm (2 in) extra all around. Measure the seat area from the bottom of the front show wood, over the seat to the bottom back rail, and from one side rail over the seat to the other side rail. Measure the inside arms and inside back from the top of the show wood to the seat rails. Measure the outside arms and outside back. Transfer all the measurements to a cut sheet. Cut and mark all the pieces from the top fabric. Mark the top of the pattern with an arrow on the wrong side.

4 Cover the seat with a piece of wadding from the show wood of the front rail to the back and inside arms, enough to tuck through to the back and arm rails. Feather the front.

5 Lay the top fabric on the seat and temporary tack along the front rail just above the show wood. Ease the fabric towards the back and make cuts to take the fabric past each back upright. Push the fabric through and temporary tack on to the top edge of the bottom back rail. Make a cut into the uprights at the front, push the fabric through and temporary tack on the bottom side rails. Staple down and remove all temporary tacks.

Dimensions

height: 69 cm (27 in)
width: 59 cm (23 in)
depth: 61 cm (24 in)

Materials

- calico 2 m (2¼ yd)
- staples 10 mm (³/₈ in)
- fine tacks 13 mm (¹/₂ in)
- machine thread
- top cover fabric 3 m (3¹/₂ yd)
- skin wadding 1700 g (48 oz), 4 m (4¹/₂ yd)
- hot adhesive sticks
- gimp 7 m (7¹/₂ yd)
- black bottom 1 m (1¹/₄ yd)

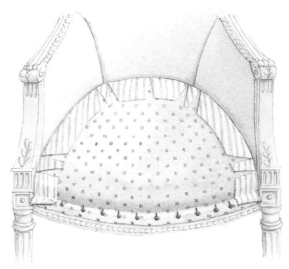

NEEDLES

Although needles are now taken for granted, in Norman Britain, ownership of a needle was a privilege only enjoyed by royalty. Only three 'legal' needles were in use—one in the medicine cabinet of the palace doctor, one kept by the chief huntsman to stitch wounded dogs, and the third was reserved for the Queen's needlework. Needles at that time were crudely made of iron, causing threads to shred and break regularly. Steel needles were not introduced into more widespread use until the sixteenth century. Since then they have developed apace. By the nineteenth century, needles were being manufactured for every imaginable specific task, leading to the wide range available for upholstery today.

6 Tack home the calico on the inside back and arms. Place the inside back and inside arm cover sections on the chair and secure with pins. Pin the back section to the arm sections to create two seams. If the fabric will not turn with the contour of the chair, make cuts to allow it to spread. Trim the seams back to 1.25 cm (½ in) and make a few notches in each seam.

7 Push the fabric just into the space where it meets the seat and make a series of cuts all around. Trim the fabric back to 1.25 cm (½ in).

8 Remove the fabric and machine stitch the seams, using the notches to match them. Cut fabric on the cross to make a collar, 15 cm (6 in) wide and of

a length to fit from the front of one arm, around the inside back to the front of the other arm. The collar can be cut in two pieces and joined in order to avoid waste. Starting from the centre back, pin the collar to the bottom edge of the inside back and arm sections, right-sides together. Machine the collar to the inside back and arm sections.

9 Place a sheet of wadding over the inside arms and back of the chair. Then place the top fabric sections back on the arms and back and secure with pins at the top.

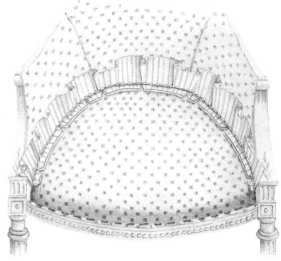

10 Cut the collar to allow it around the back uprights. Push the rest of the collar through between the seat and back, cutting again at the front uprights. Secure the collar to the bottom side and back rails using a staple gun. Trim off excess fabric, turn the edges over and staple down.

11 Temporary tack the top fabric all around the rebate on the top of the back and arms. Then staple home as close as possible to the show wood

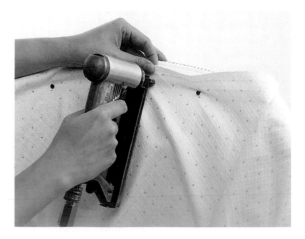

Left: The gold dots on the fabric complement the beautiful gilded woodwork on the frame of the chair.

EXPERT TIP
Never cut gimp to length in advance, as you always use more in practice than you anticipate. If you do need to make a join, do so at one of the mitred corners.

and trim the fabric. If the fabric tends to fray, trim it back and turn it under before stapling.

12 Using a glue gun or adhesive, glue the gimp close to the show wood all around the inside, tucking it down into the front of the seat to start and finish. Trim the front edge of the seat with gimp in a similar manner. It is advisable to protect the top cover while working in case the glue drips.

13 Back up the outside arms and back with calico, securing it just inside the edge of the rebate. Pin the top cover for the arms and back on the chair, making seams following the lines of the

back uprights. Remove these sections and machine stitch the seams.

14 Place wadding over the calico on the outside back and sides of the chair and put the fabric back on over it. Temporary tack the fabric, following the line of the show wood all around. Staple it in place and remove the temporary tacks. Trim off the excess fabric with a craft knife.

15 Using a glue gun, glue the gimp all around the outer edges, mitring the corners. Place the black bottom on the underside of the chair, trim to size and tack home.

⦿ *Quick Reference*
Estimating top fabric, page 78

Machine stitching, page 30

Trimmings, fixing gimp with hot adhesive, page 102

SELF-PATTERN FABRICS

As with any patterned fabric, the positioning of a self-patterned fabric is of utmost importance. The fabric used on the padding of this romantic headboard has been carefully placed to ensure that the headboard looks symmetrical. The same fabric is used in the pleating, which gives a softer look than a plain fabric would.

THIS TYPE OF fabric has remained justifiably popular for its ability to add the feel of luxury without ostentation, ever since damasks were used in the fifteenth century. As well as the traditional damasks, modern methods of weaving, printing and embossing create a diverse repetoire that can be a real discovery.

Patterns and weaves

Single-colour damasks in silk, linen and cotton have matt sateen motifs on a shiny satin woven ground. Light reflects off these different planes to create a subtle and elegant patterning so that the traditional motifs of stylized, curvilinear flowers and foliage add interest without drawing attention to themselves.

There are other one-colour weaves which, because of their rather complex structure, can be classed as self patterned. A cotton herringbone or a solid-coloured cotton and linen mix with a tiny repeated woven motif provide discreet patterning that conveys calm and dignity.

Similar patterning to damasks can now also be produced by embossing, flocking or printing tone on tone, simulating the same contrast of matt on sheen. Modern methods have evolved to such a degree that these fabrics are much more affordable than costly damasks and make a viable alternative, especially for larger furniture.

The discreet choice

Self patterns make a discreet decorating choice, adding richness and depth whilst retaining a certain subtlety. They can be used to emphasize existing patterns or motifs in a room without either detracting from the original inspiration or becoming too overbearing. For example, using a single-colour damask with an acanthus leaf motif on chairs to complement a sofa dressed in a heavily patterned and multicoloured fabric incorporating the same leaf produces a richly layered look without becoming a fussy and overwhelming jumble.

Any decorating theme can be subtly reinforced in a similar way by choosing self-pattern fabrics. Try using an upholstery fabric with swirling paisley shapes to enhance an eclectic, exotic theme, or use disciplined geometric patterning to add cool modernity to a laid-back, contemporary scheme. There is such a feeling of satisfaction in finding the fabric that incorporates just the right pattern or motif.

Only a fabric with a simple overall effect will suit a chair with an elaborately carved, gilded frame such as this Louis XVI tub chair. The subtly textured cream fabric with its tiny gold dot makes a beautiful partner for the gilded frame and really enhances its quintessential style.

167

Bucket Chair

This smart little chair is a thoroughly modern piece. Upholstered with modern techniques and foam padding, it is covered in a black and white dog-tooth check that would look good in any stylish environment.

Dimensions

height: 84 cm (33 in)
width: 74 cm (29 in)
depth: 76 cm (30 in)

Materials

- rubber webbing 8 m (9 yd)
- staples 14 mm ($^5/_8$ in)
- jute webbing 10 m (11 yd)
- hessian 1 m (1$^1/_4$ yd)
- staples 10 mm ($^3/_8$ in)
- chip foam 7.5 cm (3 in) thick, 61 x 61 cm (24 x 24 in)
- spray adhesive
- foam 2.5 cm (1 in) thick, 210 x 60 cm (84 x 24 in)
- calico 1 m (1$^1/_4$ yd)
- top cover fabric 4 m (4$^1/_2$ yd)
- polyester wadding 113 g (4 oz), 5 m (5$^1/_2$ yd)
- fine tacks 13 mm ($^1/_2$ in)
- piping cord 2.75 m (3 yd)
- machine thread
- slipping thread
- black bottom 1 m (1$^1/_4$ yd)

THE BUCKET CHAIR, although bought as a standard frame, is made of attractive wood, so when the legs were rubbed down and waxed, the natural grain shone through and made a distinctive contribution to the overall effect. It is a good example of the use of modern techniques, where jute and rubber webbings are stapled to the frame and various types of foam are used to create the upholstered base.

The clean lines of the chair are complemented by the choice of a traditional checked woollen fabric and emphasized by smart single piping. The fabric was easy to handle, with the added benefit of being hard wearing, and has a soft touch that enhances the comfort of the chair. Often associated with the business world, the dog-tooth pattern would add a modern statement to a home office or study. However, the frame is extremely adaptable and would look equally stunning in a different guise. With luscious velvets and a deep skirt, this chair could take on the splendour of the Victorian era or make a vibrant impact in a solid jewel-like colour.

1 Start on the seat, placing five rubber webs from back to front, keeping them evenly spaced, closer on the back rail and wider apart at the front. Stretch each web with the web stretcher by about 10 per cent, but avoid overstretching them or they will lose their elasticity. Secure each web with two rows of 14 mm ($^5/_8$ in) staples. Cut the ends of each web and leave them flat. Weave four webs across the seat and fix in the same manner.

2 Use jute webbing on the inside back and arms, placing three webs on the back and two webs on each arm. Staple these webs in place on the inside of the frame, turning the ends over and stapling them down as for traditional webbing. Place a final jute web around the back of the chair, halfway down the frame. First staple it to the outside of a front arm upright, strain it to the next back upright and staple it there. Repeat on the next upright and finish on the outside of the second arm upright. Turn over the ends and staple them down. This web helps take the strain from the upright webs.

3 Place hessian on the inside back and arms in three separate sections. Pull the hessian taut as you staple it to the frame with 10 mm ($^3/_8$ in) staples, folding the raw edges over to the front. Place hessian on the seat. Staple the front edge to the top of the front rail. Fit the hessian to the other seat rails. Leave it slightly slack so it will give a little as the webbing stretches when the seat is sat on. Staple all around.

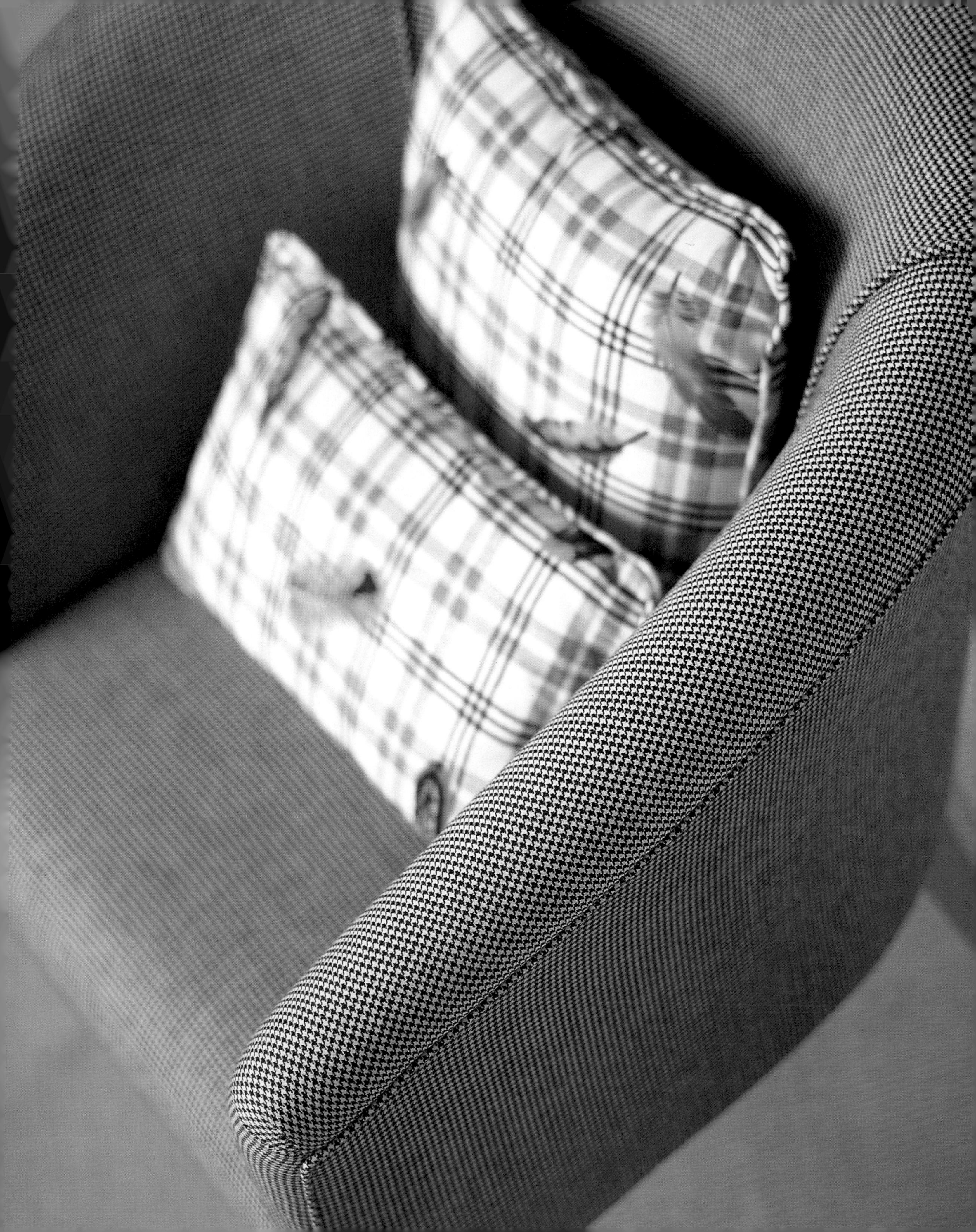

4 Make a template of the seat on a piece of paper and then transfer this shape to the chip foam. Draw around the template and cut to size using a foam cutter or a bread knife. Place the chip foam on the seat.

EXPERT TIP

If it is difficult to know where to join the inside and outside arm sections, make a guide line, that can be removed later. Place one tack at the top and one at the bottom of the arm upright and then wind a piece of twine between the two.

5 Staple the bottom edge of the chip foam to the top of the seat frame. Spray adhesive on the top edges and centre of the chip foam and cover with the thinner foam, folding it over the front and down to the bottom of the front rail. Cut the foam to fit around the uprights. Staple the edge of the thinner foam on to the back of the seat rails.

6 Cover the seat with calico, pulling it over the foam foundations, and staple it to the underside of the front rail. Cut the calico around the front uprights and, pulling it to the back of the seat, staple it all around the bottom rails. The seat should now have a soft curve over the front and a slight dome in the centre.

7 Fit the thin foam to the inside back and arms. Staple it to the outer edge all around the top rails and pull it down over the inside back and arms. Ease the foam around the front uprights and

Right: The fabric must be carefully aligned with the contours of the chair.

staple it to the outer edge of each one. Cut into the foam from top to bottom down each back upright to the bottom rail. Lift out the now separate back section and smooth both arm sections back into position. Reposition the back section and remove the overlapping foam so that the three pieces butt together along the back uprights.

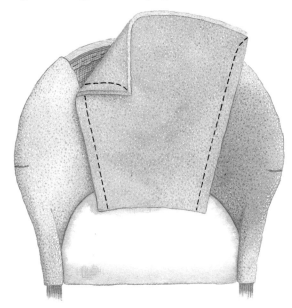

8 Spray adhesive on the back of the foam sections and press into place on the hessian. Push the foam through the gap around the seat and secure all around the underside of the bottom back and side rails with staples. The chair should now have a smooth-fitting piece of foam moulded to the shape of the back, arms and seat, ready to cover.

9 Make a cut sheet and mark out all the pieces on the wrong side of the top fabric. Label each piece and mark the top of each one as you cut it. Also measure and cut lengths of fabric for piping on the cross grain.

10 Lay a piece of wadding over the whole seat, tucking it down between the rails. Cut around the front uprights and lay the wadding over the front down to the front rail. Tear the edge away to avoid a sharp line.

11 Place the top fabric on the seat, keeping the pattern and weave straight. Make a 'Y' cut into the two back uprights and push the fabric through to the seat rails. Secure to the top of the rails with temporary tacks. Cut into the front uprights at an angle to allow the fabric around to the front. Cut into the uprights again to allow the fabric through to the side rails. Temporary tack on top of the rails all around the seat.

12 Pull the fabric over the front edge and temporary tack to hold. Smooth it around the front of the arm uprights. Staple it on the outside of the uprights and underneath the front rail. At the top of the legs, trim the fabric back and turn under straight across the top of the legs. Staple the rest of the fabric in position on the other seat rails, removing the temporary tacks.

13 Pin the inside back and arm sections on the chair right-sides down, allowing enough fabric to tuck in below the seat and fasten to the bottom back and arm rails. Pin the inside back temporarily, matching the pattern with the seat. Skewer the fabric over the back and pin it temporarily to the fabric on the seat. Now position the fabric on the inside arms, matching the pattern with the inside back, allowing enough to wrap around to the outside edges at the front. Pin to the foam to hold the fabric in place.

14 Pin the back section to the arm sections along the line of the back uprights to create two seams. If the fabric will not turn with the contour of the chair, make cuts to allow it to spread. Trim the seams to 1.25 cm (1/2 in) and make notches in each seam.

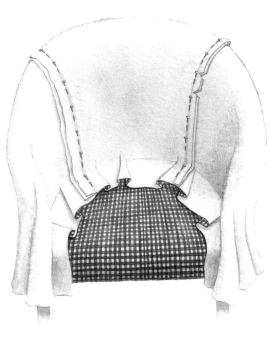

15 Make up enough piping to go down the two seams just pinned and also from the outside edge of one of the front legs, along the top of the leg to the front, up the outside of the upright, along the top of the arm and back, and down to the other front leg, with enough for finishing off and joining.

WOOL

Since the Middle Ages, wool has been widely used as an upholstery fabric. The lengthy, labour-intensive processes originally used to make wool into fabric were eventually mechanized, leading to increased production of a surprisingly diverse range of woollen upholstery fabrics, including velvets, moquettes and worsteds. Then, as now, wool was often combined with other fibres. For example, sheep's wool mixed with Angora goat hair produces mohair, particularly well suited to upholstery use because of its strength and resilience. Insulating, durable, naturally flameproof, as well as good looking and comfortingly textural, the appeal of wool and wool mixes is timeless.

16 Remove the inside back and arms cover from the chair. Undo the pinned seams and stitch piping down both sides of the inside back, using the turning allowance as a guide. Stitch the inside arm sections to the inside back, matching the notches and using a grooved machine foot, if you have one, to fit over the piping.

17 Place a layer of wadding over all the exposed foam on the inside of the chair, using spray adhesive to hold it in place. Place the top fabric on the inside back and arms. Temporary tack the top edge all around the back of the top. Cut into the back uprights in the same manner as for the seat, fold the raw edges under and pull the back fabric through to the bottom back rail. Temporary tack to the top of the rail.

18 Make cuts into the arm uprights to match the cuts made for the seat. Trim the fabric, leaving enough to turn under, and take it over the seat fabric on the uprights in a straight mitre to join the edge of the outside arms. Secure the fabric with temporary tacks on the outside of the uprights. Pull the fabric from the inside arms through to the back and temporary tack on to the top of the bottom side rails.

19 Staple the front edge of the top fabric to the outside of the arm uprights, starting at the bottom and continuing up to the top. At the top, cut away the excess fabric and make a pleat with the fold facing down. When all of the fabric is in position around the uprights and back rails, staple to secure all around and remove all of the temporary tacks.

20 Staple the piping on, starting at the back outside edge of one of the front legs, securing it on the bottom side rail. Position the piping with the cord tightly up against the outside edge of the chair. Staple the piping along the top of the leg to the front, up the outside of the upright, along the top of the arm and back, and down to the other front leg. Staple the end securely.

21 Back up the outsides of the chair with hessian. Pin the top fabric to the outside arms, starting with the grain straight along the bottom edge of each seat rail, and then pin up the arm and back uprights. Pin the outside back section to the outside arms section, matching the pattern to make seams up the back uprights. Cut off the excess fabric and make notches in each seam. Remove the fabric from the chair and stitch the two seams.

22 Lay wadding on the hessian and, using pins and skewers, fit the fabric back on to the chair, trimming away the excess. Fold the top and front edges of the fabric under, pinning it right up to the piping. Pull the fabric down and staple it on the underside of the chair, cutting in to the legs and folding the fabric as you staple. Slip stitch the fabric to the piping using a circular needle and slipping thread.

23 Finish the underneath of the chair with a piece of black bottom. Cut in to the legs to allow the cloth to lie neatly. Turn the cloth under and staple all around just inside the bottom edge, covering the previous staples.

Left: The checked scatter cushions on the chair echo the dog-tooth check of the top fabric and create an inviting seat.

EXPERT TIP
You will need a long length of piping for this type of chair, so plan the joins so that they occur in inconspicuous places, such as around the outside back.

☯ *Quick Reference*

Webbing, page 51

Estimating top fabric, page 78

Machine stitching, page 30

Trimmings, single piping, page 97

173

Victorian Dining Chair

The fabric on this chair is a brocade with a blue and gold floral motif on a bright golden yellow background that complements the tone of the wood. Although it looks delicate, this is a hard-wearing fabric with a close weave.

Dimensions

height: 84 cm (33 in)
width: 38 cm (15 in)
depth: 38 cm (15 in)

Materials

- English webbing 4 m (4¹/₂ yd)
- hessian 1 m (1¹/₄ yd)
- improved tacks 10 mm (³/₈ in)
- fibre 1.4 kg (3 lb)
- twine
- cotton felt 1 m (1¹/₄ yd)
- calico 1 m (1¹/₄ yd)
- fine tacks 13 mm (¹/₂ in)
- skin wadding 1700 g (48 oz), 1 m (1¹/₄ yd)
- top cover fabric 1 m (1¹/₄ yd)
- hot adhesive sticks
- braid 2 m (2¹/₄ yd)
- antique nails

THIS ELEGANT VICTORIAN chair was found in a second-hand furniture shop. Single chairs are usually easier to acquire, as sets of chairs tend to become separated, unless very valuable.

The condition of the upholstery was poor. The chair was covered in the original Rexine, an imitation leather cloth, and had a flat banding with studs around the base. Now restored and completely reupholstered, it makes a very dainty chair.

The gimp chosen echoes the colours in the fabric and the spaced antique nails are reminiscent of the original trimming.

1 Carefully strip off the old cover and stuffings to leave the bare frame.

2 Web the seat on the top of the rails, placing four webs front to back and then weaving four webs across. Cut a piece of hessian to cover the webs and go past the rails with 10 cm (4 in) extra allowed all around. Tack the hessian to the seat near to the edge of the rails, placing 10 mm (³/₈ in) tacks 1.2 cm (¹/₂ in) apart. Cut into the back uprights so that the hessian can go around to the back rail and tack it down. Turn the edges of the hessian back into the centre of the seat.

3 Make a tack roll, starting at the centre front, by pushing fibre tightly under the hessian turning. Roll the hessian over the fibre, and fold the raw edge under. Place a tack through the folded edge of the hessian, forcing it against the front edge, and tack it to the front rail. Continue to make the tack roll around all the edges. Fold and mitre the corners as you go, cutting the excess hessian away and tucking the ends in neatly. Each corner must be very firm, so add more fibre if necessary.

4 Stitch bridle ties in the centre section of the seat and stuff with fibre until it is higher than the top of the tack roll. Place two layers of cotton felt over the fibre, taking it right to the edges.

Step 3

Below: The antique nails are positioned evenly around the chair, on top of the braid.

5 Cut enough calico to cover the seat and down the sides. Place 13 mm (½ in) temporary tacks in the rails, one on each side and one at the front. Cut into the back uprights on each side to allow the calico to spread around. Pull the calico tight to mould the stuffing to shape, and temporary tack on the back rail. Temporary tack around the rails. When the calico is smooth, tack home and trim off the excess. Leave the edges raw to prevent a line showing.

6 Place wadding over the calico and feather the edge to just above the seat rails. Place the top fabric on, keeping the pattern central. Secure with temporary tacks on the seat rails, keeping the line very straight if the braid used to cover them is narrow so that any tack holes will be covered later. Cut into the back uprights. Trim and fold the fabric under around the uprights. On the front corners, fold the excess fabric into a double pleat. Tack the temporary tacks home.

7 Trim the fabric on the bottom edge with a craft knife. Glue braid on the bottom of the back edge, then glue it along the side edge, starting at the back and continuing around the front and along the other side. Keep some tension on the gimp so that it remains straight.

8 Complete the trimming with antique nails. Using a padded hammer, place a nail on each front corner and then at equal intervals of approximately 5 cm (2 in) along the centre of the gimp on the front edge. Repeat with the sides and back.

Piano Stool

Usually a piano stool cover would be damask or velvet, but this stool looks stunning in a rich blue textured cotton embellished with bright, modern trimmings. The sharp contrast of the orange tasselled fringe is softened by the addition of a braid on top.

Dimensions

height: 46 cm (18 in)
diameter: 31 cm (12 in)
seat depth: 6 cm (2½ in)

Materials

- scrim 50 cm (20 in)
- improved tacks 10 mm (³/₈ in)
- fibre 1 kg (2 lb)
- twine
- fine tacks 13 mm (½ in)
- hair 450 g (1 lb)
- calico 50 cm (20 in)
- skin wadding 1700 g (48 oz), 50 cm (20 in)
- top cover fabric 50 cm (20 in)
- nylon twine
- fringe 1.75 m (2 yd)
- hot adhesive sticks
- braid 1.75 m (2 yd)
- 5 tufts made to match braid

THIS OLD PIANO stool belonged to my mother, but was in a poor state. It had been painted white and the mechanism was broken, so it was no longer used as a piano stool. Now, however, with the wood returned to its true colour and the mechanism mended, it has been given a new lease of life with really fun upholstery.

The plain fabric chosen for the cover provided the perfect opportunity to have fun with the trimmings. Tufts are used instead of buttons and they are made from the fringe tassels with embroidery silk added in the centre to give extra colour. The tufts are a purely decorative touch and are not strong enough to hold down the pleating, which is kept in place with stitches.

Restored to its original use, this stool would have made my mother smile and will certainly make piano practice a much more enjoyable experience.

TUFTING

As upholstery techniques improved towards the end of the seventeenth century, stitching methods to hold stuffing in place were being devised. Tufting ties, small bunches of unspun linen threads, prevented the securing quilting thread from wearing back through the cover into the padding. Gradually, the decorative potential of tufts became recognized, and the tufts were arranged in attractive patterns, to great effect. Throughout history, many materials have been used, such as leather washers and ribbons, as well as the more familiar thread tufts. Tufts were largely superseded in the mid nineteenth century by the metal button, which even held thick stuffings in place with ease. However, tufts have now become very popular again.

Right: The orange tassel fringe looks superb covered with a matching braid.

1 Strip the old upholstery off the stool, removing any old tacks. The stool was originally stuffed with alva, a traditional seaweed stuffing, which was too frail to reuse. Chamfer the edge of the stool top all around, using a rasp, to improve the surface on which to tack the scrim and support the stitched edge. If there are no original button holes, drill them into the seat base now, one central hole and four more at equal distances apart, 4 cm (1/2 in) from the edge.

2 Draw a circle on the seat base, two thirds of the distance from the centre to the outside edge, ready to make a stitched edge. Cut a strip of scrim wide enough to cover from the drawn line to 7.5 cm (3 in) past the outer edge, and long enough to go around the outer edge plus 10 cm (4 in) overlap.

3 Fold under a turning along one long edge of the scrim. Divide the seat base and the length of scrim into equal quarters and place one temporary 10 mm (3/8 in) tack to attach the scrim to each quarter of the circle, turning under the scrim to overlap at the join. Pleat the scrim evenly between the first tacks and tack down all around the pencilled circle. Pull the scrim towards the outer edge, then tease and stuff fibre under the scrim until it is evenly distributed and firm.

4 Tuck the scrim under the fibre around the outside edge. Place a temporary tack on the chamfered edge and another on the opposite side. Place two more tacks equally spaced between the first ones. Work in this manner until the scrim is temporary tacked all the way around the stool.

5 Hammer all the tacks home and add more so that they are close together. Regulate the stuffing towards the edge. Blind stitch all around the edge, keeping the needle very close to the row of tacks. Regulate again, and then make a row of top stitches all around. Regulate again and make a second row of top stitches, producing a very firm edge.

end of twine around the tack and tack it home. Pull the other end of twine down tightly while pushing down on the stitch made through the fabric with your thumb. Wind this length around the second tack and tack home, making a tie. Repeat the process on the four other holes.

6 Make two rows of tack ties across the centre circle with 13 mm (¹/₂ in) tacks, and stitch bridle ties around the top of the stuffed outer edge.

10 On the top of the seat, fold the resulting pleats between the holding ties, using the spade edge of the regulator. Fold the fabric from the outer four holding ties over the edge of the seat. Tack off the fabric all around the stool close to the plinth. Trim off the excess fabric with a craft knife, close to the tack line.

EXPERT TIP

When buttoning, always progress out from the first button to the next one diagonally, rather than along vertical or horizontal lines. This ensures that there is enough fabric to arrange it evenly into the pleat pattern, without pulling it too tightly over the padding.

7 Tease and stuff the ties with hair so that the centre circle is slightly higher than the top edge of the scrim.

8 Place calico over the seat and prepare for tufting by positioning small washers of calico where the tufts will go. Pull the calico over the edge of the seat and tack just above the bottom plinth. Trim off the excess calico. Place a layer of wadding on the calico, and break it open at the tufting marks.

11 Trim the stool with a tassel fringe, using a glue gun and starting with the end of the fringe folded in. Glue all around and fold the other end in, butting the ends together where they meet. Position a length of braid on top of the fringe and glue it in the same manner.

9 Cut a piece of top fabric. Measure the markings for the tufts and transfer them to the back of the fabric, marking them with a cross. Pull out the calico washer in the centre buttonhole, and lay the fabric over the seat. Push a double-ended needle, eye-end out, into the top of the seat through the mark on the fabric. Thread a length of nylon twine through the needle and push through the drilled hole. Remove the needle and leave the nylon twine hanging on the underside. Thread the needle with the twine lying on top and make a stitch on the top fabric, pushing the needle through to the underside again. Place two tacks near the hole on the underside. Wind the first

12 To attach the tufts, take a double-ended needle threaded with nylon twine through the loop at the base of the tuft. Thread both ends of the twine through the drilled hole with the needle. Pull the twine down hard and fasten it with tacks in the same way as the holding ties. Fluff out the tufts.

∞ Quick Reference

Ripping out, page 50

Stitched edges, page 65

Bridle ties, page 60

Deep buttoning, calico, page 70, top cover, page 80

Trimmings, attaching fringe, page 103

BLUES

For a restful, soothing combination, match blue tones with green tones. These neighbours on the colour wheel are perfect partners for the diamond pattern chosen for the traditional Louis XV carver.

MANY PEOPLE HAVE a passion for blue and it is always popular in the home. Choosing just the right shade for your upholstery can help to take the colour scheme for a room in either a fresh or a soothing direction.

Creating different moods

Colour therapists use blue to focus and relax the mind, and, in a religious setting, it is the colour of serenity and meditation. Think of a clear blue lake or a cloudless summer sky and you will be able to appreciate how it calms and refreshes the senses, aiding concentration and making it the perfect

restorative choice for bathrooms, bedrooms and studies.

Blue can also be brisk and invigorating, with clear, unmuddied versions such as cobalt, sky blue and cerulean conjuring up the freshness of the sunny seaside.

For dramatic schemes, think of the sea turned stormy or star-spangled midnight skies. Navy blue, especially reproduced in a rich fabric such as a velvet with the mysterious impact of golden embroidered stars, has a darkly opulent note.

Vibrant blues, like the turquoise of the Agean, can be a little too lively, exhausting the mind, if overused, so reserve these shades for accenting a scheme with throws, cushions and trimmings.

Combining blue with other colours

Blue has long been used with yellow, its near complementary, for schemes that are both lively and calming—a perfect balance. The cool clarity of the blue is countered by the warmth of the yellow, producing an ever-popular combination that has a gentle effect and is easy to live with.

Warm browns also offset blue well. For example, mellow pine furniture looks good upholstered with Swedish-style checks in clean or pastel shades of blue.

When combining blue with other colours, take care to consider the underlying tones. A blue fabric that tends towards green is at the brighter end of the spectrum, and would look stunning combined with green trimmings. However, a blue with mauve undertones is closer to red on the colour wheel, and accessorizing it with lavender, lilac or purple will produce a calm, composed scheme.

Enhancing the underlying tones of your blue with adjacent shades will result in schemes that are visually arresting and work quite effortlessly.

The monocoloured blue fabric makes a bold statement on this prie-dieu chair, developing the theme of meditation. This fabric is also the perfect background for the elaborate braid, and makes a dramatic statement in a terracotta interior.

Picture-back Chair

The stuff-over dining chair with a sprung seat remains the best chair for learning most of the upholstery processes for stuffing and stitching in the traditional manner. This type of chair can be found with a back pad, called a picture back, as here, or without.

Dimensions

height: 89 cm (35 in)
width: 46 cm (18 in)
depth: 40 cm (16 in)

Materials

- English webbing 5 m (5½ yd)
- improved tacks 13 mm (½ in)
- 5 double-cone springs 10 cm (4 in) gauge 10
- twine
- laid cord
- hessian 50 cm (20 in)
- fibre 1.8 kg (4 lb)
- scrim 75 cm (30 in)
- improved tacks 10 mm (³⁄₈ in)
- hair 900 g (2 lb)
- calico 75 cm (30 in)
- skin wadding 1700 g (48 oz), 1.5 m (1¾ yd)
- top cover fabric 1 m (1¼ yd)
- gimp pins 13 mm (½ in)
- fine tacks 10 mm (³⁄₈ in)
- gimp 4 m (4½ yd)
- hot adhesive sticks

TONES OF GREENS and yellow in the fabric make a pleasant, fresh contrast to the dark wood. The trailing design follows up the seat and over the back pad and lightens what might otherwise be a rather sombre chair. A touch of red in the gimp brings out the colour of the wood and cleverly ties the scheme of the whole chair together.

1 Strip all the old cover and stuffings from the chair using a mallet and ripping chisel. Before starting to upholster, use a rasp to chamfer the top edge of the seat, ready for tacking the scrim down. Although the seat will have been chamfered originally, it is important to improve the edge after removing the old tacks.

2 Place four webs from front to back and weave four from side to side on the underside of the seat rails. Do not place the webbing too near the outer edges of the rails, or they will show on the finished chair. Secure with 13 mm (½ in) improved tacks.

3 Place five double-cone springs on the webbing, two at the front, two at the back and one in the centre. Leave a slightly larger gap between the back springs and the back rail as most weight will be placed in the centre and front of the seat.

4 Sew the springs in position on the webbing from underneath the chair, using a spring needle threaded with twine. Lash the springs down using laid cord.

5 Place hessian over the springs and tack down all around, folding the raw edges upwards. Sew the springs in through the hessian, in the same pattern and using the same method as in step 4. Stitch five rows of bridle ties across the seat, using a spring needle and twine.

6 Tease and stuff fibre under the ties until a thick pad is formed. Cover with scrim, adding extra fibre to make the edges firm as you temporary tack the scrim to the chamfered edge. Stitch stuffing ties through the seat, using upholstery twine. Knot it off temporarily, ready to tighten up after the stitched edges are sewn.

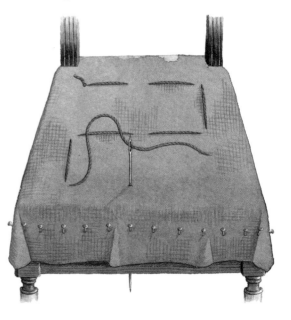

7 Tuck the scrim into the front corners and add extra fibre to make them firm. Cut into the back uprights and fold the excess scrim under. Place more 10 mm (³⁄₈ in) improved tacks so that they are close together and tack home all around.

SPRINGS

Springs were not a common feature of upholstered furniture until the 1840s, although some pioneering efforts towards developing springing systems had been attempted at various times since the 1760s. The widespread use of springs grew from an unlikely source—an exercise chair, with waisted spiral springs, which was popular in England during the latter part of the eighteenth century. These springs then began to be used in bed manufacture, and were eventually widely absorbed into upholstery techniques, after an initial scepticism.

8 Blind stitch all around, keeping close to the tack line. Then work two rows of top stitches around the seat. If you want a higher seat, do two rows of blind stitch and two rows of top stitch. Stitch rows of bridle ties across the seat. Tease hair under the ties and stuff the seat to make a good mat of hair right to the edges, adding more in the centre to give a slight dome shape.

9 Cover with calico, pulling tight and moulding the shape of the seat as you temporary tack to the front, side and back rails with 13 mm (½ in) improved tacks. Tack above the show wood, allowing space for the next tacks in the top fabric, which will be tacked close to the show wood. Trim off the front corners and fold under. Cut into the back uprights and fold under. Tack home and trim off all excess calico.

10 Place a piece of wadding over the entire seat and tear it at the bottom edge. Place the top fabric over the seat, keeping the pattern central. Place one temporary tack just above the show wood on the front, side and back rails. Cut into the back uprights, and trim off the excess fabric, leaving a turning of 1.25 cm (½ in). Fold this under. Continue to temporary tack on the back rail just above the show wood. Pull the top cover towards the front and temporary tack. Cut the fabric on the corners, allowing 1.25 cm (½ in) to fold under, and mitre the corners. Place a gimp pin on each side of the corner at the bottom of each fold.

11 Finish temporary tacking the two sides along the edge of the show wood with 13 mm (½ in) tacks. Tack home all around with 10 mm (⅜ in) fine tacks. Trim the excess fabric with a craft knife, cutting it right back to the edge of the show wood just under the line of tacks.

12 Trim the edge with a length of gimp, starting at one of the back corners. Fold the end of the gimp under and secure it with a gimp pin. Glue the gimp a few centimetres at a time and press on to the fabric, covering the line of tacks. Continue around the front and other side of the seat. Finish the end by cutting slightly longer, folding the gimp under and gluing securely. Tap gently all along the length with a cabriole hammer to make sure that the adhesive has adhered to the chair. Attach another piece of gimp across the back of the seat.

13 Cut a piece of top fabric slightly bigger than the aperture on the picture back, keeping the pattern central to match the seat. Place the fabric into the aperture from the front with the right side of the fabric facing the frame. Using gimp pins (because the rebate is very narrow), pin the fabric

so that it fits very tightly. Place a block of wood under the section you are pinning to absorb the shock and prevent damage to the frame. You could use a staple gun, if you prefer, as it will cause even less damage. When the fabric has been pinned or stapled all around, turn the edges in towards the centre and cut off the excess.

14 Place a piece of wadding to fit inside the rebate. Add a layer of hessian, secure with gimp pins and fold the excess towards the middle. Place a piece of webbing in the centre and fix top and bottom, keeping the ends flat.

15 Sew bridle ties into the hessian, making sure they do not penetrate the outside back. Tease a layer of hair under the ties to form a pad 1.25 cm (1/2 in) deep. Cover with calico and pin around the edges with gimp pins. Trim back, leaving a raw edge.

16 Place a layer of wadding over the calico, and tear the edges just short of the edge. Place a piece of top fabric, with the pattern central to match the seat, on the front of the pad. Temporary

tack all around. Fill in with gimp pins just inside the edge of the rebate and tack these home, removing the temporary tacks as you go. Trim the fabric close to the edge with a craft knife.

17 Using a glue gun, attach the gimp around the picture back, starting at the bottom left. Mitre each corner so the folds face each other. Fold the gimp at an angle to make a mitre on the last corner.

✇ Quick Reference

Ripping out, page 50

Webbing, page 51

Springing, page 54

Hessian, page 58

Bridle ties, page 60

Securing the first stuffing, page 62

Stitched edges, page 65

Trimmings, fixing gimp with hot adhesive, page 102

Below: The gimp gives a lovely finish to the chair, linking the bright fabric with the dark show wood.

GREENS

The soft green fabric of the picture-back chair is framed by an elaborately carved dark-brown wood, reminiscent of the green leaves of trees stemming from their dark-brown branches and trunks. The colours used on the chair subtly echo the decoration of the interior.

ALTHOUGH NOT ACTUALLY a primary colour, green often assumes an equal importance in interior decoration. This is probably because it is the colour of nature, with its balance and harmony, and so it creates feelings of calm, contemplation and restfulness.

Research has shown that green has the power to restore equilibrium and the ability to bring the mind, body and soul together into comfortable alignment. We need only to think of the serene greens on rolling fields to understand why the tranquil power of this undemanding colour has been recognized in homes for centuries. It is even

frequently used in decorating public buildings specifically for its calming effect.

Complementing green with red

Green partners many other colours well in the home, just as in nature. Red, its complementary and opposite on the colour wheel, makes a good companion, each colour enhancing, not fighting, the properties of the other. Think of a deep-red rose or scarlet geraniums amid green foliage.

Red and green combinations work very well in living rooms where, for example, the cool, mid-green fabric for a sofa will be warmed by dusky pinks or glowing apricots in the pattern, cushions or trimmings. Alternatively, green can be used to bring a balancing coolness to a vibrant red scheme; for instance, a moss-green tartan used to upholster chairs in a fiery-red dining room would be dramatic and yet harmonious.

Zingy combinations

The greens of nature might be deeply restorative, but nature can also evoke a sense of zing. Think of new green shoots emerging from the wintry soil in spring and you can anticipate the immediate sense of springtime that sharp, lime greens can

bring to a room. Acid-green florals in a teenager's bedroom could be the answer in the quest to combine youthfulness with a soothing influence. Take care, however, that the same look does not create too chilly a feel in a room that faces north or receives little natural light.

Greens can be used comfortably with many colours, especially red, or in glorious profusion on their own. Whichever green you choose, you will be tapping into a rich vein of design culture. Green brings nature and the comforting rhythm of the changing seasons into the home to great decorative and psychological effect.

Green is often used with red to create a festive feel, but it also creates a welcoming look on this easy chair. The teal scatter cushions provide the perfect link between the blue and green in the pattern.

Louis XV Carver

Silks are fine fabrics and the threads have a tendency to pull into tight lines, or to 'girt',

unless you are careful. This type of fabric is perhaps best reserved for a piece that will

not receive a lot of wear and tear and for when you have some experience of upholstery.

Dimensions

height: 69 cm (27 in)
width: 56 cm (22 in)
depth: 54 cm (22 in)

Materials

- English webbing 4 m (4½ yd)
- improved tacks 13 mm (½ in)
- hessian 1 m (1¼ yd))
- fine tacks 13 mm (½ in)
- twine
- fibre 1.8 kg (4 lb)
- scrim 1 m (1¼ yd)
- improved tacks 10 mm (3/8 in)
- hair 900 g (2 lb)
- calico 1 m (1¼ yd)
- top cover fabric 2 m (2¼ yd)
- skin wadding 1700 g (48 oz), 2 m (2¼ yd)
- cotton felt 50 cm (20 in)
- gimp 6 m (6½ yd)
- hot adhesive sticks
- gimp pins 13 mm (½ in)

FEW OF US are lucky enough to own an original Louis XV chair, but, if you like a particular style of antique furniture, an alternative is to buy a well-made reproduction. Choose a sturdy-looking frame with a good rebate to which the upholstery can be fixed.

This reproduction chair is mahogany and it is an easy matter to sand down and wax the wood to give it a richer appearance, resulting in a pleasing patina that makes the frame look antique.

The cover fabric is a shot silk in a diamond pattern, which complements the grain and colour of the wood. It is a glamorous fabric that gives the chair a luxury look befitting a genuine antique.

1 Chamfer the top edge on the seat rails to take a stitched edge later. Place five webs from back to front on top of the seat rails and weave four webs across, securing with 13 mm (½ in) improved tacks.

2 Place hessian over the webbing on the seat and tack down with fine tacks. Turn the edges over towards the centre and tack home. Stitch bridle ties in the hessian. Tease and stuff fibre under the ties.

3 Cover the fibre with scrim and stitch stuffing ties through the seat. Temporary tack down the scrim on the chamfered edge all around the seat with 10 mm (3/8 in) improved tacks, adding more fibre and regulating the stuffing to keep it even all around. Cut into the front and back legs, and turn the scrim under. Make a stitched edge all around the seat with two rows of blind stitch and one row of top stitch. Fasten off the stuffing ties.

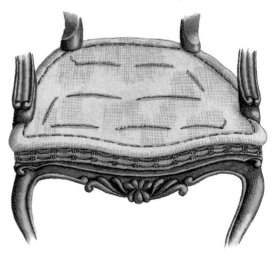

4 Now start the back pad. Place enough hessian on the front rebate of the back pad to fill the gap and give a turning of 2.5 cm (1 in). Tack the hessian on with fine tacks, pulling tight so that it is very taut and then tack home. Fold the turnings towards the centre and tack home. Draw a line 10 cm (4 in) from the rebate around the inside back, following the contour of the frame.

5 Measure all around the rebate, add 10 cm (4 in) to the measurement, and cut a strip of scrim this length and 15 cm (6 in) wide. Fold one long edge of the scrim under and pin the folded edge to the line drawn on the hessian. Using a circular needle, start in the middle of the lower edge and backstitch the scrim to the hessian. Gather the scrim on the curves so that it will spread on the outer edges. Turn the end under and overlap where the scrim meets.

GIMP

The word gimp describes a thread comprising a core yarn wound on the outside with a good-quality yarn, for example wire or stiff cord covered with silk. Over the years, this definition has come to incorporate openwork braids, which are now commonly referred to as gimp. Unlike braids, their flat counterparts, gimps have a three-dimensional framework, and are generally more flexible. Scroll gimp, with its sinuous serpentine structure, is particularly useful for curves, while straight-edged gimps work well when mitred.

Gimp has long been used to cover tacks and raw edges unobtrusively and stylishly. It may be glued, sewn, or nailed in place with decorative nails or gimp pins.

6 Start stuffing fibre under the scrim, turn the scrim under and temporary tack to the rebate just inside the show wood. Continue until a firm pad is formed. Tack home and remove temporary tacks. Regulate the stuffing. Using a curved needle for ease and to prevent damage to the show wood, stitch one row of blind stitch and one row of top stitch, starting close to the tack line.

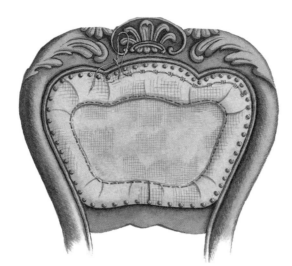

7 Make both arm pads at the same time to keep them the same size. Measure the length and depth of the arm pad, allowing an extra 10 cm (4 in) all around. Cut two pieces of scrim to size. Turn one long edge of scrim under and tack it to the inside edge of the arm frame. Make tack ties on the wood and tease fibre under them to make a firm pad. Pull the scrim over the fibre and tuck it under on the outside edge. Temporary tack along this edge, adding more fibre if necessary. Tack home. Tuck the front corners into a fold and tack them home on each corner and along the front edge. Repeat at the back of the arm pad.

8 Regulate the stuffing towards the edges of the arm pads. Then make one row of blind stitch, and one of top stitch around the tops of the arm pads to create a firm edge.

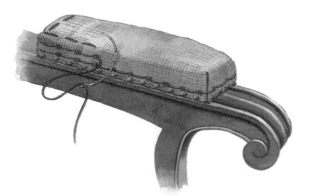

9 Stitch bridle ties across the pads and tease hair under them, making a slightly rounded centre. Cover with calico, pleating the back and front corners and trimming off the excess calico.

10 Sew bridle ties across the seat and tease a layer of hair under them until a firm pad is formed. Cut a piece of calico and place it over the seat. Temporary tack just short of the rebate on the front, sides and back of the seat. Cut into the arm and back uprights and tack home. Fold the front corners into a pleat and trim off excess calico.

11 Sew bridle ties across the back pad and add hair as for the seat. Cut a piece of calico and temporary tack all around just short of the rebate. Tack home and trim off the excess calico.

12 Measure the seat, back and arm pads and make a cut sheet for the top fabric, keeping the pattern central and leaving enough turning allowances to handle the fabric. Cut the sections out and mark them on the wrong side.

13 Place a length of wadding over the seat and trim the edges with your fingers. Place the

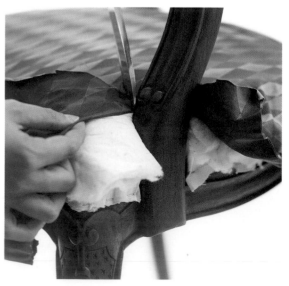

fabric on the seat and temporary tack the back, sides and front, cutting into the back uprights and the front arms to allow the fabric around them.

14 Trim back the main excess, leaving approximately 2.5 cm (1 in) to work with. Double pleat the front corners and tack home on the rebate just above the show wood. Trim back to the rebate using a sharp knife.

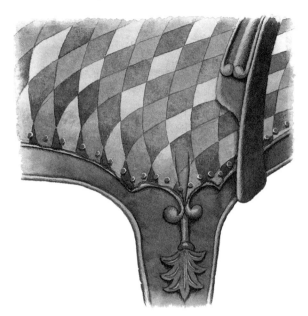

15 Place a piece of wadding on the back pad and tear the edges just inside the rebate. Place the top fabric on the back pad, lining up the pattern with the seat. Temporary tack in position just inside the rebate. Fill in with more tacks, and tack home. Trim back to the rebate.

16 On the outside back, lay cotton felt over the hessian to bring it level with the outside of

the frame. Place a piece of calico over the top to back up and cover the padding. Add wadding, tearing it around the edges. Position the top fabric and temporary tack in place, keeping the pattern in line. Add tacks and tack home just inside the rebate. Trim back to the rebate.

17 Cover the arm pads with wadding and then the top fabric, pleating the excess fabric at the corners. Tack home. Trim back to the rebate.

18 Trim the seat with gimp. To start, glue the raw end of the gimp to the rebate and secure it with two gimp pins, then fold the gimp back on itself to run right up to the edge of the rebate, following the curved line of the show wood. Glue about 15 cm (6 in) at a time, hammering it lightly as you work. Fold the gimp under at the other end and glue down. Use a gimp pin to hold until the adhesive dries. Repeat on all sides of the seat.

19 Trim the inside and outside back pads in the same way, joining the gimp in the centre of the bottom of the pad, turning the ends under and butting them to make the join invisible. Trim the arm pads in the same way, joining the gimp at the backs of the pads.

Above: The fabric has been carefully positioned so that the diamond pattern on the arms runs in the same direction as on the seat of the chair.

Quick Reference

Webbing, page 51

Bridle ties, page 60

Securing the first stuffing, page 62

Stitched edges, page 65

Estimating top fabric, page 78

Trimmings, fixing gimp with hot adhesive, page 102

Nursing Chair

Nursing chairs were traditionally used in a feminine setting, so a vibrant pink cotton was chosen for the top cover. The colour is sure to enliven any room without looking too outrageous and can be dressed up or down with different trimmings.

THIS OLD CHAIR frame was in very bad condition and had to be repaired before any upholstery could be done. However, it was obvious that with a certain amount of skill and effort it could be made into a very striking piece of furniture.

The distinctive pink of the top fabric cried out for dramatic trimmings. Here the elaborate cord in strongly constrasting colours, with its matching rosettes and tassels, makes a strong statement that is both elegant and slightly formal. The pink fabric could also have been complemented with frivolous trimmings that would look pretty in a bedroom.

1 Rip out the fabric, all stuffings and springs back to the frame. Remove any old tacks, and, using a rasp, chamfer the edges of the frame along the tack lines. Re-glue and cramp the frame if it is loose. Clean the legs and, if you wish to paint them, sand and undercoat them at this stage.

2 Web the underside of the seat using five webs each way and securing with 13 mm (1/2 in) improved tacks. Web the inside back of the frame, placing two webs close together 7.5 cm (3 in) from the bottom rail, one web across at the top of the back uprights and four webs evenly spaced between.

3 Spring the seat with six double-cone springs, three in a row towards the back and three at the front, using the following working order. Position the springs, sew them to the webbing, and lash them down. Apply hessian, attaching it to the back, side and front rails. Sew the springs to the hessian. Sew in bridle ties. Tease in fibre to cover the seat area. Cover with scrim. Stitch in stuffing ties. Sew two rows of blind stitch and one of top stitch on the sides and front. Bridle stitch across the scrim and tease hair under the ties.

4 Cover the seat with the calico, cutting into the back uprights and tacking home on the back rail using fine 13 mm (1/2 in) tacks. Make a pleat on the front corners. Cut away the excess calico before tacking home along the face of the side and front rails.

Dimensions

height: 66 cm (26 in)
width: 52 cm (21 in)
depth: 54 cm (22 in)

Materials

- English webbing 8.5 m (9 1/2 yd)
- improved tacks 13 mm (1/2 in)
- 6 double-cone springs 15 cm (6 in) gauge 10
- twine
- laid cord
- hessian 1 m (1 1/4 yd)
- fibre 3.6 kg (8 lb)
- scrim 1 m (1 1/4 yd)
- hair 1.8 kg (4 lb)
- calico 1 m (1 1/4 yd)
- fine tacks 13 mm (1/2 in)
- improved tacks 10 mm (3/8 in)
- top cover fabric 2.25 m (2 1/2 yd)
- skin wadding 1700 g (48 oz), 2 m (2 1/4 yd)
- gimp pins
- machine thread
- back tack strip 60 cm (24 in)
- black bottom 1 m (1 1/4 yd)
- cord 4.5 m (5 yd)
- 2 tassels
- 2 rosettes
- panel pins

5 Place hessian over the webbing on the inside back and build up the stuffing from the hessian in the same manner as the seat. Shape the upholstery by following the contour of the back uprights and adding extra fibre in the lumbar region. Place scrim in position and tack home using 10 mm (³/₈ in) tacks. Stitch two rows of blind stitch and two rows of top stitch to make an edge along each upright, creating a contour. Stitch bridle ties into the scrim.

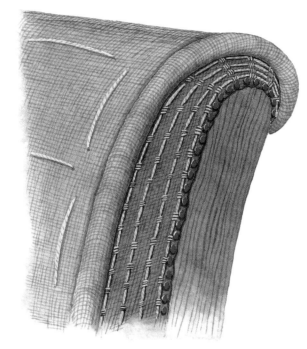

6 Add a layer of hair and cover in calico. Make a pleat at the two top corners, cutting away excess calico. Tack home on the side face of the upright rails using 13 mm (¹/₂ in) fine tacks and finish over the top on the back of the head rail.

7 Measure the seat from under the front rail, over the seat, to the back rail and from under one side rail, over the seat, to under the other side rail at the widest part of the seat. Measure the inside back from the base of the head rail, over the inside back to the back rail and from side to side, starting and finishing on the outside of the upright rails at the widest point. Measure the outside back area. Transfer the measurements to a cut sheet, allowing enough for turnings. Cut out and label the pieces from the top fabric.

8 Lay a piece of wadding over the calico on the inside back and feather the edges. Lay the top fabric in place over the head rail and temporary tack it to the base of the head rail. Pull the fabric over towards the seat and cut into the inside of the two uprights.

9 Push the fabric through to the back, and then trim away excess fabric and temporary tack on the bottom of the back rail. Pull the fabric around to temporary tack on the back of the uprights. At the top of the uprights, cut off the excess fabric, fold under and make a pleat. Finish tacking home the top and sides.

10 If you are painting the legs of the chair, give them a top coat of paint now and allow to dry before continuing. Wrap the legs in stockinette or something similar to prevent damage while working.

11 Place wadding on the seat, feathering the edges just above the seat rails. Place the top fabric over the seat and secure with temporary tacks underneath the seat rails. Cut into the inside of the upright rails, matching the cuts on the inside back. Push the fabric through between the seat and the back, and secure to the back seat rail. Make another cut to the outside of the upright rails to allow the fabric around. Turn the fabric back to create a mitre down to the back corner of the frame, lay this over the inside back fabric and tack to the underside of the seat rails.

12 Cut into the back legs, trim away excess fabric and fold under, level with the bottom edge of the frame. Secure with tacks on the back uprights. Pull the fabric under the side rails and temporary tack. Cut into the side of the front leg and trim off the excess fabric. Fold under so that

the fabric is level with the frame and tack along the edge. Pull the cover over the front of the seat and secure under the front rail. Cut into the leg in the same way as at the side and trim back. Pin down the front corner, making a pleat. Cut away the excess fabric and turn the edges under. Fold the bottom edges under and secure on the bottom corner with a gimp pin. Slip stitch neatly down the two front pleats, starting at the top. Continue to secure the fabric under the base rail all around.

13 Place the outside back fabric over the inside back of the chair, with right sides facing. Position the top of the fabric along the underside of the head rail on the outside back and temporary tack to hold. Put back tack strip along the head rail on top of the fabric and tack it in place, removing the temporary tacks.

14 Pull the fabric back over the strip and position wadding on the outside back underneath the fabric. Turn in the sides of the fabric and pin just in from the edges. Cut into the legs and turn the fabric under level with the frame. Pull the fabric under the frame and tack home along the base rail. Slip stitch down the edges of the outside back.

15 Turn the chair over, and finish the underneath by covering with a piece of black bottom. Cut into the legs and fold the turnings under neatly around the bottom rails. Tack the black bottom in place.

16 Turn the chair upright again to add the trimming. Stitch cord along the bottom edge of the chair, starting by securing it on the outside back with a tack. Finish by laying the ends of cord over each other and sewing them together to stop the edges fraying and disguise the join.

17 To trim the back of the chair, take an end of cord and make a coil. Slip stitch to the left side of the chair using a small circular needle, making sure that the centre of the coil is well secured. Drape the cord across the front of the inside back, making sure it hangs in a position that is comfortable to sit against. Place pins in the cord and the fabric to mark where to start slip stitching again. Coil the cord into a mirror image of the first coil. Trim the end, tuck it in and secure. Slip stitch the coil to the right side of the chair.

18 Thread the cord of one of the tassels through one of the rosettes and knot it at the back to hold securely. Position the rosette over one of the cord coils on the chair and secure to the frame with a padded hammer and panel pin. Invisibly slip stitch the rosette in place. Repeat with the second tassel and rosette, making sure both tassels hang at the same height.

19 For an alternative idea for trimming a chair like this, see page 40. A pleated ribbon was gathered and slip stitched in place around the base of the chair. The same ribbon was formed into small bell shapes around a stamen made of gold cord and stitched in place of tassels. These trimmings would not withstand much wear and tear, but, for occasional use, give a lovely frivolous feel in a boudoir setting.

EXPERT TIP

On an old frame, chamfer the rails with a rasp where the upholstery will have a stitched edge. This will give the tacks a better grip, create a clean line and avoid the tacks wearing through the top fabric.

Below: The tassels are threaded through a rosette and stitched in place over the coiled cord.

TRIMMINGS *the finishing flourish*

TRIMMINGS ARE THE icing on the upholsterer's
cake—tempting confections of colour and texture.
With so many to choose from, it is easy to become
confused into dazed indecision.

Choosing trimmings

Allow as much time to select the trimmings as you
took to choose the main fabric. Before you set off,
consider the overall impression you want to
create. The shape, function and period of the
piece of furniture will have steered the choice of
top fabric, and trimmings are equally important in
contributing to the finished look.

Most manufacturers produce rosettes, tassels,
braids and fringing in complementary colourways
for an effortlessly co-ordinated look. However,
what looks striking in a small swatch can be too
overpowering en masse, so obtain a generous
sample and try it against the top fabric on the
furniture to avoid expensive mistakes, especially
if your project needs large quantities.

Using a whole colour-matched range is not
always the most appropriate or stylish choice.
You could put together your own combinations
or have trimmings specially made to pick out
colours in the top fabric. If an exact match cannot

be found, go for a slightly darker shade of the desired colour, rather than a tonally accurate, but clumsy, colour match. If in doubt, pick out the underlying, rather than the prominent, colours in the top fabric to achieve a look of depth and subtlety.

Dramatic differences

Whether you use understated trimmings in subdued tones, simple shapes and matt textures, or go crazy with glossy, show-stopping tassels, rosettes and braids, make a well-considered and appropriate choice.

The purity of a chaise lounge covered in unbleached linen could be effectively contrasted with glamorous ivory silk tassels and matching silk tufts, each material emphasizing the qualities of the other. The same chaise would probably look disastrous with bright red trimmings, but put them on the chaise covered in a fabric of similarly hot colours and the result will be a stunning success. Trimmings certainly do not need to be discreet. When a rosette and tassel is added to a beautifully pleated bolster, they lead the eye to a point deserving special attention.

The trimming makes all the difference.

On a piece that is not likely to receive much wear and tear, you can afford to choose trimmings that are a little more elaborate and even fragile. The bright orange tassels on the piano stool are frivolous and fun, but they were also tested before being applied to make sure they were robust enough for the job.

197

Prie-dieu Chair

The fabric used is a plain but richly coloured hand-woven cotton, with a raised texture that gives a self-patterning effect and catches the light. A wide, wired braid emphasizes the ecclesiastical look in a sumptuously stylish way.

ANTIQUE PRIE-DIEU, or prayer, chairs are sometimes lavishly decorated. They often have beautifully carved frames, and are upholstered in heavily embroidered fabric and exquisite trimmings. They are usually heirlooms, and the chance of finding one in your local antique shop is probably remote. However, this need not stop you enjoying upholstering a prie-dieu, as reproduction frames are available. This frame is upholstered using modern materials and technique, but you can upholster the chair in the traditional style.

The real beauty of the chair lies in its simple shape, which provides the basic canvas, so your imagination can dress it with extravagance.

1 Wax and polish the legs of the chair before you start to upholster.

2 Web the seat on the top of the seat frame with three webs front to back and two woven across, securing with improved tacks. Web the inside back with two vertical webs and four woven across. Place a piece of hessian on the seat, allowing 5 cm (2 in) extra all around. Tack the hessian down, keeping it taut. Turn the edges towards the centre and tack down again. Attach hessian to the inside back in the same way.

3 Make a template of the head rail. Transfer this pattern to the chip foam and cut out using a foam cutter or bread knife. Reposition the chip foam on the head rail and lay a piece of the 2.5 cm (1 in) thick foam on the inside back, adding an extra 15 cm (6 in) on the height to cover the 'T' shape. Make a template of the top of the seat frame on a piece of paper. Transfer this pattern to the remainder of the chip foam and cut out the shape for the seat.

4 Spray adhesive on the hessian on the seat, and press the chip foam to it, lining up the edges with the frame. Spray adhesive on both the chip foam and a sheet of 1.25 cm (½ in) foam. Lay the sheet foam over the chip foam and fold it down the sides and front of the seat, entirely covering it. Cut away the excess on the front corners, and glue the corners down to butt neatly. Trim the foam level with the bottom edge of the frame.

Dimensions

height: 99 cm (39 in)
width: 51 cm (20 in)
depth: 71 cm (28 in)

Materials

- English webbing 5 m (5½ yd)
- improved tacks 13 mm (½ in)
- hessian 1 m (1¼ yd)
- chip foam 5 cm (2 in) thick, 55 x 90 cm (22 x 36 in)
- foam 2.5 cm (1 in) thick, 75 x 200 cm (30 x 80 in)
- spray adhesive
- foam 1.25 cm (½ in) thick, 75 x 200 cm (30 x 80 in)
- top cover fabric 2.5 m (2¾ yd)
- polyester wadding 56 g (2 oz), 3.5 m (4 yd)
- fine tacks 13 mm (½ in)
- gimp pins 10 mm (3⁄8 in)
- slipping thread
- machine thread
- calico 2 m (2¼ yd)
- fine tacks 10 mm (3⁄8 in)
- black bottom 1 m (1¼ yd)
- wired braid 4 m (4½ yd)

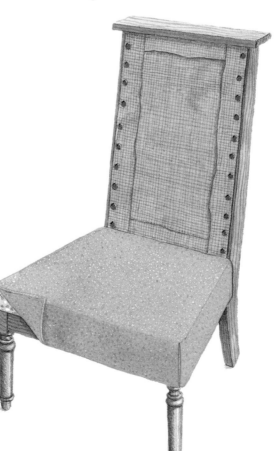

5 Spray adhesive on the head rail and press the chip foam on. Draw a straight horizontal line 2.5 cm (1 in) from the top front edge of the chip foam. With the knife or cutter held against the front edge of the frame, cut down along the line, taking the front corner in line with the inside back.

6 Spray adhesive on to the hessian on the inside back and fit the 2.5 cm (1 in) thick foam to the back. Glue the foam over the chip foam on the head rail, folding it neatly around the ends. This process should give the inside back of the chair a smooth, sloping outline.

7 Fit a layer of 1.25 cm (½ in) thick foam over the inside back in the same manner, covering the existing foam. When you reach the top section, cut a straight line across each side of the foam to allow it to fold around to the sides underneath the head rail. Trim the foam off level with the uprights at the back.

8 Measure for the inside back top fabric around the widest part of the head rail and from the underside of the head rail on the outside back, over the top, and down to underneath the bottom back rail. Measure the seat across the widest part from the underside of one side rail to the other, and from underneath the front rail, over the seat, to the back rail. Measure the outside back from under the head rail to underneath the bottom back rail and from one upright to the other. Measure the strip down the side of the chair back across the widest part and from the top of the head rail, around the 'T' shape and down the side of the chair to the bottom rail. Add turning allowances of 5 cm (2 in) to all measurements and transfer them to a cut sheet. Cut out and label the pieces.

9 Lay a piece of wadding over all the foam on the seat and tear just above the bottom edge. Lay the top fabric over the wadding, lining up the pattern centrally. Temporary tack underneath the bottom rail all around using 13 mm (½ in) fine tacks. Cut into the back uprights, push the fabric through between the back rails and temporary tack. Cut into the corners on the outside of the back uprights and temporary tack to the side rail. Pin the front corners and cut away the excess fabric, remove the pins and turn the edges under to make a fold. Pin, ready to slip stitch. Cut around the legs, trim and turn the fabric under. Fasten at the bottom corners with a gimp pin, and slip stitch the front corner folds. Add extra tacks and tack home underneath the frame.

Right: The braid is mitred to match exactly at the corners of the chair.

10 Lay the fabric on the inside back and hold in position with upholstery pins. Pin one of the side strips to the inside back from where the inside back meets the seat to underneath the head rail on the outside back, matching the pattern across. At the corners where the strip turns under the head rail, cut right into the corner and pin the fabric pieces together, following the line of the frame. Repeat on the other side with the second strip.

of the uprights. Where the seat meets the back, fold the side strips under and tack the bottom edge of the fabric underneath the inside back rail.

12 Tack home all around, adding more tacks where necessary. Back up the outside back with calico, leaving a raw edge all around. Cover with wadding. Pin the top cover in position and slip stitch around the top and sides.

BRAIDS

In the seventeenth century, top cover fabrics were hand woven on narrow looms, approximately 52 cm (21 in) wide, necessitating the joining of fabrics on wider chair backs and seats. Braids, which are tightly woven, flat bands, were used to conceal joins on fabric-covered walls and then used on seat upholstery in the same way. They increasingly became used in purely decorative, as well as practical, ways. Braids continue to play a vital role in concealing and embellishing seams and joins to this day, as well as defining and accentuating shapes. They are available in many designs, from simple to complex. Even today, a passementière working to traditional designs and methods will take one day to produce 3.5 m (4 yd) of braid.

11 Trim and notch both seams, remove the fabric from the chair, and machine stitch the sections together. Place wadding over the inside back and cap the fabric back on. Temporary tack under the head rail at the back and down the back

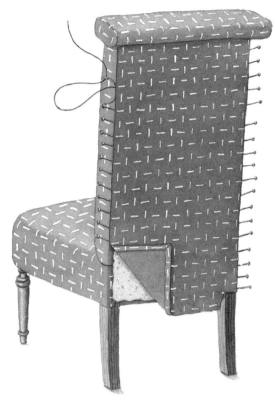

13 Cut into the legs and fold the fabric under around the top of them. Tack the rest of the fabric along the underside of the back rail and trim with 10 mm (3/8 in) fine tacks. Position a piece of black bottom and tack in place, turning in the edges and cutting round the legs.

14 Start attaching the braid just under the head rail, turning a small amount under. Using a circular needle, stitch the back edge for a short distance, then stitch the front edge, keeping the braid flat. Continue stitching down the side. At the bottom corner, stitch the back edge first and keep the needle in the braid at the point you want it to turn. Fold the braid under until the bottom edge is level with the bottom of the seat and the top edges of the mitre match exactly. Tap the mitre gently with a covered hammer to flatten it, and stitch in position. Continue stitching around the bottom of the seat. Match the mitre on the other side and continue up the second side. Cut the braid at the head rail, leaving a small allowance to turn under. Stitch it down securely.

Modern Sofa

Two-seater sofas can be found in many homes and, if well constructed, can be well worth giving a new lease of life. On this sofa, the basic upholstery was sound and only the seat cushions had suffered, so they and the top cover needed replacing.

Dimensions

height: 62 cm (25 in)
width: 1.47 m (60 in)
depth: 86 cm (34 in)

Materials

- top cover fabric 9 m (10¾ yd)
- lining 1.05 m (1¼ yd)
- platform cloth 75 cm (30 in)
- polyester wadding 56 g (2 oz), 12 m (13 yd)
- fine tacks 13 mm (½ in)
- staples 10 mm (⅜ in)
- machine thread
- cotton tape 30 mm (1¼ in) wide, 2 m (2¼ yd)
- calico 1 m (1¼ yd)
- back tack strip 5 m (5¼ yd)
- slipping thread
- black bottom 1.5 m (1¾ yd)
- 2 foam seat cushions 10 cm (4 in) deep (75 cm²/8 ft² cut to size)
- stockinette 2 m (2¼ yd)
- 4 zips 60 cm (24 in) each

THIS TWO-SEATER sofa has an entirely modern structure, consisting of a wooden frame with zigzag springs in the seat and webbing on the arms and back. The shape is moulded from fire-retardant foam. The two back cushion pads are filled with man-made filling, that still has plenty of bounce, and do not need replacing.

The fabric in smart charcoal grey and cream is made of mixed fibres. The small check suits the straight lines of a modern sofa and yet there is a more subtle interest added by the slightly ribbed texture and a soft sheen on the surface of the fabric, that bring it to life in different lighting conditions.

1 Rip off all the old cover using a mallet and ripping chisel or staple remover and pincers. Clean off all the debris and check the frame to see if it needs any repairs. The caster blocks on modern frames usually need repairing.

2 If the webbing is loose or needs replacing, tighten or replace it at this stage. To gain access, carefully lift the foam back from the bottom of the seat and arms and fold it back. Hold the foam back firmly with a skewer, but do not overstretch it, and avoid making any holes. When the webbing is back in place, lay the foam back in position and staple down to the bottom rails.

3 Measure the sections to be covered and make a cut sheet, allowing an extra 5 cm (2 in) for turnings and matching the pattern all around. The outside back is wider than the width of the fabric, so allow for a join on each side, with seam allowances. Cut the pieces out from the top fabric, label them and mark the direction with an arrow on the wrong side.

4 Also cut fabric for the kick pleats, cutting five pieces 21 cm (8 in) deep across the width of the fabric, matching the pattern. Cut five widths of lining 19 cm (8 in) deep. Cut strips on the cross for piping, making enough to go along the front and top of the two outside arms and the outside back, and around the top of the kick pleat on the front, sides and back. Also cut enough piping for the four cushions. Cut a piece of platform cloth to cover the seat area, including 5 cm (2 in) extra all around.

5 Cover the original foam on the inside back with wadding, lining it up along the outside back edge. Place the top fabric over the wadding and

LEATHER

Just as deeply buttoned Chesterfields in a gentlemen's club speak discreetly of elitism and affluence, early leather coverings proclaimed their owner's prosperity with considerably less subtlety. Seventeenth century leather was gilded, painted and embossed to produce the ultimate in status symbol upholstery. In the eighteenth century, 'Damask leather' featured scorched patterns, stamped into the surface. Today, plain finishes are subtly elegant, as well as durable. Leather hides are being so thinly cut that they are much more workable than the thicker skins of old, and with the emergence of buffalo hide onto the market, it has never been easier to incorporate this wonderfully tactile covering into upholstery.

temporary tack just over the back of the head rail. Make two cuts into the top corner and one at the bottom to allow the fabric through to the upright.

6 Pull the fabric underneath the inside back rail and temporary tack to this rail. Check that all the pattern lines are straight, then staple to secure, removing the temporary tacks as you go.

7 Position the top fabric for one of the inside arms so that it hangs slightly over the arm rail and wraps around the front upright. Pin it in position. Cut into the front corner to allow the fabric to spread, ready to meet the front border and platform. Position the outside arm fabric and pin it to the inside arm fabric from the bottom edge at the front, following the outside edge of the frame along the arm to the outside back. Pin along the top of the front, making a dart to take up the excess fabric. Trim the seams, keeping a 1.25 cm (½ in) seam allowance. Notch the seams.

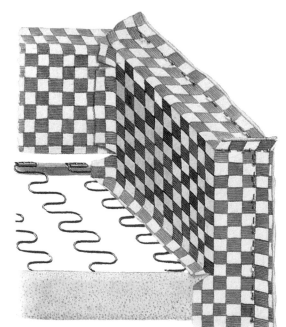

8 Remove the cover from the sofa and unpin it. Lay it on the other inside and outside arm sections, right-sides facing, and transfer all the shaping and notching. With a matching thread, machine the darts on the two arms and press them open.

9 Make up enough single piping for the outside arms. Sew the piping along the front and top of both the outside arms sections. Lay the outside arm on the inside arm section, right-sides together. Machine stitch, matching all the notches. When you reach the corner, make sure the dart is right on the corner, then cut into the corner, leave the needle in the fabric, lift the machine foot to turn the fabric and continue stitching.

10 Lay wadding over the inside arm, trimming away the excess with your fingers. Cap on the arm section over the wadding. Make cuts on the inside arm to match those on the inside back,

pull the fabric through and secure it on the back upright. Temporary tack the outside arm fabric on the back upright. Secure the section on top of the inside back fabric with a temporary tack.

11 Cut the inside arm into the front upright to allow the fabric to pass between the arm and seat rails. Temporary tack it to the arm rail. Fold back the front inside and outside arm fabric and wadding where it meets the front border on the side rail, and pin out of the way. Staple the rest of the arm fabric in position, removing the temporary tacks. Place wadding on the outside arm from the top arm rail to the seat rail and staple it onto the wood. Repeat on the other arm.

12 Turn and stitch hems on the platform cloth on the two side and back edges. Mark the centre front of the platform with a notch. Take one full width of fabric for the front border and mark the centre with a notch. Pin the top cover and the platform cloth together, right-sides facing, matching the notches and leaving the fabric wider than the platform cloth. Machine stitch the seam. Cut a length of cotton tape 20 cm (8 in) longer than the front border. Stitch it to the unopened seam, starting and finishing securely and leaving an equal length unattached on each side.

Smooth the fabric over the front border and secure with staples underneath the bottom rail. Cut into the border where it meets the inside arms, and staple to the front upright.

14 Pull the outside arm fabric back down and staple underneath the side bottom rail and around on to the outside of the back upright rail. Finish the top by folding the fabric under and stapling on the back of the head rail. Pull the wadding and fabric on the inside arm back down. Cut in to the front border and fold the edges under to sit neatly over the border. Secure with staples underneath the front and side rails. Repeat on the other arm.

15 Back up the outside back with a piece of calico. Place wadding over the calico and feather the edge. Stitch the pieces of top fabric for the outside back together, matching the pattern. Position the top edge of the fabric along the top edge of the head rail, matching the pattern, and then lay the bulk of the fabric over the inside back. Place back tack strip on top of the fabric just below the top edge of the head rail and staple it in place. Pull the fabric back over the outside back, turn it under down both sides and pin in place. Staple the fabric underneath the bottom rail. Slip stitch the sides.

13 With the front of the arm sections pinned out of the way, place wadding on the front edge of the seat and front border. Position the seat section on the sofa, pulling the platform cloth over the springs and tacking it on the back rail. Pull the top fabric down over the front lip and border. Pull the cotton tape tightly down on both sides and secure with staples on the top of each arm rail.

16 Remove the casters from their sockets. Place a piece of black bottom on the underside of the sofa, turn under and staple all around. Cut a cross in the black bottom over the socket holes and replace the casters.

17 To make the kick pleat and cushions, see pages 96 and 107.

∞ Quick Reference

Ripping out, page 50

Estimating top fabric, page 78

Machine stitching, page 30

Trimmings, single piping, page 97

Covering the outsides, page 86

Base finishes, kick pleats, page 96

Cushions, page 107

NEUTRALS

This sofa is an example of how contemporary decoration often relies more on pattern and form than colour for interest. With its straight lines and checked fabric, it complements its setting and the striped artwork perfectly, but the whole scheme is softened by the plump scatter cushions.

THIS PALETTE COMBINES the tried and trusted staples of the contemporary decorator. Quietly reliable, neutrals are certainly not dull, and exude an air of quality. Now the neutral palette is well and truly in the spotlight, with a newly discovered appreciation of natural materials.

Practical considerations are still important when choosing from the palest end of the neutral spectrum, although modern fabrics often have better crease resistance and stain retardance. While a cream linen looks amazingly chic on a chair in its virgin state, it may look rather grubby a few months later. Be realistic about your

lifestyle and choose fibres and shades that will withstand whatever your life, family and pets throw at them.

Choice of fabrics

Once pure, untouched colours predominated and unbleached calicos and linens, complete with nobbly raw fibres, were an affordable choice for furniture requiring an elegant, if primitive, feel. They still lend themselves to stylish upholstery, perfect for town or country, contemporary or traditional interiors. Hessian, cotton duck, ticking and unbleached linen are all suitable choices. Try accessorizing them with even more natural, comforting textures in materials not hardy enough for upholstery, such as knitted cushion covers or raffia tassels.

Recently, the whole natural colour range from milk, through putty, oatmeal and sand, has been replicated in all manner of fabrics, creating new and exciting visual effects. Further evolution has taken the simple features of natural neutrals into yet more sophisticated shades of minerals, metallics and even neutralized colours, such as silvery lilac and pewtery purple, all particularly suitable for town and city living. Look closely at the iridescent tones of a seashell and you start to realize just how colourful non-colour really is.

The dimension of texture

These subtle choices of colour give texture and form, and the way light interacts with them, a definite impact. The difference in the way light glances over a silky smooth fabric pulled into sharp shapes and the softened shadows it creates on a piled fabric folded into the curves of a chair is vitally important to the overall effect. Play with layers of textured neutrals in this way and you will discover many different effects.

Texture plays a pivotal role in neutral decorating schemes, introducing another dimension to what might otherwise be rather dull. The cream pile fabric chosen for the button-back chair imparts a richness and the texture is further enhanced by the double-piped edge.

Day Bed

The Jacquard weave fabric was chosen for its many facets. It gives the impression of a quilted background with an embroidered design. It also has distinctive colourful stripes, with subtle cross bands and a rambling floral motif.

Dimensions

height: 94 cm (37 in)
width: 81 cm (32 in)
length: 1.7 m (67 in)

Materials

- English webbing 24 m (26 yd)
- improved tacks 16 mm (⁵⁄₈ in)
- 27 double-cone springs 17.5 cm (7 in) gauge 9
- twine
- laid cord
- hessian 2 m (2¹⁄₄ yd)
- fine tacks 13 mm (¹⁄₂ in)
- fibre 9 kg (20 lb)
- scrim 2.5 m (2³⁄₄ yd)
- improved tacks 10 mm (³⁄₈ in)
- hair 6 kg (14 lb)
- calico 2 m (2¹⁄₄ yd)
- top cover fabric 6 m (6¹⁄₂ yd)
- skin wadding 1700 g (48 oz), 4 m (4¹⁄₂ yd)
- machine thread
- cord 8 m (9 yd)
- 2 tassels
- 4 rosettes
- 2 panel pins
- black bottom 1.5 m (1³⁄₄ yd)

DAY BEDS WERE very popular in Victorian times, but modern reproductions, with their generous proportions, are probably more practical for use today. The tall back and rounded end give this day bed a pleasing line, and a bolster adds to both its comfort and style.

The Jacquard weave fabric is not an easy fabric to work with because the stripes are not symmetrical and work independently of the floral pattern. Here the stripes run down the length of the bed and around the border, giving continuity to the whole piece. The scroll is kept flat, rather than pleated, and that clean approach is followed through to a simple mitre on the bottom corner. So with careful planning, especially on the borders and scrolls, great results can be achieved.

1 Chamfer all around the top edges of the seat and the scroll edges on the back of the frame using a rasp. Wrap the legs at this stage, leaving them to be polished later.

2 Place webbing on the underside of the seat, using three single webs down the length and eighteen across the width, woven together in pairs for extra strength. Secure with 16 mm (⁵⁄₈ in) tacks. Place eight webs from side to side across the inside back, keeping them closer together over the scroll area and placing the last one underneath the scroll.

3 Position twenty-seven double-cone springs at the intersections of the webs on the seat and sew them in position. The back of the day bed is not sprung.

Step 3

TASSELS

Throughout history, tassels have been used in costume and interior decoration to add individuality, and denote status. Fifteenth and sixteenth century portraits show sumptuous tassels made of gold thread, interwoven with black or red wool, adorning the furniture of the sitter's home. Not only does this unashamed display of wealth emphasize the subject's position in life, but tassels are used in these portraits as they are today on upholstered furniture to draw the eye to a particular point of interest, such as a scroll, or bolster end, and encourage it to dwell there most pleasurably.

4 Place 16 mm (⅝ in) improved tacks at an angle around the top of the frame in line with each row of springs. Lash the springs across and lengthways, using laid cord. Knot each spring on each side and across the centre to keep them from moving out of line. Place a piece of hessian over the springs, leaving enough to turn back. Tack the hessian down all around with 13 mm (½ in) tacks.

5 Turn back the edges of the hessian and tack down all around. Cut in to the back upright and push the hessian through to the bottom back rail. Tack home on the top of the rail, fold the hessian over and tack home again.

6 Place hessian over the inside back, covering the edges of the webbing. Finish under the scroll, tack the hessian on to the rail, fold the edge over and tack home again. Cut into the upright at the bottom of the back and push the hessian through. Tack home on the top of the bottom back.

7 Sew the springs in the seat in place through the hessian, using a spring needle and twine, in the same manner as the underside. Sew bridle ties across the seat in rows. Tease fibre into the seat

under the bridle ties until the whole seat is covered, and add more in the middle section to make a slight dome.

8 Cut enough scrim to cover the seat, tuck under the fibre all around, and down between the back and seat rails. Stitch stuffing ties through the scrim and fibre down the length of the seat and tie off temporarily. Tuck the scrim under and temporary tack to the chamfered edge. Add more fibre to make the edge firm, removing the temporary tacks and replacing with 10 mm (⅜ in) improved tacks. Tack home as you progress. Ease the scrim around the bottom curves, pleating it so that the height and density of the stuffing remains constant. Finish all around the edge, then push the scrim through at the back, adding fibre to keep the seat level. Temporary tack to the bottom back rail.

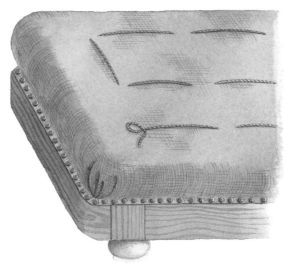

9 Regulate the seat edge and sew two rows of blind stitch and two rows of top stitch, starting and finishing at the point where the back meets the seat.

10 Sew bridle ties, evenly distributed, across the inside back. Stuff with fibre, cover with scrim, sew in stuffing ties and tack home all around the inside back, following the scroll line and keeping the edges even and firm. Regulate one edge and blind stitch, starting under the scroll and proceeding down to meet the seat. Add another row of blind stitch, regulate, then stitch two rows of top stitch. Repeat on the other side to match. Pull up the stuffing ties and fasten with a knot.

11 Sew bridle ties in rows in the scrim on the seat. Tease in a layer of hair to cover right to the edges on the seat. Cover with calico, using skewers to hold the calico in place just under the stitched edge. Sew a blind stitch along under the edge, using slipping thread and a circular needle. Trim the excess calico. Repeat exactly the same process on the inside back. Sandpaper and polish the legs at this point. Do not rewrap them as you need access while top covering.

12 Make a basic plan of how the pattern of the top fabric will work around the day bed, but cut the pieces as you go. Lay the fabric over the seat to decide where the pattern will be placed, making sure that the design is balanced. Mark on the underside of the top cover, then remove the piece of fabric and cut it following the marks. Place a sheet of wadding over the calico, feathering the edge of the wadding just above the stitch line. Place the fabric over the seat and skewer it under the stitched edge. Blind stitch one row just under the stitches on the calico, using a circular needle and slipping thread. Cut into the inside back upright, push the fabric through, and secure on the bottom back rail with 13 mm (¹⁄₂ in) fine tacks. Remove the skewers as you work.

13 Measure the inside back. Cut the back section out, matching the pattern on the seat and allowing extra for the pattern repeat. Place a sheet of wadding over the back and position the fabric, matching the pattern. Skewer each side, pleating around the scroll to ease the excess fabric in. Cut into the back uprights to allow the fabric through and tack down on the back rail. Continue to fit the back fabric around the scrolls. Blind stitch under each edge, removing the skewers as you work.

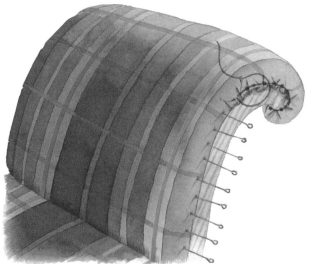

EXPERT TIP

Allow plenty of time to plan the placement of the pattern. Pin the fabric in place to see where the main features of the pattern fall and the best way to match them, particularly on the side and scroll borders. Draw a rough sketch to keep a record of your ideas.

14 Plan the border and scroll sections so that they match at the mitre. Cut the border lengthways from the fabric. Cut the scroll sections, allowing enough for the fullest width and 30 cm (12 in) longer than the height of the scroll. Secure the border to the seat with upholstery pins, from the outside back on one side, around the end of the bed to the other side. Temporary tack the ends of the border on the back of each upright. Temporary tack the bottom of the border underneath the bottom rail to keep the line of the pattern straight.

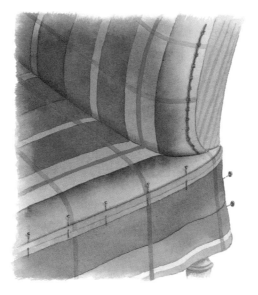

15 Pin the scroll fabric temporarily in place, checking the position of the pattern. Make a

mitre across the bottom edge from the seat to the bottom of the frame, matching the pattern on the border. Pin across the mitre, trim back to a 1.25 cm (½ in) turning, and notch. Repeat on the other scroll. Remove the fabric from the bed and machine stitch the mitres. Lay wadding on the border and the scroll area. Pin the top cover back in place, turning the top edge under. Temporary tack under the bottom rail all around, keeping the pattern level.

16 Pin the scroll under the stitched edge, turning under the edges, and slip stitch in place. Continue slip stitching all around the top of the border and repeat the process on the other scroll. Turn the back edge of the scroll fabric around the back uprights and temporary tack down the outside back. Tack home the border under the bottom rail.

17 Cut a piece of fabric for the outside back, matching the pattern. Tack home any tacks on the rails and then back up with calico. Place a piece of wadding on the calico, and pin the top fabric under the rail and down the two sides. Slip stitch in place with a matching thread. Tack just underneath the bottom rail, cutting around the legs if necessary.

18 Start attaching the cord by tucking it under the base on the outside back and securing with a tack. Using a circular needle and slipping thread, slip stitch the cord around the outline of the scroll and border to finish on the opposite side. Secure the cord underneath with a tack.

19 Knot one tassel through one of the rosettes. Position them on the scroll to give a well-balanced effect. Place a panel pin in the centre of the rosette, part the silk with the point of a skewer, and hammer the panel pin into the wood. Push the silk back in place. Repeat on the other scroll.

Step 18

20 To make up the bolster, see page 110. Make sure that the pattern runs around the bolster to match the seat and the back. Trim the bolster as you wish. Here, the bolster is finished with a rosette.

21 Place the black bottom on the underside of the bed. Cut into the legs and turn a small turning under around them. Turn the rest of the edges under and tack home all around. Re-fit the casters and buff the legs to remove any blemishes.

Above: The bolster has been trimmed to match the rosettes and cord on the bed.

REDS

Many reds can be quite brash, but something more subtle was needed for the day bed in its softly striped setting. The blue pattern on this fabric softens the red to create a purple-pink tinge and still looks dramatic. The cord, twisted in red, burgundy and burnt orange, draws attention to the elegant lines of the bed.

POWER AND SUCCESS are universally associated with red, so its use in the home makes a very definite statement.

The power of red

Red is quite literally the colour of earth and fire. Natural red earth pigments have long been used to produce tones of incomparably rich fabrics, producing effects that are strong and intense, warming and comforting.

It is not surprising that red is symbolically very important in many cultures. The Chinese regard it as so auspicious that wedding and birthday greetings are printed in red to promote health, good fortune and happiness. The Victorians, key celebrants of the hearth as the centre of the home, chose to emphasize this theme by decorating their sitting rooms in vermillion red, adding sumptuous velvets in cranberry, wine and rose to amplify the message. The desired effect reflected their ideas of status and success.

So red speaks of affluence and makes a bold, confident statement. Contemporary Feng Shui recommends using red in rooms used chiefly by the breadwinner to encourage prosperity.

Using red successfully

These days, few of us can afford the luxury of decorating a room for sole occupancy or just one purpose. It is more likely that a dining room, for example, will also be used as an occasional home office. Even so, the positive power of red can be introduced in a more restrained way.

Red is often used in dining rooms, and, given that research proves this colour increases the respiratory rate and accelerates brain activity, meals in a red room should prove to be lively and convivial. By upholstering the chairs in red and leaving the rest of the room fairly neutral, it will also work on an everyday level, leaving you free to turn up the heat later with vibrant red table linen, flowers and candles.

A greater concentration of red can still work well. Mix tomato, chilli and fuchsia for a scheme that really sizzles or use them as distinctive accents to set the pulse racing. Alternatively, use rich reds and terracottas with subtle shades of olives and lichens for a combination that is both warm and nurturing.

However you incorporate red in your upholstery and room schemes, it is sure to make a dramatic impact.

Red is not a colour choice for the faint-hearted. Any piece upholstered in red will undoubtedly become the focal point of the room in which it stands. Gold and red make the richest companions, and, combined in silk on this Georgian chair, they guarantee meals will be classy affairs.

Sprung-back Easy Chair

Chairs with fluted backs used to be very popular and this style still provides interesting detail. This particular chair has only three flutes, although usually there were more, closer together, as seen in car upholstery.

THIS CHAIR DATES from the 1950s and was covered in red moquette, which was very fashionable then. There was little of the original upholstery worth saving, so the chair was stripped to the frame and totally reupholstered. The new spring unit is a standard size, but they can be made to order if necessary. The back is hand sprung, as was the original. This chair has a double front border, the lower border being fixed while the upper part moves up and down when the spring unit is sat on.

The fabric used on the chair is linen and features a richly coloured design that makes this chair something really special. The bold pattern of the fabric and distribution of colour suits the style and frame of the chair well. The fluting breaks up the design a little, but does not detract from the effect, and the chair has acquired a great presence in its new upholstery.

On a chair like this, the order of upholstering needs to be planned carefully so that parts of the chair are not made inaccessible. The order below may seem to be haphazard, but keep to it and you will find the processes slot in easily.

1 Measure the chair and make a cut sheet for the top fabric. Plan the pattern so that it runs centrally down the inside back, seat and front border, and runs in line around the arms. Cut the sections as you need them, to allow for adjustments in the pattern and the extra padding of the flutes.

2 Rip the old upholstery out right back to the frame. Chairs of this style and age usually had card in the inside arms, as well as wire outlining the springs, so leave the card in place and retain the shaped wire. Strip and repolish the wood on the arms and legs at this stage if necessary.

3 Fit the spring unit on to the seat first so that its sharp coils of wire and metal bands do not damage the top fabric. Bend the metal bands of the spring unit over the front, side and back rails. Secure the metal bands to the wood with clout nails hammered through pre-drilled holes. Hold the front edge of the spring unit firm with laid cord ties secured to the front rail with fine 13 mm (½ in) tacks.

4 Now start on the back. Place two webs together in the centre, securing them on the inside back at the top and the outside back at the bottom with improved tacks, to preserve the contour of the chair back. Place one web across, just above the arms. Place three springs across the head rail, securing them to the wood with a strip of webbing laid under the base of the spring wire. Tack through the webbing close to the spring to trap it. Place another three springs on the cross webbing. The two outer ones will be partly on wood, so trap the edges with webbing and tacks to hold them in place; the part of the spring resting on webbing is sewn in place. The middle spring is sewn directly to the webbing.

5 Place the edge wire around the outer edges of the springs. Lash the springs across and down, including knots on the wire to hold it firmly in place. Add an extra lashing in between the springs,

Dimensions

height: 80 cm (32 in)
width: 70 cm (27 in)
depth: 67 cm (27 in)

Materials

- top cover fabric 5.5 m (6 yd)
- spring unit to fit seat
- clout nails 25 mm (1¼ in)
- laid cord
- fine tacks 13 mm (½ in)
- English webbing 4 m (4½ yd)
- improved tacks 13 mm (½ in)
- 6 double-cone springs 15 cm (6 in) gauge 12
- twine
- galvanized wire staples 20 mm (¾ in)
- hessian 2 m (2¼ yd)
- spray adhesive
- cotton felt 3 m (3¼ yd)
- skin wadding 1700 g (48 oz), 5 m (5½ yd)
- staples 10 mm (⅜ in)
- piping cord
- machine thread
- hot adhesive sticks
- hair 2 kg (4 lb)
- calico 1 m (1¼ yd)
- slipping thread
- needle felt 1 m (1¼ yd)
- rubberized hair
- black bottom 1 m (1¼ yd)

both down and across as an extra support for the wire. Secure the wire along the inside back rail with wire staples hammered into the wood, to trap it.

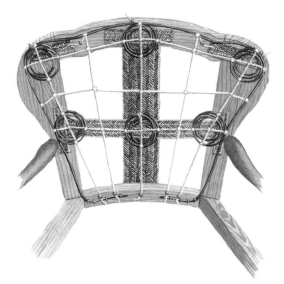

6 Cover the inside back with a piece of hessian. Cut it into the arms and push the hessian through to the back, temporary tacking it to the back upright with fine tacks. Tack the hessian around the back of the head rail, pleating on the corners to make a good fit. Tack all the tacks home, turn the raw edges back and tack home again. Stitch a row of blind stitch around the back, catching in the wire. Then sew a row of top stitch to define the contour on the front edge of the inside back. Sew the springs in from the front through the hessian and sew in bridle ties.

7 Now work on the inside arms. Spray adhesive on the backing-up card and pad with a layer of cotton felt, then add a layer of wadding. Measure

top fabric for the inside arms and cut to size. Temporary tack the fabric in position, then staple it close to the rebate under the arm. Trim the edge of the fabric back to the staples with a craft knife. Push the fabric through the gap between the arm and inside back. Pull the fabric under the bottom arm rail, wrap it around the rail and secure on the top with temporary tacks.

8 The inside arms are trimmed now when access is easiest. Make up a length of double piping and glue it in place from under the seat at the front, around the rebate on the inside arm close to the polished wood to the back upright. Finish at the back with a tack through the piping. Repeat on the other arm.

9 Now continue with the inside back, filling the bridle ties with a thin layer of hair. Cover with calico, cutting in to the top and bottom arm rails and pushing the calico through to the back. Pull the calico over the top and side edges and, with a circular needle and slipping thread, back stitch all around just behind the contour of the front edge. Trim off the excess calico.

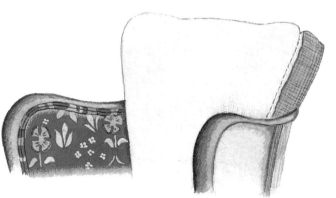

Step 9

Step 10

10 Return to working on the seat. Cover it with a piece of hessian and tack home all around the bottom rails, pleating at the corners to lose the fullness. Turn the raw edges over and tack again. Using a large circular needle and twine, sew the hessian to the spring unit by making a stitch along the top edge, knotting it and continuing in the same way all around.

11 Lay a piece of needle felt over the top of the hessian to prevent the springs wearing into the hair. Cut a piece of rubberized hair 10 cm (4 in) bigger all around than the seat and place it on top of the needle felt. Stitch stuffing ties through the middle of the seat to hold the hair. Place cotton felt along the recessed line of stuffing ties to keep the whole seat at the same height. Bring the hair over the front edge, and to meet the arms and inside back. Secure with a line of stitching under the edge of the spring unit, folding the front corners in and continuing to stitch around the corners to meet the arms.

12 Place another layer of cotton felt over the whole seat and front edge. Next cover the seat in calico. Temporary tack the calico to the side and back rails and stitch it under the edge on the front border and around the corners to meet the arms.

13 Cut the top fabric for the seat and both front borders, making sure that the pattern is central and matched. Pin the seat fabric just overhanging the front edge. Pin the top border to the seat fabric, following the line of the frame and taking it around the front corners of the seat to just beyond the junction with the arms. Pin the lower border to the top border, creating the double border. Notch all the seams and remove the cover from the chair.

14 Make up a length of single piping. Machine stitch one length of piping between the seat and top border, and another between the top and lower borders. Machine stitch all the sections together. Place cotton felt on the double border and then a layer of wadding on the seat and double border. Replace the top cover on the seat and skewer to hold in place. Cut into the front corners and around the legs, fitting the fabric around the front corners into the arms. Temporary tack under the front rail. Push the fabric through to the outside back and cut into the back uprights. Push the fabric through to the outside arms. Secure the fabric all around the base rails with temporary tacks and tack home when it is all in place.

15 Return to the inside back and make the fluted section. Cut a piece of hessian, sufficient to cover the back plus an overlap to meet the border. Skewer it in place on the back and, with a marker pen, mark the centre line for guidance and two equally spaced lines at an angle, where the flutes will be stitched. Take the hessian off the chair.

16 Find the centre of the top fabric and mark it with a line on the wrong side. Measure across the centre flute on the hessian from one stitch line to the other and add 3 cm (1½ in) to allow for the thickness of the padding. Using this measurement, mark two stitch lines on the wrong side of the top cover at an angle to match those on the hessian. The centre flute on the top fabric is now 3 cm (1½ in) wider than on the hessian.

LINEN

Linen is an immensely durable fabric. Pieces up to seven thousand years old have been discovered in archeological digs, so it is hardly surprising that it remains a favourite upholstery fabric. Naturally strong and luxuriously smooth to the touch, linen has a subtle texture that takes printed patterning particularly well. The designs seem to be integrated into the cloth, rather than sitting brashly upon the surface, making linens and linen unions a popular choice for schemes where a sophisticated, restrained look is desired.

17 Fold the fabric along one stitch line with the right sides facing. Pin the fold on the corresponding line on the hessian. Machine stitch down the line on the hessian very close to the fold. Cut a piece of cotton felt to the shape of the centre flute and lay it on the hessian. Cover with a layer of wadding.

18 Fold the top fabric along the second stitch line and pin this to the corresponding line on the hessian, encasing the padding. Machine stitch down the line as before.

20 Sew a row of blind stitch with slipping thread and a circular needle, removing the skewers. Cut the fabric around the back uprights and tack home. Pull the arm fabric tight and tack home on the uprights as well. Pull the calico and hessian through between the back and the seat and tack home on top of the inside back rail, cutting away excess. Pull the bottom of the fabric through and tack home on the same rail.

21 Cut a piece of fabric for the back border, temporarily pin it in position and mark the shape of the front edge on it. Remove the border, make a series of cuts on the curves and machine stitch a length of piping along the front edge. Pad the back border on the chair with cotton felt and place the fabric section on, skewering it in place. Turn the front edge under and slip stitch along the

19 Pad the outside flutes from the stitched lines to the outer edges and secure with pins. Place the fluted section over the calico on the inside back and skewer in place just behind the stitched edge.

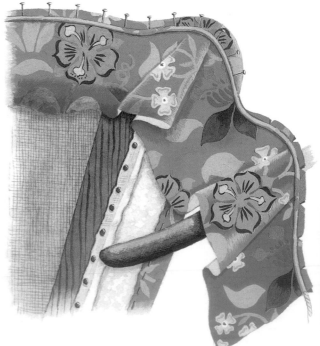

front edge. Turn the edges under where they meet the arms and slip stitch in place close to the show wood. Pull the fabric to the outside back and tack home around the frame. Cover the outside arms in the same manner as the inside arms, matching the fabric and trimming with double piping. Tack the bottom of the fabric underneath the bottom rail.

22 Back up the outside back with hessian and place wadding over it. Pin the outside back fabric in place and slip stitch all around. Cut around the legs and tack underneath the bottom rail. Finish with black bottom on the underside. Cut the cloth into the legs, turn under and tack all around just inside the edge.

Above: The padded flutes and rounded contours of the arms complement each other well.

Wing Chair

A rigid checked pattern like this may make an upholsterer's heart sink at first, but, with careful planning to make sure the lines run and match around the chair, checks can work well, even on curved shapes.

Dimensions

height: 100 cm (40 in)
width: 78 cm (31 in)
depth: 65 cm (26 in)

Materials

- top cover fabric 6 m (6½ yd)
- fine tacks 13 mm (½ in)
- jute webbing 7 m (7½ yd)
- hessian 1 m (1¼ yd)
- staples 10 mm (³⁄₈ in)
- spray adhesive
- foam 2.5 cm (1 in) thick, 115 x 125 cm (45 x 50 in)
- cotton felt 2 m (2¼ yd)
- polyester wadding 115 g (4 oz), 7 m (7½ yd)
- machine thread
- piping cord 10 m (11 yd)
- platform cloth 1 m (1¼ yd)
- back tack strip 80 cm (1 yd)
- slipping thread
- black bottom 1 m (1¼ yd)
- foam seat cushion 10 cm (4 in) deep, cut to fit
- stockinette 75 cm (30 in)

THIS WING CHAIR had been reupholstered before, so the remains of two former coverings were evident. The frame of the chair was in good condition and the tension springs on the seat were sound, but they needed a new platform over them to prevent damage to the new cushion.

The fabric chosen for the chair is a woven wool plaid, which is pliable, easy to handle and also very hard wearing.

The subtle colours of the checks help to play down the formality of the pattern and create an inviting chair. The piping cut from the bias of the plaid defines the chair's contours to give extra interest, and a toning chenille cushion adds comfort and a contrast in texture.

1 Measure the chair and make a cut sheet for the top fabric. Allow at least one extra repeat of the pattern on each piece to adjust the pattern to match all around the chair. Cut out and label the pieces.

2 Rip out the back and wings and remove all the staples from the rest, but leave the old fabric lying on the arms to avoid disturbing the padding at this stage. Tack three webs down the inside, and weave four across, two close together across the lumbar region and two evenly spaced between the arms and the head rail.

3 Place hessian over the inside back and staple it to the head and inside back rails. Spray adhesive on the hessian and place a layer of foam over the inside back, cutting into the wings at the top to make it lie flat. Cover with a sheet of cotton felt, then wadding.

4 Place the top fabric over the inside back and secure with staples on the back of the head rail, over on to the top of the inside wing. Cut into the upright below the top of the wing frame, above and below the arm rail and into the seat rail. Push the fabric through to the back all around. Secure with staples on both the uprights and under the back rail.

PIPING

Piping emphasizes the outline of upholstery, as well as providing protection and stability to vulnerable edges. Sophisticated and sleek, it can provide discreet added interest, while not detracting at all from the curvilinear appeal of a piece.

Single piping is machine stitched between two sections of fabric, whereas double piping is attached directly along the edges of show wood. Piping fabric may be cut from a top cover in a number of ways. Bias-cut fabric, applied over a cotton twist cord, makes the most pliable piping, but needs a lot of fabric. However, its pliability more than justifies the expense if it is being used on curved work. Piping may be used as a smart, subtle finish against show wood with the main cover fabric slip stitched to it.

5 Web the inside of the wing, using the fine tacks, with one web down the centre and a second one almost touching the inside back, so it can be used as a rail. Cover the inside wing with hessian and staple all around.

6 Place foam over the inside wing and secure with staples on to the wood around the top edges. Cut to match the inside back cuts at the top corner. Push the foam through the gap between the web and the back. Place a piece of cotton felt, then wadding, over the inside wing and trim off the excess with your fingers.

7 Place the top fabric over the wadding and line the pattern up with the inside back. Cut into the top corner and secure with temporary tacks around the outside of the wing. Pull the fabric through the gap at the back of the wing and secure with staples on the back upright, making sure that the pattern is still level. Staple home around the wing, then remove the temporary tacks.

8 Pin back the old cover and padding on the arm and make a series of cuts to allow the fabric to spread at the bottom of the wing where it meets the inside arm frame. Secure with staples to the frame. Repeat on the other wing.

9 Remove the old cover from the arms. If the padding is in good condition, lift it off and retain. Renew the webbing and hessian on the inside arm. Replace the padding and add another layer of wadding. Repeat the process on the other arm. If the padding on your chair is unusable, renew it now with cotton felt and a layer of wadding.

10 Lay the top fabric in place on the inside arm, lining it up underneath the scroll on the outside arm and taking it down to the seat. Pin it in place, keeping the pattern in line with the inside back. Pin the front scroll section of fabric in place so that the pattern matches accurately. Pin the inside arm to the front scroll fabric, following the front edge of the scroll from underneath the scroll to the top of the seat. Trim back to leave a 1.25 cm (1/2 in) turning, and notch. Remove the section from the arm, unpin it and make a mirror-image copy for the other arm. Machine stitch piping around the scroll, leaving a length hanging to go down the outside arm. Sew the inside arm and scroll sections together from under the scroll to the seat.

11 Cap the cover back over the inside arm and secure under the side rail and under the top arm rail with temporary tacks. Cut into the fabric, matching the cuts on the base of the wing. Push the fabric through at the back and temporary tack on the back upright, matching the cuts on the inside back to gain access. Trim back the excess fabric around the wing, and turn under neatly.

12 Remove the stuffing from the seat. Cut into the front scroll fabric where it meets the front rail and staple the raw edges to the frame. Tack home the lower edge of the inside arm underneath the side rail and the top edge under the top arm rail. Staple the outer edge of the scroll down the outside of the arm upright. Staple the piping down the edge of the upright. Remove all temporary tacks. Repeat the processes on the other arm.

13 Place a piece of hessian over the lip of the seat and front border. Then place a layer of cotton felt, and then wadding, over the top.

14 Pin the top fabric over the lip and front border, making cuts to match the front scrolls. Pull the fabric down the sides of the border, wrap it around the front and, bringing the seat fabric over the front of the border, pin a dart to fit each front corner.

15 Cut enough platform cloth to cover the seat. Place it on the seat and mark the position of the back tension spring. Cut two strips of top fabric to the length of the seat from front to back and 12.5 cm (5 in) wide. Stitch the strips on each side of the platform cloth and fold them back. Hem the top fabric and platform cloth together down each side edge. Turn a wide hem on the back of the section where it was marked for the spring, creating a slot big enough to thread the spring through later. Pin the platform section to the front border fabric, right-sides facing, and notch the seam. Remove the border and platform cloth from the chair. Stitch the two front darts on the front border. Stitch the platform cloth to the front border.

Below: The piping has been cut from the bias to contrast with the straight lines of the plaid.

Above: The seat cushion is cut from a template of the seat for a perfect fit.

16 Cap the whole seat section on the chair. Turn the sides under around the bottom of the scrolls. Staple the front border underneath the front and side rails, turning the edges under around the top of the legs. Staple the sides of the platform on the side and back rails. Turn the chair over and remove the tension spring nearest the inside back. Thread this through the slot on the platform and replace the spring. The platform will now move with the weight of a person sitting in it without splitting.

17 Position the top fabric for the outside arm down the front edge, right-sides together. Place a length of back tack strip tight against the piping on the edge and secure.

20 Back up the outside back with hessian and place wadding on top. Position the outside back fabric on the chair and secure by stapling back tack strip along the top edge. Pull the fabric back over the outside back and pin the side edges under. Pull the fabric under the bottom rail, cut around the legs and staple to the rail. Slip stitch the sides.

18 Back up the outside arm with a piece of hessian. Lay wadding on the hessian and pull the fabric back over it. Turn the top edge under and pin it to the inside arm fabric under the scroll. Temporary tack the back edge on to the outside of the back upright. Take the bottom edge under the side rail, cut around the legs, turn under and staple home.

19 Back up the outside wings with hessian. Make a length of piping long enough to go from the bottom edge of one wing, across the back, to the bottom of the other wing. Staple this to the edge all around, making sure you start and finish securely. Lay wadding on the outside wing and pin the cover to fit the wing, leaving a turning to attach to the outside back. Trim away excess, turn under and slip stitch in place around the top and front edges of the wing. Lift the temporary tacks from the outside arm fabric to allow the wing fabric to be stapled to the arm rails. Staple the outside arm fabric on the back upright and trim off excess fabric. Slip stitch the outside arm and wing fabrics together.

21 Place black bottom on the base of the chair, turn in the edges, and staple all around.

22 To make the cushion, take a 'T'-shaped template of the seat and cut out the cushion foam to fit. Make the cushion cover in exactly the same way as for a seat or back cushion with a border (see page 107), cutting into the seam to allow it to spread smoothly around the shaping at the front of the cushion.

✇ *Quick Reference*

Estimating top fabric, page 78

Ripping out, page 50

Webbing, page 51

Trimmings, single piping, page 97

Machine stitching, page 30

Covering the outsides, page 86

Cushions, page 107

CHECKS

THERE IS NO doubt that checks, and the more sophisticated plaids and tartans, make a statement. Tartans have always had undeniable potency for the Scots and are symbolic of a rich heritage and strong sense of identity. Queen Victoria also popularized the use of tartans in interiors when she used them on every surface, from furniture to carpets, of her Balmoral home.

Classic dependability

Plaids and tartans seem to have a feeling of dependability about them. True tartans seem to fall outside the whims of fashion, making them perfect for rooms such as studies that need a serious, yet inviting atmosphere. Even so, some of these classics are still susceptible to new trends and you can now find plaids in pastels and other prettier blends of colours.

No matter how traditional or modern the colour combination, the linear form of checks, plaids and tartans will give a piece of furniture a look of geometric order. For example, woollen dog-tooth checks, traditionally worn by the sober and discreet, still retain a certain quiet presence even when they are woven in the most unexpected and daring of colours.

The elongated checks of the fabric in the child's headboard demonstrate an unusual combination of colours, in association with carefully planned buttoning. The result is crisp and fun—perfect for a child's room.

A talent for blending

Since so many colours can be incorporated in plaids and tartans, they are extremely useful for pulling together a scheme by weaving the various strands of colour from other furnishings into a cohesive whole.

On the other hand, checks may or may not be multicoloured. Ginghams and other larger, open checks in single colours on natural grounds create a crisp look that works well with many other patterns. Even a difficult subject such as toile de jouy looks good partnered with a cotton check and gives summer freshness to a scheme that could otherwise easily be cloying.

There are few rules governing the use of checks and related patterns, although their regular patterning looks particularly good viewed flat rather than being pulled into deep buttoning or around curves. Also take care to match, align and centre these fabrics on furniture with great precision as any mismatches will show up alarmingly and spoil their intrinsic orderliness.

Checks, plaids and tartans are some of the most enduring and best loved of patterns and are destined to clothe our homes as well as our bodies for years to come.

This cosy chair is covered in a traditional plaid, but uses a modern pastel, combining Scottish design with the colours of the heathers of the glen. On a complex piece of furniture such as this, careful matching of the checks is crucial for a professional and satisfying result.

229

Button-back Chair

This Victorian button-back chair is covered in a linen velvet that is a joy to handle, allowing the folds on the buttoning to stay straight once put in place. The buttons are shown tied from the front, an alternative to the other methods in the book.

Dimensions

height: 90 cm (36 in)
width: 61 cm (24 in)
depth: 53 cm (21 in)

Materials

- top cover fabric 2.75 m (2³/₄ yd)
- skin wadding 1700 g (48 oz), 3 m (3¹/₂ yd)
- fine tacks 13 mm (¹/₂ in)
- staples 10 mm (³/₈ in)
- nylon button twine
- calico 75 cm (30 in)
- 13 button forms size 24
- gimp pins 13 mm (¹/₂ in)
- piping cord 15 m (16³/₄ yd)
- hot adhesive sticks

THE CHAIR HAS very attractive mahogany show wood and, with its well-padded back, is extremely comfortable to sit in. The upholstery was in good condition and the stitched edges in good shape, so it was only necessary to renew the top cover to transform the chair.

The reflection of light on the cut pile makes the linen velvet fabric look lively, and its colour of soft champagne yellow makes a good contrast to the dark wood. Double piping outlines the contours and gives the chair an understated elegance.

1 Strip the outside back off carefully, cut the button ties and remove the buttons from the front. Remove any trimmings and then the covers on the seat, inside back and arm pads. Even if the underlying upholstery seems to be in good condition, check the stitched edges by undoing the top corner of the calico on the back and peeling back the layers of upholstery underneath to check them. Then replace the layers and tack back in place.

2 Make a cut sheet and cut out and label the top fabric pieces. Add new skin wadding to the seat and place the top cover in position, making sure that the grain is straight. Temporary tack the fabric under the side rails. Make a 'Y' cut into the front corner to the arm upright. Fold a small turning under to fit the fabric snugly around the base of the upright. Repeat on the other side. Temporary tack the front edge of the fabric under the front rail.

3 Push the fabric towards the back of the seat and cut into the back uprights. Push the fabric down between the seat and inside back and temporary tack it to the back rail. Staple securely and remove the temporary tacks. Staple underneath the side rails and ease any excess fabric towards the front. Pull the fabric over the front edge, removing the temporary tacks, and staple it on the front rail just above the show wood.

4 Mark the position of the buttons on the wrong side of the fabric for the inside back, taking measurements from the existing upholstery to incorporate an allowance for the padding. Position the fabric on the inside back. Push a double-ended needle threaded with button twine through one of

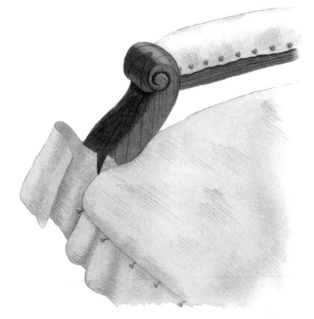

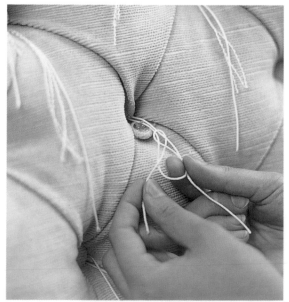

DEEP BUTTONING

Contrary to popular opinion, deep buttoning did not develop as a functional fixing method for the increasingly thick stuffings of the 1840s. It evolved purely as a styling feature, since the stuffing beneath is already held securely by bridle and stuffing ties. Deep buttoning satisfied the Victorian taste for opulent and voluptuous upholstery. Surprisingly, although upholstery of this period is traditionally thought of as being luxuriously comfortable, most of it would have been exceptionally rigid. It would have needed 'breaking in', in the same way as a saddle, the manufacturing techniques of which had, ironically, formed the basis of fixed stuffing upholstery techniques.

the button positions from the inside to the outside back. Now return the needle through the same hole to the inside back, but place a washer of calico under the twine to retain a stitch on the outside back. Slip the button on to one end of the twine, secure it with an upholsterer's knot and pull the button nearly home. Continue in the same manner until all the buttons are in place, regulating the folds as you go. When you are satisfied that the fabric is evenly tensioned between the buttons, tie the buttons off, cut the excess twine and tuck the ends under the buttons.

5 Pleat the folds around the edge of the inside back, holding the fabric in place with the tip of the regulator. Secure the folds with tacks or staples to the rebate. Pleat the folds over the lumbar area,

pull through to the back and tack home on the top of the bottom rail.

6 Cover the two arm pads with the skin wadding. Then temporary tack the top fabric in place using gimp pins, pleating the front and back corners to match each other. Alternatively, staple the fabric all around.

Left: The fabric is pleated out from the buttons and then secured to the rebate.

7 Back up the outside back of the chair with calico and then with the wadding. Place the fabric in position, temporary tack to make sure that the grain is straight and then tack home or staple to secure the fabric.

8 Make a length of double piping long enough to go around the front edge, the inside and outside back, and right around the arm pads, plus enough extra for cutting and finishing. Using a sharp craft knife, cut the fabric cover on all the edges to be trimmed right back to the rebate. Start to attach the double piping under the arm on the inside back by turning under and securing with a tack. Glue the piping on, keeping it in a smooth line close to the show wood all around. Repeat the same process on the seat front, outside back and arm pads. Butt the edges together on the back of the arm pads to make a neat join.

Quick Reference

Ripping out, page 50

Estimating top fabric, page 78

Deep buttoning, top cover, page 80

Trimmings, double piping, page 100

233

PLAIN FABRICS

Plain fabrics are the ideal choice for those who like to adorn their upholstery with lavish trimmings. The shocking pink nursing chair lends itself beautifully to the elaborate cord and tassels. On a busy, patterned fabric, these trimmings may well look overdone, yet here the effect is one of sophistication and elegance.

HERE IS THE store cupboard stand-by of the home decorator. Plain fabrics may not have the visual interest of pattern, but they are not dull and will never let you down, providing a never-ending supply of possibilities to bridge the gaps between other busier fabrics or make a fine decorative feast in themselves.

Creating harmony

Plain fabrics are particularly useful for restoring order to the sort of incohesive look that develops in most homes where furniture and soft furnishings accumulate over the years.

How would you decide on a fabric for an armchair surrounded by printed, patterned curtains, a sofa in a different print and an antique footstool with a needlepoint cover? Simply pick a colour from one of the other patterned fabrics, preferably one that occurs in the other fabrics, too, and select a plain fabric in the same colour for a result at once harmonious and imaginative. Choose a quiet, darker tone in a matt, uniformly textured fabric that will not draw attention to itself, if you want the patterned fabrics to remain dominant. Alternatively, choose a lighter, brighter shade on a more dramatically textured fabric that will draw the eye to the upholstery, if you want the patterned pieces to recede.

Creating variety

The choice of fabric type is as crucial as the choice of colour. A vast range of materials is available, from flat cottons and silks, to woven linens and wools, to piled cords and velvets. Choose a fabric for practical reasons, of course, but also for the opportunity to experiment.

You can completely alter the feel of a piece of furniture by re-covering it in a different type of fabric, even if it is the same colour as before.

Consider a well-loved chaise lounge covered in a favourite colour that matches the room well, but that definitely needs a new lease of life. The familiar, but faded, blue velvet might be replaced by a smart new cover of deep indigo cord. It will then retain something of the original with its deeply emotional connotations, please the most conservative taste with its rich blue and yet give the classical lines of the chaise a new modernity.

Careful consideration is just as important in choosing trimmings, whether you go for plain on plain or you choose a plain colour to contrast a patterned fabric.

Plain colours are often used to create harmony by linking different patterned items together. However, they can also be used with other plain colours to create a bold, striking effect. Take a tip from nature—the inky purple of an aubergine makes a dramatic foil for the brilliant colours to be copied from flowers.

235

USEFUL INFORMATION

Glossary

This glossary provides a quick and easy reference for many of the terms used in the book and includes instructions for making the stitches, knots and ties recommended for use in upholstery.

adhesive
a substance used to secure foam and/or trimmings (see also fabric adhesive, glue gun, hot adhesive sticks, spray adhesive)

alva
a traditional seaweed stuffing

antique nails
see decorative nails

arm rails
the horizontal bars at the top and bottom of the arm on a chair or sofa frame

back rail
the bottom horizontal bar along the back of a chair or sofa frame

back scroll
the shaped panel on each side of a chair or sofa back

back tack strip
a strip of purpose-made card used to give a straight edge along the top fabric tack line

back up
fill in an area on the frame before final covering

backstitch
forms a continuous row of stitches used for sturdy hand-sewn seams

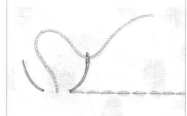

Working from right to left, make a stitch twice as long, pulling the needle through. Make the next stitch, starting at the end of the previous one. Repeat to produce a continuous row of stitches.

base finish
fabric finish around the base line of a chair or sofa frame (see also box pleat, kick pleat)

base rails
the front, back and side horizontal bars around the base of a chair or sofa frame

Bergère
a style of armchair, originating in the Louis XIV and XV periods,

with upholstered backs and arms and carved show wood

bias
the diagonal line or cut across the weave of the fabric, at a 45° angle

bias seam
a seam, sewn at a 45° angle, joining two lengths of fabric that have been cut on the bias

black bottom
see bottoming cloth

blanket stitch
hand-sewn stitch overlocking two edges together

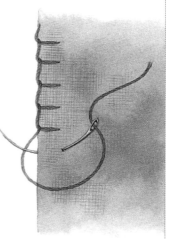

Secure the twine and bring it out on the edge of the fabric. Make a 1 cm (¹/₂ in) stitch, 1 cm (¹/₂ in) to the left. Take the thread around the back of the needle. Pull the needle through and proceed to the next stitch.

blind stitch

a row of blind stitches is used to create a firm wall in a stitched edge (see pages 65–66)

a) Push the needle up at an angle from just above the tack line to 10 cm (4 in) in from the top edge. Pull the needle up so the threaded end is just below the surface. Push it down to above the tack line, 2cm (3/4 in) to the left. Pull it out, tie a slip knot in the ends of the twine and finish with a locking knot.

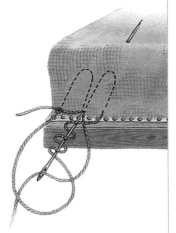

b) Push the needle in 4cm (1¹/2 in) to the right. Make a stitch as before. Pull the needle halfway out and wrap one end of twine around it three times.

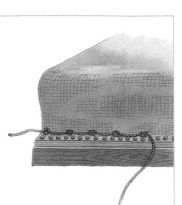

c) Pull the needle and twine through the loops. Pull the twine to the left, then right to lock. Stitch along the whole edge. Wrap alternate ends of twine around the needle, pull left and right to lock and tie a locking knot.

bolster

a cylindrical cushion often used as a feature on sofas, chaise, etc

bordered cushion (box cushion)

a seat or back cushion with a border between the top and underside

bottoming cloth (black bottom)

a slightly stretchy, finely woven black cloth used to cover the underside of furniture, to catch the dust and give a neat finish

box cushion

see bordered cushion

box pleat

a base finish consisting of fabric sections that hang as pleats at intervals around the base of a sofa or chair

bradawl

an awl with a pointed end used for making pilot holes or for marking in timber

braid

a flat, usually woven, trimming used for decorating edges

bridle ties

overlapping loops of twine sewn into hessian and scrim to hold fibre and hair stuffings in place

brocade

fabric, usually floral patterned, with a rich sheen on the surface

brocatelle

a self-patterned fabric with a surface of light and shade, and a quilted effect

bump interlining

soft interlining usually used for padding soft furnishings

button forms

the metal button shapes, for covering with top fabric, to make buttons

buttoning

a method used to make indentations in the upholstery with buttons (see also deep buttoning, float buttoning)

cabriole hammer

a hammer with a very small tip on one end, used for working on show wood or delicate areas

calico

a cotton fabric, usually unbleached, used to cover and mould the stuffings to shape, prior to top covering

campaign chair

a style of light, foldable chair probably taken on army manoeuvres

cap on

the process of stitching fabric sections together on a sewing machine and then pulling the whole construction on to the furniture

chamfer

to cut or grind a flat surface at an angle as on chip foam or along the edge of a frame

chintz

a heavy-glazed cotton

chip foam

a firm foam used as a padding on modern upholstery

chipboard

a thin stiff sheet made of wood chips bound by a synthetic resin

circular needle (cording needle)

needle used for stitching against

a firm surface, the half circular shape being better suited to the task than a straight needle

claw hammer

a narrow-headed hammer, with a claw at one end for removing tacks or nails, and a blunt end for work such as webbing

close nailing

decorative nails butting up to each other to form a continuous line

coir

made from coconut husks, it is ginger in colour, used as a first stuffing

collar

an extra piece of top fabric sewn to the main section of top fabric to give a good line around curved sections

cord

trimming of twisted threads (see also laid cord, piping cord)

cording needle

see circular needle

cordless driver

a rechargeable tool that has
different attachments, allowing it
to be used as a screwdriver or drill

cotton

fabric made from the cotton plant

cotton felt

a thick sheet of cotton linters,
held together between sheets
of paper that are removed
before use

craft knife

a retractable knife used for
cutting into edges and trimming
excess fabric away

cut sheet

diagram, with measurements, of
top fabric sections, used for
estimating and cutting top fabric

cuts

see straight cut, 'T' cut, 'Y' cut

damask

a self-patterned fabric with a
light and shaded effect

**decorative nails
(antique nails)**

nails with large, shaped heads
used, either spaced or close
nailed, as a trimming and to
secure fabric edges

deep buttoning

a buttoning technique of
traditional upholstery where
buttons are secured through all
the layers, making deep indents
and folds between the buttons

**double-cone springs
(waisted springs)**

hour-glass shaped springs used
for traditional upholstery

**double-ended needle
(mattress needle)**

a needle with a round or bayonet
point at each end, and an eye at
one end, used for stitching
edges, stuffing ties and buttoning
through thick padding

double-grooved foot

a sewing machine accessory,
ideal for making double piping

double piping

a trimming made of two lengths
of piping cord encased in one
piece of top fabric

drop-in seat

a seat that is separate to the rest
of the frame, can be upholstered
independently and then dropped
into the frame

English webbing

a traditional webbing, with a
black and white herringbone
weave

estimating sheet

diagram, with measurements, of
fabric sections, used for estimating
and cutting plain top fabrics

fabric adhesive

a substance that glues fabrics
together on contact

fibre

long black curly strands used
mainly for first stuffing in
traditional upholstery

fine tacks

tacks with a small head that can
be easily removed, and are
unlikely to split threads in finer
cloths, used for attaching calico,
black bottom and top fabric, and
for temporary tacking

first stuffing

the main stuffing in traditional upholstery, usually of fibre, held in place with bridle and stuffing ties

flange cord

a decorative cord stitched during manufacture to a cotton tape or flange that enables it to be inserted between sections of top fabric

flax line twine

widely used, but not recommended, for stitching

float buttoning

a technique where buttons are secured through the top layers of upholstery, making a slight indent in the top fabric

flock

a traditional padding, often found but not recommended for use now, made of waste fibres

flutes

separately padded panels in a top covering

fly

an extra piece of fabric added to the top fabric sections to extend them down to the rails

foam

see chip foam, pincore latex foam, polyurethane foam

frame

the supporting structure of a piece of furniture

fringe

trimming with a heading like gimp or braid with a hanging fringed edge, which can be cut or uncut

front border

surface from the front seat to the base rail on a chair or sofa

front rail

the bottom horizontal bar along the front of a chair or sofa frame

front scroll

shaped panel on the front of each arm of a chair or sofa

G-cramp

an adjustable, solid metal, G-shaped tool used to hold pieces of wood together

gimp

a narrow, woven trimming, typically incorporating bound wire, used for decorating edges

gimp pins

small fine pins with a flat head, used for attaching gimp and braids, as well as for delicate areas where a tack would be too heavy

girt

a thread pulled tight by a tack causing an unsightly indentation in the fabric, most commonly in silk

glue gun

a tool that melts solid adhesive and ejects it as a trigger is pushed

hair

long curly animal hair used mainly as a second stuffing in traditional upholstery

half hitch knot

used for knotting laid cord around springs

Bring the cord over the top of the spring wire. Take the end underneath the wire, over the cord and back under the wire. Pull the knot tight.

handling allowance

extra fabric added to allow for handling and fitting

head rail

the horizontal bar across the top of the back of a chair or sofa frame

hessian

a loosely woven cloth made from jute that is used for the foundations of upholstery, holding the stuffings in place (see also spring canvas)

hide (leather)

treated cow or buffalo skin used as a top cover

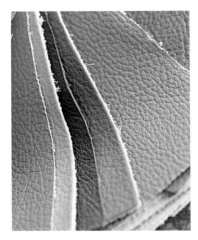

hitch knot

a knot used in securing springs with laid cord

Bring the cord over the top of the spring wire. Take it around underneath and back over the top of the wire. Wind it around underneath and over the wire again, taking the end through the second loop. Pull the knot tight.

holding twist

a technique used to hold one laid cord in place as it crosses another

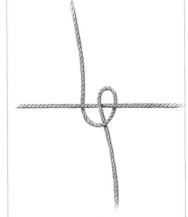

To hold one cord in position as it crosses another, take it over and around the existing cord, pull tight and continue lashing.

horsehair

long curly hairs from the mane and tail, recognised as the best type of second stuffing in traditional upholstery

hot adhesive sticks

solid sticks of adhesive that are used in a glue gun

improved tacks

tacks with a large head used for attaching scrim and webbing

inside arm

the area on the inside of the arm measured from the base rail, over the top of the arm to the top arm rail

inside back

the area on the inside of the back measured from the base rail, over the top to the back of the head rail

interlining

see bump interlining

jacquard
fabric with a pattern woven
into it

jute
a natural fibre used to make
string, webbing and hessian

jute webbing
a strong, beige webbing, widely
used on backs, arms and some
seats

kick pleat
a base finish consisting of fabric
sections that hang as pleats at
each corner of a sofa or chair

lacing
see lashing

lacing cord
see laid cord

laid cord (lacing cord)
a heavy cord used for lashing
springs

lashing (lacing)
a technique for knotting springs
with laid cord to hold them
in position

leather
see hide

linen
fabric made from flax and often
mixed with other fibres to give
it strength

lining cloth
see platform cloth

locking knot (single knot)
a single knot that locks off a
previous knot

*Take the end of the twine and
loop it over itself at the base of
the previous knot. Take the end
through the loop and pull the
knot tight.*

machine thread
blended polyester cotton or clear
nylon machine threads can be
used for machine stitching

magnetic hammer
a hammer with a magnetic end
to pick up tacks

mallet
a tool with either a square or
round head, used with a chisel
for ripping out

matelasse
a traditional upholstery fabric
with a raised textured surface

mattress needle
see double-ended needle

mesh top spring unit
see spring unit

mitre
to fold fabric or a flat trimming
under at an angle so it turns, to
make it turn a corner

moquette
a very hard-wearing fabric made in wool, cotton or man-made fibres; has a looped pile that can be left uncut or cut

nails
see decorative nails

needles
see circular needle, double-ended needle, sacking needle, sewing needles, spring needle, tapestry needle

notch
a v-shaped cut made in seams while they are still pinned together, so they can easily be matched together again

nursing chair
a nineteenth century term for a chair with a low seat

nylon buttoning twine
a very strong, white twisted twine most suitable for buttoning, but sometimes used for stitching

outside arm
the area on the outside of the arm measured from the base rail to the top arm rail

outside back
the area on the outside of the back measured from the base rail to the head rail

passementerie
a term for trimmings, taken from the French

passementière
a professional maker of passementerie

pattern sheet
diagram, with measurements, of top fabric sections, allowing for matching of the pattern, used for estimating and cutting patterned top fabrics

pile fabric
a fabric with a surface of looped or cut threads, such as velvet and velour

pilot hole
holes marked into a piece of wood in order to guide where to place the screws

pincers
a tool used for removing tacks and nails; some have a claw end for reaching into awkward places

pincore latex foam
a firm foam used for padding seating and cushions

pins
see upholstery pins

piping
a trimming made of piping cord encased in top fabric (see also double piping, single piping)

piping cord
a twisted cotton cord for making piping

piping foot
see double-grooved foot, single-grooved piping foot, zip foot

pirelli webbing
a rubber webbing used as a flat spring on seats and backs, fixed to the chair frame with clips, wire hooks or tacks

platform cloth (lining cloth)
a cotton cloth used as a platform under a seat cushion, over tension springs

245

pliers
a tool similar to pincers, used to remove old tacks and nails

plywood
comprised of an odd number of thin layers of wood glued together, with the grain of one layer at right angles to the grain of the adjoining layer

polyester cotton thread
thread used for machine and hand sewing

polyester wadding
a wadding often used in modern upholstery between the calico and top fabric instead of cotton wadding where hair has not been used as a stuffing; also used to wrap foam cushions

polypropylene webbing
a webbing used on modern furniture

polyurethane foam
foam, available in different densities, used for padding modern upholstery and cushions

presser foot (running foot)
a sewing machine accessory used for straight stitching

prie-dieu
a chair with a high and 'T'-shaped back, also called a prayer chair

rails
the uprights and cross bars that make up the frame of a piece of furniture

rasp
a coarse file used to chamfer the edges on chair frames, prior to tacking down scrim

rebate
a recess or groove cut into the surface or along the edge of a piece of wood

regulator
a large needle-like tool with a sharp end useful for holding fabric in place while tacking, as well as regulating stuffing, and a flat blade used for arranging pleats when deep buttoning

retractable steel measure
a rolled-up steel rule, enclosed in a case, used mainly for measuring larger areas

rip out
to remove the old cover and stuffing from a chair frame prior to reupholstering

ripper
see ripping chisel

ripping chisel (ripper)
a type of chisel used with a mallet to remove tacks; straight or cranked chisels are available

rolled edge
firm edge made with hessian or scrim rolled tight around fibre and secured with tacks to the edge of the frame

rosettes
circular trimmings used on their own or with tassels

rubberized hair

a mixture of animal hair bonded by a rubber solution and made into sheets; used as a padding on modern upholstery

ruche

a strip of pleated fabric used as a trimming

running foot

see presser foot

sacking needle

similar to a spring needle, but is straight with a curved top end

sash cramp

an adjustable tool used to hold a frame together or joints in place while adhesive is drying

scissors

long bladed-scissors are used for cutting fabrics on a flat surface; shorter blades are used for general cutting and shaping fabric on the furniture

scrim

a very loosely woven linen cloth used to mould the first stuffing and stitched edges on traditional upholstery

scroll

the curved upright on the front of an arm or up the side of a chair or sofa back

seam allowance

extra fabric added to allow for seams

second stuffing

the soft padding, usually of hair, under the calico on traditional upholstery

serpentine springs (sinuous springs, zigzag springs)

zigzag-shaped springs, cut to length and fixed with clips to the seat or back frame; used in modern upholstery

sewing needles

short straight needles with sharp-pointed ends, used for hand-stitching tasks

sheet wadding

see skin wadding

show wood

the visible polished wood on a frame, often with carved decoration

side rail

the bottom horizontal bar along each side of a chair or sofa frame

silk

fabric woven from the fibres produced by silkworms

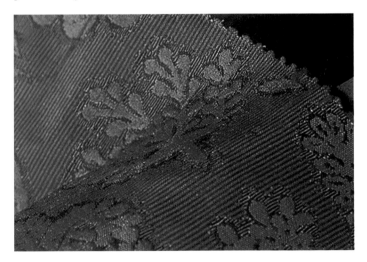

single-grooved piping foot

a sewing machine accessory used for making accurate single piping, double piping, and for sewing on flange cord

single knot

see locking knot

single piping

a trimming made with a single cord encased in top fabric

sinuous springs

see serpentine springs

skewers
long steel pins with a circular end, used to hold calico and top fabric temporarily in place

skin wadding (sheet wadding)
a wadding made of cotton, with a fluffy layer between two skin-like layers that hold it together

slip knot
see upholsterer's slip knot

slip stitch
a hand-sewn stitch used to almost invisibly join two pieces of fabric or attach trimmings to top fabric

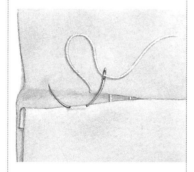

Working from right to left, make a stitch along the seam line in the underlying piece of fabric. Start the next stitch directly opposite the end of the first, along the fold in the top piece of fabric. Continue making stitches on alternate sides, pulling them up and the fabric together, so the stitches are concealed.

slipping thread
waxed linen thread used for hand stitching fabrics and trimmings

spray adhesive
an adhesive in an aerosol can, useful for attaching foam

spring canvas (tarp, tarpaulin)
a heavy-weight tarpaulin that can be used over springs instead of hessian

spring needle
a curved needle with a bayonet end used to sew through webbing and hessian when sewing in springs

spring unit
a unit of springs to cover a whole seat or back in traditional upholstery; available off the shelf or made to measure

springs
form part of the foundation of the upholstery, used on the seat and back of chairs to add depth and comfort; held to the frame with lashings (see also double-cone springs, serpentine springs, spring unit, tension springs)

staple gun
a power tool used to fire staples accurately into wood

staples
metal fixings fired from a staple gun, for use in modern upholstery, on delicate frames and fine fabrics

steel rule
a steel measuring stick used when cutting out on a flat surface

steel wool
see wire wool

stitched edge
a firm walled edge around the exposed contours of upholstery; formed by blind and top stitches moulding the first stuffing

stockinette
a stretchy, net-like fabric made of a cotton or polyester mix, used over foam cushion pads

straight cut
a cut to allow cloth to go in different directions

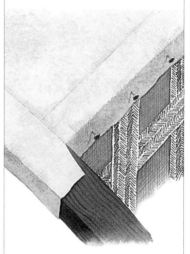

Make a straight cut to the point where two rails meet, to allow the cloth to spread.

stuffing
the materials used to pad a piece of furniture under the cover (see also coir, fibre, hair)

stuffing ties

ties made with twine to hold the scrim and first stuffing in place

suede

the inside of a hide, treated and shaved to an even surface

'T' cut

a cut to allow cloth to spread around two sides of a rail

Fold the cloth back on itself diagonally across the corner, lining the fold up close to the rail. Make a straight cut to the corner edge of the rail. Fold the cloth under or pull down around the rail.

tack home (tack off)

to tack the heads of the tacks right to the frame

tack lifter

a tool with a metal end that is split into a fork shape, which tucks under the tack to remove it

tack line

the line on the frame along which the tacks are inserted

tack off

see tack home

tack roll

firm edge made with hessian or scrim rolled tight around fibre and secured with tacks to the edge of the frame

tack ties

loops of twine tacked onto the frame with tacks to hold the stuffing in place instead of bridle ties

tacks

used in traditional upholstery to attach all the materials and top fabric (see also fine tacks, improved tacks)

tailor's chalk

used for marking the wrong side of top fabric

tape measure

a flexible tape useful for measuring over and around objects when estimating for coverings

tapestry

originally a wool fabric woven or stitched by hand or, more recently, a fabric designed to give a similar effect

tapestry needle

a needle with a rounded, blunt end

tarp

see spring canvas

tarpaulin

see spring canvas

tassel

a trimming that hangs from cord; can be used singly or in pairs on upholstered furniture

tease

the action of separating the strands of fibre and hair stuffings to ensure they are free of knots and tangles

temporary knot

a locking knot that has been left as a loop so that it is easily undone and tightened later

temporary tack

to hammer tacks in just far enough to hold upholstery materials and fabric to the frame before either removing them or tacking home

tension springs

consist of a long coil with a hook at each end that is usually slotted into a spring plate fitted to the side rails; used in modern upholstery

thread

see machine thread, slipping thread

tie off

knot the ends of twine or laid cord to make a secure fixing

top cover (top fabric)

the fabric used for the main finishing cover

top fabric

see top cover

top stitch

used after blind stitching to create the firm, sharp roll on a stitched edge

trim off

cut the upholstery materials or fabric back to the tack line

trimmings

the materials used to decorate and finish a piece of furniture

tub chair

a chair with a concave back and arms

tuck-in

fabric or calico pushed out of sight below the inside back, arms and seat, and tacked to the frame

tufts

made from leather or strands of wool or silk; used as decoration and to hold stuffing in place

turning allowance

extra fabric added to allow for turnings

tweed

fabric made from cotton, wool or a mixture of yarns; can be woven in plain or twill weave structure

twine

see flax line twine, nylon buttoning twine, upholstery twine

upholsterer's slip knot

a knot made to secure an end of twine or thread

a) Make a stitch with twine from right to left. Keeping the long right length taut, loop the left end under and then over it, taking it through the gap and back under itself.

b) Cross the same end over the front of both twines, creating a second loop.

c) Take the end round the back of the right twine and through the lower loop to the front. Pull the knot up tight.

upholstery pins

thick and strong, sharp steel pins, used for pinning and positioning fabric

upholstery twine

used for bridle ties, stuffing ties and edge stitching; available in various thicknesses

upright rails

the vertical bars at the front and back of a chair or sofa frame

velour

see pile fabric

velvet

see pile fabric

vinyl

a cloth that imitates leather, with graining and plain colours; has a knitted backing to give it extra flexibility

'W' formation

pattern of tacks placed on webbing

wadding

material used over the stuffing or over the calico to prevent the stuffing from wearing up through the top fabric (see also cotton felt, flock, polyester wadding, skin wadding)

waisted springs

see double-cone springs

warp

the thread running along the length of the fabric

web stretcher

a tool used for stretching webbing tight before it is tacked to the frame; the most common type is a bat and peg

webbing

strong strips, traditionally woven, stretched over the frame to support the springs and stuffing (see also English webbing, jute webbing, pirelli webbing, polypropylene webbing)

weft

the thread that forms the cross threads in the fabric

white wood

a new bare frame prior to being stained or polished

wings

parts of a chair or sofa frame protruding from the back to provide a head rest

wire cutters

used to remove staples by cutting them and then pulling them out of the wood

wire wool (steel wool)

an abrasive pad made of fine steel fibres

wood rule

a wooden measuring stick used when cutting out on a flat surface

wool

fabric woven from the fleece of sheep, wool is often mixed with other fibres to make it more versatile

'Y' cut

a cut to allow cloth to spread around three sides of a rail

Fold the cloth back on itself so the fold butts the rail. Make a straight cut towards the centre of the rail, stopping 2.5 cm (1 in) short. Cut to each side edge of the rail. Turn the centre flap of cloth under and take the two sides round the rail.

zigzag springs

see serpentine springs

zip foot

a sewing machine accessory used to insert zips, and also used as a piping foot

Suppliers and Institutions

The listings below give contact details for suppliers of fabrics, trimmings and upholstery materials, as well as professional bodies and related institutions. When locating supplies, contact the companies below for information on local suppliers or mail order arrangements. All details are current at the time of publication, but neither the publishers nor those listed can be held responsible for subsequent changes.

FABRICS

Abbott & Boyd
8 Chelsea Harbour Design
Centre
London
SW10 OXE
United Kingdom
Tel: +44 20 7351 9985

**Andrew Martin
International Ltd**
200 Walton Street
London
SW3 2JL
United Kingdom
Tel: +44 20 7584 4290

Also available from:
Halogen International
8 Kramer Road
Kramerville 2147
South Africa
Tel: +27 11 448 2060

Kravet Fabrics Inc
225 Central Avenue South
Bethpage
NY 11714
USA
Tel: +1 516 293 2000

Unique Fabrics
301 Auburn Road
Hawthorn East
VIC 3123
Australia
Tel: +61 3 9882 0727

Unique Fabrics
19 Garfield Street
Parnell
New Zealand
Tel: +64 9 377 8444

Arthur Sanderson & Sons
100 Acres
Sanderson Road
Uxbridge
UB8 1DH
United Kingdom
Tel: +44 189 523 8244

Also available from:
A Sanderson & Sons Ltd
3 Partiot Center
285 Grand Avenue
Englewood
NJ 07631
USA
Tel: +1 201 894 8400

A Sanderson & Sons Ltd
Suite 403
979 Third Avenue
New York City
NY 10022
USA
Tel: +1 212 391 7220

A Sanderson & Sons Ltd
160 Bedford Road
Unit 301 Upper Level
Toronto
Ontario
M5R 2K9
Canada
Tel: +1 416 944 3337

The Fabric Library
Stand 61 Old Pretoria Road
PO Box 912
Halfway House 1685
Johannesburg
South Africa
Tel: +27 11 805 4211

Maurice Kain Textiles Ltd
PO Box 2846
Woollahra
NSW 2025
Australia
Tel: +61 2 9326 1455

Maurice Kain Textiles Ltd
Textile Centre, Kenwyn Street
Parnell, PO Box 4050
Auckland
New Zealand
Tel: +64 9 309 0645

Baumann Fabrics Limited
41/42 Berners Street
London
W1P 3AA
United Kingdom
Tel: +44 20 7637 0253

Also available from:
Creation baumann
114 North Centre Avenue
Rockville Centre
NY 11570
USA
Tel: +1 516 764 7431

Creation baumann
Australia Pty Ltd
87 King William Street
Fitzroy
VIC 3065
Australia
Tel: +61 3 9419 6799

Brian Yates Interiors (Ltd)
3 Riverside Park
Caton Road
Lancaster
LA1 3PE
United Kingdom
Tel: +44 15 243 5035

Also available from:
A Sanderson & Sons Ltd
Englewood, USA
(see under Arthur Sanderson
& Sons)

Ashcraft Fabrics
19a Boundary Street
Rushcutters Bay
NSW 2011
Australia
Tel: +61 2 9360 2311

The Silk Company
3rd Floor, RBC Building
8 Kramer Road
Kramerville 2148
South Africa
Tel: +27 11 448 2578

Brunschwig & Fils
10 The Chambers
Chelsea Harbour Drive
London
SW10 OXF
United Kingdom
Tel: +44 20 7351 5797

Also available from:
Brunschwig & Fils Inc
75 Virginia Road
North White Plains
NY 10603-0905
USA
Tel: +1 914 684 5800

Brunschwig & Fils Inc
320 Davenport Road
Toronto
Ontario
M5R 1K6
Canada
Tel: +1 416 968 0699

Halogen International
Kramerville, South Africa
(see under Andrew Martin
International Ltd)

St James Furnishings (NZ) Ltd
The Foundation
8 George Street
Parnell
New Zealand
Tel: +64 9 303 3915

St James Furnishings Pty Ltd
142–144 Burwood Road
Hawthorn
VIC 3122
Australia
Tel: +61 3 9819 1569

Chelsea of London Ltd
Springvale Terrace
London
W14 0AE
United Kingdom
Tel: +44 20 7602 7250

The Designer's Guild
3 Olaf Street
London
W11 4BE
United Kingdom
Tel: +44 20 7243 7300

Also available from:
Wardlaw Pty Ltd
100 Harris Street
Pyrmont
NSW 2009
Australia
Tel: +61 2 9660 6266

GP & J Baker Ltd
PO Box 30
West End Road
High Wycombe
HP11 2QD
United Kingdom
Tel: +44 149 446 7467

Also available from:
The Fabric Library
Johannesburg, South Africa
(see under Arthur Sanderson
& Sons)

Lee Jofa Inc
Bethpage, USA
(see under Lee Jofa
International Ltd)

St James Furnishings Pty Ltd
Hawthorn, Australia
(see under Brunschwig & Fils)

HA Percheron Ltd
6 Chelsea Garden Market
Chelsea Harbour
London
SW10 0XE
United Kingdom
Tel: +44 171 349 1590

The Isle Mill Ltd
12 West Moulin Road
Pitlochry
PH16 3AF
Scotland
Tel: +44 179 647 2390

Also available from:
Charles Radford Furnishings
Pty Ltd
8–18 Glass Street
Burnley
VIC 3121
Australia
Tel: +61 3 9429 6122

Richard Gladstein
979 Third Avenue
New York
NY 10022
USA
Tel: +1 212 688 1802

Robert Malcolm Ltd
348 Manchester Street
PO Box 914
Christchurch
New Zealand
Tel: +64 3 366 9839

**JAB International
Furnishings Ltd**
1/15–16 Chelsea Design Centre
Chelsea Harbour
London
SW10 0XE
United Kingdom
Tel: +44 20 7349 9323

Also available from:
The Fabric Library
Johannesburg, South Africa
(see under Arthur Sanderson &
Sons)

JAB Anstoetz Inc
326 Davenport Road
Toronto
Ontario
M5R 1K6
Canada
Tel: +1 416 927 9192

Seneca Textiles Ltd
10–12 Adolph Street
Richmond
VIC 3121
Australia
Tel: +61 3 9428 5021

Seneca Textiles (NZ) Ltd
14 Heather Street
Parnell
New Zealand
Tel: +64 9309 6411

Stroheim & Romann Inc
155 East 56th Street
New York City
NY 10022
USA
Tel: +1 212 486 1500

Kravet London
G17 Chelsea Design Centre
Chelsea Harbour
London
SW10 0XE
United Kingdom
Tel: +44 171 795 0110

Lee Jofa International Ltd

Chelsea Harbour Design Centre
Chelsea Harbour
London
SW10 0XE
United Kingdom
Tel: +44 20 7351 7760

Also available from:
Lee Jofa Inc
201 Central Avenue South
Bethpage
NY 11714
USA
Tel: +1 516 752 7600

Mokum Textiles
98 Barchom Avenue
Rushcutters Bay
NSW 2011
Australia
Tel: +61 2 9380 6188

Mokum Textiles
11 Cheshire Street
Parnell
New Zealand
Tel: +64 9 379 3041

St Leger & Viney (Pty) Ltd
PO Box 5508
Northlands 2116
South Africa
Tel: +27 11 444 6722

Malabar Ltd

31–33 South Bank Business
Centre
Ponton Road
London
SW8 5BL
United Kingdom
Tel: +44 20 7501 4200

Also available from:
Davan Industries
144 Main Street
Port Washington
NY 11050
USA
Tel: +1 516 944 6498

Halogen International
Kramerville, South Africa
(see under Andrew Martin
International Ltd)

The Malabar Cotton Company
103–105 Regent Street
Chippendale
NSW 2008
Australia
Tel: +61 2 9310 2234

Osborne & Little Inc
Stamford, USA
(see under Osborne & Little)

Monkwell Ltd

10–12 Wharfdale Road
Bournemouth
BH4 9BT
United Kingdom
Tel: +44 120 275 2944

Also available from:
Home Fabrics
60 Old Pretoria Road
Halfway House
Midrand 1685
South Africa
Tel: +27 11 805 0300

Lee Jofa Inc
Bethpage, USA
(see under Lee Jofa
International Ltd)

Mokum Textiles
Rushcutters Bay, Australia
(see under Lee Jofa
International Ltd)

Mokum Textiles
Parnell, New Zealand
(see under Lee Jofa
International Ltd)

Telio et Cie
1407 rue de la Montagne
Montreal H3G 1Z3
Canada
Tel: +1 514 842 9116

Nobilis-Fontan

211 The Chambers
Chelsea Harbour
London
SW10 0XE
United Kingdom
Tel: +44 20 7351 7878

Also available from:
Mavromac
12D Kramer Road
Kramerville
South Africa
Tel: +27 11 444 1584

Nobilis-Fontan Inc
57A Industrial Road
Berkeley Heights
NJ 07922
USA
Tel: +1 908 464 1177

Redelman & Son Pty Ltd
96 Dalmeny Avenue
Rosebery
NSW 2018
Australia
Tel: +61 2 9313 6811

Telio et Cie
Montreal, Canada
(see under Monkwell Ltd)

Osborne & Little

49 Temperley Road
London
SW12 8QE
United Kingdom
Tel: +44 20 8675 2255

Also available from:
Osborne & Little Inc
90 Commerce Road
Stamford
CT 06902
USA
Tel: +1 203 359 1500

Wardlaw (NZ) Ltd
PO Box 9451
Newmarket
New Zealand
Tel: +64 9 520 2363

Wardlaw (Pty) Ltd
230–232 Auburn Road
Hawthorn
VIC 3122
Australia
Tel: +61 3 9819 4233

Pongees

28–30 Hoxton Square
London
N1 6NN
United Kingdom
Tel: +44 20 7739 9130

Ross & Co Ltd

Hales Road
Leeds
LS12 4PL
United Kingdom
Tel: +44 113 279 3531

Rubelli SpA
available from HA Percheron Ltd
London, United Kingdom
(see under HA Percheron Ltd)

Also available from:
Bergamo Fabrics Inc
D & D Building
979 Third Avenue
17th Floor
New York
NY 10022
USA
Tel: +1 212 888 3333

Mavromac
Kramerville, South Africa
(see under Nobilis-Fontan)

St James Furnishings Pty Ltd
Hawthorn, Australia
(see under Brunschwig & Fils)

Telio et Cie
Montreal, Canada
(see under Monkwell Ltd)

Vivace Textiles
Studio 6
125th Strand
Parnell
New Zealand
Tel: +64 9 309 6271

Sahco Hesslein
24 Chelsea Harbour Design
Centre
Chelsea Harbour
London
SW10 0XE
United Kingdom
Tel: +44 20 7352 6168

Also available from:
Bergamo Fabrics Inc
New York, USA
(see under Rubelli SpA)

Sandberg Tapeter AB
Box 69
S-523 22 Ulricehamn
Sweden
Tel: +46 321 121 15

Also available from:
Arelier Textiles, New Zealand
Tel: +64 9 373 3866

*Sandberg Tapeter United
Kingdom*
Tel: 0800 96 72 22

Sandberg Tapeter USA
Miami: +1 813 831 6230
New York City:
+1 212 838 1796
Washington DC:
+1 202 863 0606

The Silk Company
Johannesburg, South Africa
(see under Brian Yates Interiors
Ltd)

Thomas Dare
341 Kings Road
London
SW3 5ES
United Kingdom
Tel: +44 20 7351 7991

Also available from:
Fonthill
979 Third Avenue
New York
NY 10022
USA
Tel: +1 212 755 6700

The Silk Company
Johannesburg, South Africa
(see under Brian Yates Interiors
Ltd)

Turnell & Gigon Ltd
Chelsea Harbour Design Centre
Chelsea Harbour
London
SW10 0XE
United Kingdom
Tel: +44 20 7351 5142

Also available from:
Old World Weavers-Stark
979 Third Avenue
Suite 1002
NY 1022
USA
Tel: +1 212 592 6800

Warner Fabrics plc
Talbot House
17 Church Street
Rickmansworth
WD3 1DE
United Kingdom
Tel: +44 191 371 0300

Also available from:
St Leger & Viney
777 Andries Strect North
Wynberg Park
Wynberg 2090
South Africa
Tel: +27 11 887 8690

Wardlaw (Pty) Ltd
Hawthorn, Australia
(see under Osborne & Little)

Whittaker & Woods
5100 Highlands Parkways
Smyrna
GA 30082
USA
Tel: +1 770 435 9720

Zimmer + Rohde UK Ltd
15 Chelsea Harbour
Design Centre
Chelsea Harbour
London
SW10 0XE
United Kingdom
Tel: +44 20 7351 7115

Also available from:
Home Fabrics
Midrand, South Africa
(see under Monkwell)

Mokum Textiles
Rushcutters Bay, Australia
(see under Lee Jofa
International Ltd)

Mokum Textiles
Parnell, New Zealand
(see under Lee Jofa
International Ltd)

Zimmer + Rhode
37 West 17th Street, Suite S-E
New York
NY 10011
USA
Tel: +1 212 627 8080

Zoffany
Chelsea Design Centre
Chelsea Harbour
London
SW10 0XE
United Kingdom
Tel: +44 20 7349 0043

TRIMMINGS

Abbot & Boyd
(see under fabrics)

Anna Crutchley
The Frater Studio
6B Priory Road
Cambridge
CB5 8HT
United Kingdom
Tel: +44 123 332 7685

Aviamentos
457 King Street
Newtown
NSW 2042
Australia
Tel: +61 2 9550 3774

Henry Newbery & Co
18 Newman Street
London
W1P 4AB
United Kingdom
Tel: +44 20 7636 5970

Monkwell Ltd
(see under fabrics)

Troynorth Ltd
High Ardley
Hexham
NE46 2LG
United Kingdom
Tel: +44 143 460 7366

Turnell & Gigon Ltd
(see under fabrics)

VV Rouleaux
54 Sloane Square
London
SW1W 8AX
United Kingdom
Tel: +44 20 7730 3125

Wemyss Houles
40 Newman Street
London
W1P 3PA
United Kingdom
Tel: +44 20 7255 3305

Zoffany
(see under fabrics)

UPHOLSTERY SUPPLIES

Arlene's
2282 Holdom Avenue
Burnaby
British Columbia
V5B 4Y5
Canada
Tel: +1 604 292 6922

Bert Woll Fabrics
125 Glacier Street
Coquitlam
British Columbia
V3K 5Z6
Canada
Tel: +1 604 941 7774

Caddum Design Furniture Products Limited
13–14 Peter Road
Commerce Way Industrial
Estate
Lancing
BN15 8TH
United Kingdom
Tel: +44 1903 755 6064

Carr and Bury Ltd
42 North Street
Bishop's Stortford
CM23 2LR
United Kingdom
Tel: +44 127 965 4352

Chintz and Company
950 Homer Street
Vancouver
British Columbia
V6B 2W7
Canada
Tel: +1 604 689 2022

The Foam Shop
2 Montana Road
Kesgrave
1P5 7ER
United Kingdom
Tel: +44 473 624 034

The Furnishing Workshop
146 Stanley Park Road
Carshalton
SM5 3JG
United Kingdom
Tel: +44 20 8773 3950

Gatestone Upholstery
243 Carshalton Road
Carshalton
SM5 3PZ
United Kingdom
Tel: +44 20 8642 9605

Gwyder Foam
4 Dillwyn Street
Swansea
South Wales
SA1 4AE
United Kingdom
Tel: +44 1792 462 151

Ian Williams
454 Argyle Street
Moss Vale
NSW 2577
Australia
Tel: +61 2 4868 1588

JA Milton
Unit 6
Whitchurch Business Park
Whitchurch
SY13 1LJ
United Kingdom
Tel: +44 194 866 3434

Linda S Storey
69 High Street
March
PE15 9LB
United Kingdom
Tel: +44 135 465 1057

Maxwell Fabrics
188 Victoria Drive
Vancouver
British Columbia
V6M 2Z3
Canada
Tel: +1 604 253 7744

Prickett and Sons
42 Broadway
Leigh-on-Sea
SS9 1AJ
United Kingdom
Tel: +44 170 247 6966

Relics
35 Bridge Street
Witney
OX8 6DA
United Kingdom
Tel: +44 199 370 4611

Shann Accessories Pty Ltd
23–45 Gipps Street
Collingwood
VIC 3066
Australia
Tel: +61 3 9419 5640

INSTITUTIONS

The institutions below are sources of more information about upholstery, including advice on leisure and professional courses, industry standards and collections of upholstered furniture.

Association of Master Upholsterers and Soft Furnishers

Francis Vaughan House
102 Commercial Street
Newport
NP9 ILU
United Kingdom
Tel: +44 163 321 5454

British Furniture Manufacturers Association

30 Harcourt Street
London
W1H 2AA
United Kingdom
Tel: +44 1494 523 021

British Standards Institute

389 Chiswick High Road
Chiswick
London
W4 4AL
United Kingdom
Tel: +44 20 8996 9000

The Chair Frame Makers Association

Francis Vaughan House
102 Commercial Street
Newport
NP9 ILU
United Kingdom
Tel: +44 163 321 5454

Chambre d'Apprentissage

des Industiries de l'Amb
200 Bis Boulevard Voltaire
75 011 Paris
France
Tel: +33 1 43 72 22 88

City and Guilds of London Institute

76 Portland Place
London
W1N 4AA
United Kingdom
Tel: +44 20 7294 2468

Commercial Furniture Industry Association of Australia Inc

2 Humphreys Lane
Hurstville
NSW 2220
Tel: +61 2 9580 8922

Consumers Association

2 Marylebone Road
London
NW1 4DX
United Kingdom
Tel: +44 20 7830 6000

The Crafts Council

44a Pentonville Road
Islington
London
N1 9BY
United Kingdom
Tel: +44 20 7806 2500

Department of Trade and Industry

Ashdown House
123 Victoria Street
London
SW1E 6RB
United Kingdom
Tel: +44 20 7215 5000

Design Council

28 Haymarket
London
SW1Y 4SU
United Kingdom
Tel: +44 20 7420 5200

Furnishing Industry Association of Australia

129 York Street
South Melbourne
VIC 3205
Tel: +61 3 9686 1555

Furniture Industry Research Association

Maxwell Road
Stevenage
SG1 2EW
United Kingdom
Tel: +44 1438 777 700

Geffrye Museum

Kingsland Road
London
E2 8EA
United Kingdom
Tel: +44 207 739 9893

London Guildhall University

(formerly London College of Furniture)
41–71 Commercial Road
London
E1 1LA
United Kingdom
Tel: +44 20 7320 1000

The National Council for Vocational Qualifications

222 Euston Road
London
NW1 2BZ
United Kingdom
Tel: +44 20 7509 5555

National Trust

36 Queen Anne's Gate
London
SW1H 9AS
United Kingdom
Tel: +44 20 7222 9251

Victoria and Albert Museum

South Kensington
London
SW7 2RL
Tel: +44 20 7942 2000

Acknowledgements

The Publishers would like to thank the companies below that generously gave fabrics or trimmings for upholstered furniture featured in this book. Special thanks go to Rebecca Metcalfe and Lucy Meharg at Osborne & Little, London, and Melina Coffey at The Decorative Fabrics Gallery, London, for their cheerful help and tireless enthusiasm.

Contact details can be found in Suppliers and Institutions listings.

Child's Headboard (page 114): Zimmer + Rohde UK Ltd (fabric)

Romantic Headboard (page 117): Lee Jofa International Ltd (fabric); Troynorth Ltd (cord)

Four-fold Screen (page 122): Sandberg Tapeter AB (pastel fabric); Sheila Coombes at Brian Yates Interiors (Ltd) (gold/beige fabric); Wemyss Houles (braid)

Circular Stool (page 126): JAB International Furnishings Ltd (fabric)

Drop-in Seat (page 130): Arthur Sanderson & Sons (fabric)

Metal Chair (page 132): Christian Fischbacher at Chelsea of London Ltd (fabric)

Campaign Chair (page 136): Malabar Ltd (fabric); Fisco Fasteners Ltd (nails: only available from local retailers)

Chippendale-style Stool (page 139): GP & J Baker Ltd (fabric)

Georgian Drop-on Seat (page 144): Warner Fabrics plc (fabric)

Modern Dining Chair (page 146): Lee Jofa International Ltd (fabric); Fisco Fasteners Ltd (nails: only available from local retailers)

Pin-cushion Settle (page 149): Brunschwig & Fils (fabric); British Trimmings (gimp: only available from local retailers)

Blanket Box (page 154): Lee Jofa International Ltd (exterior fabric); Brunschwig & Fils (interior fabric); Henry Newbery & Co (gimp and cord)

Louis XVI Tub Chair (page 162): Baumann Fabrics Limited (fabric); Turnell & Gigon Ltd (gimp)

Bucket Chair (page 168): The Isle Mill Ltd (chair fabric); Zimmer + Rohde UK Ltd (cushion fabric)

Victorian Dining Chair (page 174): L.Rubelli at HA Percheron Ltd (fabric); Monkwell Ltd (braid); Fisco Fastners Ltd (nails: only available from local retailers)

Piano Stool (page 177): Monkwell Ltd (fabric); Wemyss Houles (braid with tassels); VV Rouleaux (striped braid)

Picture-back Chair (page 182): Monkwell Ltd (fabric); Wemyss Houles (gimp)

Louis XV Carver (page 188): Pongees (fabric); Wemyss Houles (gimp)

Nursing Chair (pages 40 and 192): Baumann Fabrics Limited (fabric); Abbott & Boyd (pages 40, right and 192: trimmings); VV Rouleaux (page 40, left: ribbon and cord)

Prie-dieu Chair (pages 41 and 198): Thomas Dare (fabric); Brunschwig & Fils (trimmings)

Modern Sofa (page 202): Baumann Fabrics Limited (fabric)

Day Bed (page 208): Baumann Fabrics Limited (fabric); Anna Crutchley (trimmings)

Sprung-back Easy Chair (page 216): Liberty at Osborne & Little (fabric)

Wing Chair (page 222): Nina Campbell at Osborne & Little (chair and cushion fabrics)

Button-back Chair (page 230): Monkwell Ltd (fabric)

Demonstration Button-back Armchair (page 89): Osborne & Little (fabric); Henry Newbery & Co (cord)

Footstool (page 36, left): Sahco Hesslein (fabric)

Footstool (page 36, right): Ross & Co Ltd (top fabric); GP & J Baker Ltd (main fabric); VV Rouleaux (fringe and ribbon)

Footstool (page 37, left): Nobilis-Fontan (fabric); Henry Newbery & Co (cord)

Footstool (page 37, right): Thomas Dare (fabric); VV Rouleaux (braid)

The Publishers would also like to thank the following companies (and others not listed) for lending items that feature in photography throughout the book, as follows:

Cushions featured on pages 38–39: De Le Cuona Designs Ltd at The General Trading Company (+44 20 7730 0411), Evertrading Ltd (+44 20 8878 4050), Nono Designs Ltd (+44 161 929 9930), Osborne & Little (+44 20 8675 2255), Sussex House (+44 20 7371 5455), The Decorative Fabrics Gallery Ltd (+44 20 7589 4778)

Fabrics featured on pages 75 and 77: Roylston House (+61 2 9331 3033); DJ's Upholstery (+61 2 9550 5946); Julie Garner Agencies (+61 2 9552 1121)

Other props: Pittards plc, for leather (+44 1935 474 321); Zoffany, for trimmings (+44 20 7495 2505); Brats, for paint (+44 20 7351 7674)

Tools featured on page 27: Webber & Sons for tack lifter (+44 1483 202 963)

Author's acknowledgements:

I would like to thank all the following for their generosity in giving their time and expertise to help me have all the projects ready on time.

My husband John, who helped repair, paint, and polish the frames.

My son and business partner, Jonathan, for his patience and sense of humour during the disruption of our workshop.

Jim Cunningham working with us at The Furnishing Workshop, who contributed a great deal to the projects, and helped keep our normal workload at bay.

My son Matthew who, in spite of his own commitments at Gatestone Upholstery, took the time and interest to help with the projects, and to make the stools in the Decorative Choices section.

Fred Garner, our very good family friend, who always comes to the rescue when needed; he was an important link in this wonderful team of master upholsterers who helped me to finish the projects and demonstration chair on time.

Thanks to my niece Tracey Croswell for the use of her hands, and for being the general 'dogsbody' during the photo sessions.

To Andrew Newton-Cox, a wonderful photographer and a very practical man, who took a great interest in the subject of upholstery.

To Deena Beverley for her contribution in styling the photographs and writing the Decorative Choices section and the Special Features.

To Carolyn Jenkins, who turned my rough line drawings into works of art.

Marylouise Brammer and Caroline Verity, who are responsible for the inspirational design and layout of the book.

Geraldine Christy and Justine Harding, who edited my manuscript, and made it fit the pages.

To Karen Hemingway, the senior commissioning editor, who asked me to write this book, in an impossibly short time, and who motivated me with her enthusiasm.

Thank you, it was a pleasure to work with you all.

Index